THE EVOLUTION
OF
AMERICAN
URBAN SOCIETY

Howard P. Chudacoff

Brown University

PRENTICE-HALL, INC., Englewood Cliffs, New Jersey

Library of Congress Cataloging in Publication Data

CHUDACOFF, HOWARD P.
　　The evolution of American urban society.

　　Includes bibliographies and index.
　　1. Cities and towns—United States—History.
2. Urbanization—United States.　3. United States—
Social conditions.　I. Title.
HT123.C49　　　301.36′0973　　　74-23558
ISBN　0-13-293688-7
ISBN　0-13-293670-4 pbk.

To my parents,
MILDRED AND IRVING CHUDACOFF,
and
to the memory of my grandparents,
JENNIE AND WILLIAM SAFERSTEIN

© 1975 by PRENTICE-HALL, INC.
Englewood Cliffs, New Jersey

Printed in the United States of America

10　9　8　7　6　5　4　3　2　1

Prentice-Hall International, Inc., *London*
Prentice-Hall of Australia, Pty. Ltd., *Sydney*
Prentice-Hall of Canada, Ltd., *Toronto*
Prentice-Hall of India Private Limited, *New Delhi*
Prentice-Hall of Japan, Inc., *Tokyo*

CONTENTS

PREFACE

This book traces the urban path of American history. Although interest in urban affairs is relatively recent, cities have existed in this country since its earliest years, and they have fostered activities and attitudes that distinctly differed from those of the surrounding countryside.

Americans have often held great expectation for their cities. Early in the 1800s, a promoter of St. Louis predicted, "We have but commenced to tell the wonders of a city destined in the future to equal London in its population, Athens in its philosophy, art, and culture, Rome in its hotels, cathedrals, and grandeur, and to be the central commercial metropolis of a continent." The fact that he expressed his dream in an urban hyperbole is significant, for he seemed to agree with the ancient Greek dramatist Sophocles who had proclaimed that the highest achievements of mankind were "language, wind-swift thought, and city-dwelling habits."

But there were others who saw things differently. Writing at about the same time that the St. Louis booster penned his panegyric, Henry David Thoreau defined city life as "millions of people being lonely together." Nearly a half-century earlier, Thomas Jefferson had announced, ". . . I view great cities as pestilential to the morals, the health, and the liberties of man."

The St. Louis promoter, Thoreau, and Jefferson were all echoing major themes of American urban development. On the one hand, cities emerged from lofty intentions; on the other, their unplanned growth and social problems created disillusion. Yet, in spite of persisting myths about the virtues and attractions or rural life, Americans have generally accepted their cities; only a few mavericks like Thoreau completely rejected urban society. As places promising the highest achievements as well as the most threatening evils, cities have directed the course of American civilization.

Today, most people have feelings about what a city is, but a detailed definition is elusive because the term implies so many different things and is used in so many different ways. Probably the most comprehensive, and currently acceptable definition would be something like the following: Cities are communities of concentrated populations that coordinate and control large-scale activities. This phrase implies four major criteria: (1) that population density is a necessary characteristic; (2) that cities are focal points, or nodes, that centralize and disperse goods, services, and communications; (3) that complex and specialized relationships characterize social life; and (4) that urban dwellers display particularly "urbane" habits and shared interests. By contrast, rural communities are less dense, contain lower proportions of wage earners, promote simpler, more close-knit social ties, and are less cosmopolitan in their outlook. These characteristics of urban density, urban functions, urban society, and urban attitudes have, for better or worse, made cities the centers of human culture and aspirations. The physical and social problems resulting from large numbers of people living in close proximity to each other have necessitated communal solutions. By bringing together people and resources, cities have encouraged the specialization that in turn has been responsible for economic and technological progress. The competitiveness and variability of urban life have often been responsible for sorrow and tragedy, but they have also meant joy and adventure. And the cosmopolitanism of cities has made them workshops for advances in the arts and education.

The above definition and its four corollaries are sufficiently generalized to be widely applied, but they raise a number of knotty questions. What is a necessary density? What are the boundaries of nodes? What kinds of social relationships are complex and specialized? How does one define "urbane"? Obviously the answers to these types of questions depend upon context—variables of time and place. Thus, in the final analysis, a definition of cities must be a flexible one that is sensitive to a variety of frames of reference.

What seems more important to the American experience than a static definition is the way in which cities have grown relative to the rest of society—the process known as urbanization. In its simplest version, urbanization occurs when the urban population of an area or nation increases at a faster rate than the rest of the population in that area or nation. The history of the United States has been one of almost consistently rising urbanization. In 1790, at the dawn of nationhood, only one-twentieth of the American population lived in cities; today, the proportion has reached above three-fourths. This rapid spread of urban life constitutes a key factor in explaining the nation's social, economic, political, and cultural history.

An urban population grows in three ways: by natural increase (excess of births over deaths); by net migration (excess of in-migration over out-migration); and by boundary changes (annexation or reclassification). Until recently, high mortality and low birth rates (relative to rural areas) have limited the amount of natural increase in American urban areas. Boundary changes have affected individual cities—as in 1898 when New

York City's population was doubled by consolidation with its surrounding boroughs—but are usually not important from a regional or national perspective—that is, the areas attached to New York in 1898 were already highly urbanized. Thus most urbanization in this country has been the result of net migration, the excess influx of people from farms, towns, other cities, and other countries. Only this kind of growth could swell the population of Chicago from a few thousand to a million in half a century or produce a string of cities and suburbs that today links Boston to Washington, D.C.

The types of migrants to a city—rural, southern, European, and so forth—and the types of large-scale activities—manufacturing, commerce, administration, or mixed—produce complex and specialized social structures. Each city contains a myriad of overlapping subcommunities consisting of neighborhoods, work groups, ethnic groups, church parishes, friendship circles, professional associations, and so on. The dynamics of urban life result from the ways in which these subcommunities interact with larger systems such as markets, politics, or communications. The mix of subcommunities and large-scale activities account for differences between cities, and the superstructure of large systems gives cities similar qualities. Thus in 1900, the combination of northern Europeans, eastern Europeans, and rural Midwesterners within an economy based on the processing and distribution of agricultural products made the city of Omaha, Nebraska, a much different community than Providence, Rhode Island, with Irish, Italians, and Yankees living in a more industrialized environment where factories produced textiles, machines, and jewelry. Yet both communities had similar patterns of activity, similar routines involving people in the quest for work, housing, consumer goods, entertainment, social relationships, and power.

Earlier in this century, when American scholars first undertook serious study of urban life, it was common to view cities in an unfavorable light. The process of urbanization that was transforming American, indeed all of Western, society, from simple, uncluttered, folk communities into a fast-paced, competitive, specialized world was believed to produce social disorganization—mental instability, family breakdown, and criminality. Today, however, scholars seriously question the causal link between urban growth and social problems. Research has shown that loneliness, impersonality, and anxiety are not uniform from city to city or neighborhood to neighborhood and that the quality of urban life may be determined as much, if not more, by age structures, educational levels, bureaucratic influence, or other characteristics as by the growth rate, size, and density of the population. Thus rather than emphasizing pathological consequences, many social scientists are now examining the ways in which urbanization has attracted and assimilated migrants, standardized principal social and economic activities, provided organizational and technological innovations, and revised the methods and effects of human communications.

I have tried to apply this more functional point of view to the following pages. My purpose is to emphasize the overriding theme of urbanization—the process of growth and evolution. It is a theme that puts people at the center and that highlights the networks of interaction between urban dwellers and their environment.

ACKNOWLEDGMENTS

In the course of this book's preparation, I have accumulated debts of gratitude to a variety of helpers and advisers. I offer first thanks to my wife, Nancy Fisher Chudacoff, whose historical insights, editorial skills, and inspirational support have made her a near-collaborator. In many ways, this book began during Richard C. Wade's American urban history courses at the University of Chicago. Professor Wade's ideas and advice have been a formative force, and his influence pervades the following pages. Among those who aided me as I struggled from chapter to chapter, I owe particular thanks to my colleague James T. Patterson who read almost the entire manuscript and provided countless perceptive comments. I may not have followed all of his suggestions, but the book would have suffered without them. Others whose work and advice have proved valuable include Melvin Feldman, Tamara K. Hareven, Stephan Thernstrom, William G. McLoughlin, Jr., Gordon S. Wood, Mary Y. Kujovich, R. Burr Litchfield, Charles Tilly, and Maris Vinovskis. I also thank all those authors and scholars whose names appear in my various bibliographies. Any errors of fact and interpretations belong to me alone.

When this book was first conceived, I received some helpful comments from Joseph Hawes, Thomas Jones, John Cumbler, Ray Shortridge, and Andrew Aschenbaum whom I consulted at the University of Michigan during the summer of 1972. At Brown University, I have also received assistance from graduate students, particularly B. Michael Zuckerman, Judith Smith, Anthony Coelho, Timothy Meagher, Bruce Tucker, Nancy Osterud, Conrad Wright, and Archie J. Powell. For their aid in selecting illustrations, I thank Marsha Peters of the Rhode Island Historical Society, Georgia Baumgartner of the American Antiquarian Society, Jeanette Black of the John Carter Brown Library, and Mary Frances Rhymer of the Chicago Historical Society. For typing and general assistance I owe a special debt to Karen Mota and Winifred Barton. Finally, I wish to acknowledge the expert and valuable contributions made to this book by Ann Torbert, Robert Fenyo, Brian Walker, and all of their assistants at Prentice-Hall.

1

URBAN AMERICA
IN THE COLONIAL AGE

From the very beginning those who colonized North America were urban-minded people. A whole continent opened before them, but the settlers needed central places for defense, for trade, for administration, and for worship. In Europe towns and cities existed in the midst of rural hinterlands. In the American wilderness, however, cities were bridgeheads, vanguards of settlement. They not only linked the Old World to the New but also contained the cultural seeds of a new nation.

Each of the major colonizing nations contributed to America's urban heritage. The Spanish, who arrived first, developed a formal system of town planning. This was the Laws of the Indies, an enactment of 1583 synthesizing earlier practices of colonial settlement. The Laws specified uniform requirements for town location, street layout, and land use, and they shaped urban beginnings in Florida and the American Southwest. In contrast to the Spanish, the early French settlers came not as government agents but as individuals seeking personal gain. As traders they needed centers for the exchange of goods, so they founded commercial posts along the waterways of America's northern and western perimeters. Their urban legacy includes such places as Quebec, Montreal, Detroit, and St. Louis. The Dutch, like the Spanish, also brought elaborate plans. New Amsterdam, their trading capital on Manhattan Island, was to be a star-shaped fortress with a twenty-five-foot main street and a central marketplace.

These projects remained as important precedents for future American cities, but the English colonies along the North Atlantic coast, more than any others, created and shaped American urban life. It was especially in the several settlements along or near the Massachusetts shore that the urban frontier began. These towns combined Puritan notions of social and religious harmony with inward, village orientation of agrarian peasant society to create a kind of corporate communalism, a collective attitude and local identification that laid the foundations for the development of an urban spirit. The town of Boston, however, recast the mold. According to the precepts of John Winthrop, the colony of Massachusetts Bay was to be "as a Citty upon a Hill," a place that bound people together in the sanctification of God. But in 1630 when the settlers relocated from Charlestown across the Charles River to Boston in order to take advantage of the excellent harbor there, they began a process that was to swell population growth and economic diversity, thus obliterating Winthrop's vision. For Boston was to become more than an agrarian-based town; its harbor and natural location as a commercial and administrative hub turned it into a prosperous, worldly city whose interests spilled over the bounds of "a Modell of Christian Charity."

In subsequent decades several other cities similarly developed southward along the Atlantic coast, all built around deep harbors and all sustained by trade. In 1639 a group of religious dissenters founded Newport on the Island of Rhode Island, ostensibly as a haven for the persecuted. The site they chose had the best harbor in southern New England, and it was this geographical advantage rather than religious tolerance that assured the town's existence. When the British took New Amsterdam from the Dutch in 1664, they inherited the finest natural port in North America and quite naturally preserved the commercial functions of the city as well as making it the capital of New York colony. In 1680 proprietors of the Carolina colony moved their chief settlement from a marshy location to a peninsula jutting out between the Ashley and Cooper rivers in order to utilize its harbor and more healthful environs. The settlement, named Charles Town (later Charleston), soon became the largest and wealthiest town of the southern colonies. And in 1682 William Penn chose the site for Philadelphia one hundred miles up the Delaware River where it was joined by the Schuylkill. This was to be not only the capital of the Pennsylvania colony and the most extensive experiment in city building that the colonies had yet witnessed, but also a place intended as "the most considerable for merchandize, trade, and fishery in these parts. . . ."

There were and would be others—Providence, Albany, New Haven, Baltimore, Norfolk, Savannah—but throughout the colonial period the five cities of Boston, Newport, New York, Philadelphia, and Charleston

Colonial New Amsterdam, 1660

This extraordinary map is a redrawing by John Wolcott Adams and I. N. Phelps Stokes of the Castello Plan of New Amsterdam, first drawn in 1660. The street leading out from the fort and into the undeveloped area is Broadway. The road along the fortification separating the settled area from the unsettled land is Wall Street. *I. N. Phelps Stokes Collection. Prints Division, The New York Public Library. Astor, Lenox and Tilden Foundations.*

were the largest and most influential. Although their origins spanned a half-century, the five resembled each other in several important ways: all were ports, all had planned beginnings, and all were products of the same civilization. Except for Newport all originated in intent and personnel in London and Amsterdam, both centers of societies that judged cities to be necessary and desirable. Thus it is not surprising that the Dutch and, particularly, the British established settlements that assumed the functions of genuinely urban places: defense, organization, population control, and accumulation and dissemination of goods and communications. The colonial cities represented for the colonizers the transfer of "civilization"—an urban environment and the activities associated with it—from the Old to the New World.

Because the major colonial cities were commercial and administrative centers, thus attracting inhabitants as much by natural economic forces as by official policy, they all grew rapidly. Boston, the largest city for over a century, had a population of 7,000 by 1690 and over 16,000 by 1742. Philadelphia and New York contained about 4,000 inhabitants in 1690, well over 10,000 by 1740, and 40,000 and 25,000, respectively, on the eve of the Revolution. Newport and Charleston grew from 2,600 and 1,100, respectively, to over 10,000 by the 1770s. These developments satisfied British mercantile objectives of centralization for the sake of control. Indeed the Crown had encouraged the growth of towns because such concentrations of population facilitated defense and government of the colonists.

But the size and economic opportunities of these cities also prompted activities that stretched the intended limits of colonial administration and eventually threatened the colonial system. As links in the mercantilist system, the colonial ports collected and dispatched raw materials needed by England and received the wares of British merchants for American consumption. Thus most lines of communication extended from individual cities to the Mother Country rather than among the colonies themselves.

It was not long, however, before the colonial towns bred their own merchants and tradesmen who began to look to the interior settlements in search of markets for locally produced as well as imported goods. Consequently each city began to cultivate its own commercial hinterland, an activity that turned the colonial ports into small mercantilist powers themselves and enabled them to expand their economies beyond English goals of simple self-support. As early as the 1640s Boston traders tightened commercial ties westward and southward to Springfield, Hartford, and along Long Island Sound, and by the eve of the Revolution inland trade had become an important concern to all urban America. In Rhode Island, for example, a Providence merchant, Welcome Arnold, shipped processed lime—a necessity for the production of mortar and plaster—not only to Boston, New York, Philadelphia, and Baltimore, but also to smaller settlements in the New England interior. Arnold added retail consumer goods to his inland lime traffic, and he helped attach a broad hinterland to Providence which choked off any potential expansion by Newport, enabling Providence to surpass Newport's size and become New England's second city by 1800. This quest for domestic markets sparked rivalries between cities that gave American urbanization a spirited quality.

Size and commercial activity, combined with benign neglect on the part of England, also forced the colonial cities into the expansion of self-government. The provincial governments were the creators of towns and therefore held ultimate authority over the form and scope of local administration. But gradually every large town except Charleston assumed self-management of local details, acquiring power either by piecemeal grant or by charter revision. Philadelphia and New York (after 1664), capitals of proprietary colonies, resembled English towns in that they were municipal boroughs, incorporated by royal charter and administered by a mayor and some kind of council. Because these officials were appointed by the governor, however, they tended to be aristocrats who acted in their own interests. Moreover, the mayors and councils had very limited taxing and spending powers so that they were slow to meet the needs of urban growth. A new charter in 1731 empowered New Yorkers to vote for their councilmen, a reform that forced local government to be more responsive to an expanded constituency and to provide better administration. In Philadelphia, change occurred more slowly. Although the powers of the council, called the Corporation, were successively diluted between 1712 and 1775 so that elected officials handled more local matters, the nature of the city's government remained exclusive and sluggish. Lack of progressive government failed to inhibit growth, however; Philadelphia was easily the largest city in the colonies by the Revolution.

The affairs of Boston and Newport were tended in town meetings, an institution that resembled the assemblies of rural England, yet grew out of Puritan congregationalism. Several times a year all male residents (freemen) of the town would meet to conduct local business—to elect officials, pass laws, levy taxes, and settle disputes. Boston's and Newport's more open structure and broader fiscal and administrative powers made their governments more efficient than those of New York and Philadelphia. Moreover, because the town meetings acted to dissolve local differences, they created a situation in which government was able to establish public facilities without much debate, and the citizens were generally willing to pay for them. Town meetings were thus symbols of order as well as agencies of government. However, they met only a few times a year. During the interims men chosen as executive officials, "selectmen," assumed governmental duties. Their power over appointments, judiciary decisions, and administration often diminished the initiative of the town meeting. The same men, usually those of high standing in both the market place and the church, tended to monopolize the councils of selectmen. Nevertheless, these men were chosen for office by their fellow townsmen and fit into the scheme of community concord.

Throughout the colonial era the government of Charleston remained in the hands of the provincial assembly that appointed commissioners to manage the affairs of the city. The assemblymen and commissioners often did not live in Charleston and represented interests that were seldom sympathetic to the city's welfare. As a result the city was burdened with the least responsive government of the five ports.

PROBLEMS OF GROWTH

Almost from their inception the local governments felt the pressures of urban growth; many of the physical and social problems that nag modern urban society appeared in every colonial city. Although the practical experience and technological tools for their solution were lacking, each town improvised, adjusted, and borrowed methods of response from England and each other. Initially, individual citizens took steps to remove inconveniences, but quite early they combined into collective efforts, often surrendering private initiative to government directive. The cities were still small enough and most of their problems so simply defined that the consequences of alternative solutions (including the alternative of neglect) could be comprehended by most people without involving the community in the dilemma of defining public interest. Thus most colonial urban dwellers could appreciate the utility of collective action and accept the exercise of regulatory powers by government.

Urban organization requires efficient transportation and communications, so it is not surprising that town governments devoted a large proportion of their efforts determining where, how, and when new streets should be constructed. In every city, including Philadelphia where gridiron street patterns had been established prior to settlement, individuals had laid out new roads and paths where they were needed without regard for a larger scheme of coordination. In the 1700s government authority intervened, and the construction of new streets became accepted as a function of public policy even though such roads were merely open stretches cleared of obstructions.

The laying of streets, however, involved more than locating a route, removing tree stumps and rocks, and, occasionally, paving with gravel and cobblestone. Mud and stagnant water impeded traffic and threatened health, causing drainage to become a related concern. Boston was most successful in meeting this problem; after 1713 the city began grading streets so that they slanted from the middle to side gutters. By the 1760s other cities had initiated drainage projects. The cities acted to solve other problems. The governments of Boston, New York, and Newport levied fines to prevent builders from erecting structures in paths of traffic. Certain towns constructed and maintained bridges over streams and marshes. These intrusions of public authority met with little resistance from private citizens.

Once the streets, sewers, and bridges were built, the difficulties were far from over, for as the colonial cities grew, so did their traffic. Not only did the streets provide transportation routes, but they also served as play areas for children and foraging ground for hogs, dogs, and cattle. By the

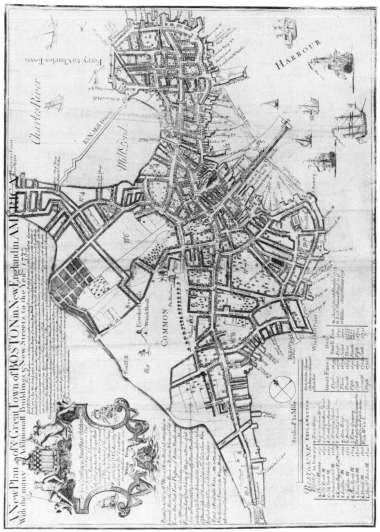

Boston, 1733

This plan, drawn by John Bonner in 1733, includes the Long Wharf, which stretched some 1,500 feet into the harbor and contained shops and warehouses. As time passed, spaces between the other wharfs and docks were filled in, and the wharfs were joined to make room for new buildings. Throughout its history, the city of Boston has constantly reclaimed space from areas formerly covered by water. *The John Carter Brown Library, Brown University.*

7

middle of the seventeenth century congestion and accidents plagued city streets. To protect pedestrians and playing children, several towns levied fines for riding at fast gaits on city streets and for failure to keep horses and other draft animals under tight rein.

Regulations could not lessen the amount of traffic, however, and in an attempt to ease the pressure, cities built more streets, undertook grading and paving projects, and paid more attention to street cleaning. The best streets were those of Boston and Newport where the town governments could levy taxes for highway improvements. Other cities had to depend upon private means or other sources of public funds such as fines, license fees, or lotteries. Where projects were elaborate, as in Boston, full-time laborers were hired at public expense. Most cities, however, followed the English custom of requiring each householder to devote a certain number of days each year to labor on public works or hire a substitute. In Charleston slaves did most of the public work, and in Boston each free Negro was forced to work on the roads eight days a year instead of doing watch duty, from which blacks were prohibited.

Tossing refuse onto the streets had been one of the bad habits of European urban dwellers, and colonial Americans were no more restrained. Their streets quickly became cluttered with waste, ashes, bones, shells, and other rubbish. The cities, beginning with Boston and New Amsterdam, responded by passing laws prohibiting the indiscriminate disposal of trash. A report from Boston in 1652 noted:

> At a meeting of all the Selckt men, it is ordered that now person inhabiting within said Town shall throw forth or lay any intralls of beasts or fowls or garbidg or Carion or dead dogs or Cattle or any other dead beast or stinkeing thing, in any hie way or dich or Common within this neck of Boston, but ar injoynened to bury all such things that soe they may prevent all anoyanc unto any. Further it is ordered that noe person shall throw forth dust or dung or shreds of Cloth or lether or any tobacco stalks or any such thing into the streets.

But such measures proved impossible to enforce and ineffective as deterrents. Only Boston made any public provision for regular street cleaning, hiring a number of scavengers to haul away street rubbish, but this service was abandoned after 1720 because of mounting costs. Nonetheless, American streets probably were cleaner, better constructed, and better lighted than most of their European counterparts. As early as the 1690s Philadelphians had begun to light lamps in front of their homes at night. Their example was followed by residents of other cities, and by the middle of the eighteenth century local governments began to raise and allocate money for public street lighting.

Streets and traffic caused only inconvenience; fire threatened existence.

Indeed fire was one of the most feared hazards of urban life, and danger of it necessitated public regulations which were less imperative on the rural countryside. Except for Philadelphia where there were many brick structures, most buildings in colonial American cities were made of wood and spaced close together, so a blaze was hard to confine. Lacking advanced technology, the best steps local authorities could take were limited and precautionary. They enacted preventive measures such as prohibiting smoking out of doors, regulating the storage of gunpowder and other combustibles, and establishing standards for the construction of roofs and chimneys. These last provisions formed the first American building codes and included prohibitions on reed and straw roofing and on wood and plaster chimneys. Authorities also attempted to confine potential fires by limiting the places in which brush or rubbish could be burned and forbidding the construction of wooden buildings in the center of town. In 1649 Boston adopted the English curfew, requiring all house fires to be covered or extinguished between 9:00 at night and 4:30 in the morning. Nearly all American towns adopted the European tradition of community responsibility for extinguishing fires. Each city contained at least one volunteer fire company comprised of private citizens and organized as a protective and social agency.

Unfortunately the towns did not react to such urban dangers as fires until after a disaster had occurred. This was to be a recurring pattern in American urban history. Destructive or disruptive events usually provoked some civic reform, but then the concern would dwindle to apathy until another disaster struck and galvanized a new spirit of action. After the first of the "great" fires struck Boston in 1653, public alarm prompted the first urban fire code in colonial America. The measure required every householder to keep a ladder, at his own expense, to facilitate fire fighting. The town also bought ladders and hooks, and officials assumed the authority to order the leveling of any burning structure. Few other precautions were taken until 1676 when another conflagration threatened to destroy all of Boston. After it was extinguished, the town bought a fire engine from England and appointed a supervisor and twelve assistants to operate it. Even these measures were not enough, for in 1679 one of the worst fires in American history swept Boston, ravaging most of the commercial section. This disaster forced officials to tighten the fire regulations and to organize the city into districts for more efficient fire control. Other towns acted similarly to meet the threat of fire, but because Boston had so many destructive fires, reactions there resulted in regulations and equipment among the most advanced in the world.

The problem of protection was another issue confronting the young cities. The wealth of people clustered in one relatively compact place naturally attracted criminal elements. Moreover, because the cities were commercial centers, they were frequented by seamen, transient laborers, pirates, and others prone to violence and disorder. Urban life necessitated some kind of agency to preserve the peace and protect property. Private citizens initially organized volunteer patrols, until most police forces copied the European system of daytime constables and night watches appointed daily and paid by the public. As James Richardson noted for New York, "The quantity and quality of (the) watch varied considerably over the years depending upon whether the citizens' fear for their saftey or reluctance to pay taxes was greater." Although duties differed from town to town, they consisted mainly of apprehending criminals, maintaining order—especially controlling brawlers and drunks—and watching for fires.

Constable and watch duty, required of every citizen, proved to be a thankless and dangerous job, and as time passed increasing numbers of townsmen tried to evade service. The wealthy could hire a substitute or pay the fine for not serving; thus, most early police were comprised of laborers, tradesmen, and artisans who could least afford to contribute time from their daily livelihoods. Since Americans mistrusted arbitrary authority and were becoming increasingly wary of anything that resembled a standing army, they were not willing to create a permanent, professional police force. By the middle of the eighteenth century the average city dweller faced rising danger to person and property from street riots, drunken brawls, and petty thievery, but he or she did not yet perceive the situation as a significant threat. Commitment to a formal agency of law enforcement remained unformed. Although crime in the colonial towns seems to have been less severe than in English cities and on the Continent, the failure to establish a discipline and institution of urban order has haunted American cities to the present.

Notions of public health in the seventeenth and eighteenth centuries were probably more primitive than those of fire and police protection. The germ theory of disease had not yet been established; most people believed noxious vapors from stagnant water and decaying material caused sickness. Nevertheless, regulations that attempted to eliminate these vapors by controlling garbage disposal—at first left to hogs that roamed the streets — and prohibiting pollution of streams and ponds removed some of the breeding places of disease-carrying pests. Local laws were enacted prohibiting citizens from dumping refuse and filth in certain public places, and men were hired to carry away trash and human waste. Most cities eventually passed measures that regulated the location and depth of privies and graves and confined tanneries and slaughterhouses to one part of town. In each instance measures to control the disposal of waste were enacted with little, if any, objection to the use of public power.

Town dwellers feared infectious diseases as much as fires, and once an epidemic began it was hard to stop. All the colonial cities, except Charleston, were located away from the climate and diseases of the tropics, but all were seaports and therefore vulnerable to epidemics brought in by infected seamen, vermin, and insects. Smallpox was the most frequent and dreaded danger, threatening every city. Boston and Charleston suffered most severely, experiencing epidemics which killed hundreds at a time. But as with fire, misfortune helped to create progressive policy, for by the 1760s Americans were beginning to accept inoculation as the best preventive measures. Fever, dysentery, and other diseases were also prevalent, and the cities combatted them by requiring inspections of entering ships and refusing landing to those on which sickness was found. Boston was the first city to establish quarantine regulations, and by the early 1700s most other cities had followed its lead. In spite of limited medical knowledge, by 1770 city officials had succeeded remarkably well in controlling most major scourges except yellow fever, which remained to plague eastern and southern cities until the twentieth century.

Another problem of urban growth was the large number of indigent residents whose care became a major responsibility of each city. Poverty has never been a problem peculiar to cities, but it has taken on new meaning in the urban context. As towns grew, their increasing economic complexity brought uncertainty—good and bad times, high and low wages, periodic unemployment. A drop in business could crush those on the lower economic rungs with particular force. In the cities, where populations concentrated more densely than in the country, the poor became a more visible element, a threat to established society. But cities also had the resources, both human and material, to relieve—or to control—the poor.

The colonists brought with them the seventeenth-century English notion of public responsibility for the support of dependent classes; thus poor relief accounted for a good proportion of local taxes. Public expenditures for the poor in Boston rose from £500 in 1700 to £4,000 in 1736 and in New York from £250 in 1698 to £5,000 in the 1770s. Most assistance was given in the form of outdoor relief—money, food, clothing, and fuel granted to dependents to be used in their own homes. Many cities, however, also constructed almshouses or poorhouses which provided food and shelter in return for some kind of labor. These institutions also housed the sick poor who could not work and the "Vagrant & Idle Persons" who would not work and were therefore classed as criminals. Some officials stigmatized those on relief by requiring them to wear or carry badges designating their status as paupers. Another form of relief consisted of assigning (binding out) the needy to private businesses in a form of indentured servitude. Finally many cities tried to minimize pauperism—as well as their taxes for poor relief—by restricting immigration. Philadelphia, New York, and nearly all the New England towns had provisions requiring the registration, bonding, or inspection of all newcomers. Those who had no friends or relatives to vouch for them or who lacked visible means of support were ordered away. As the cities grew in size, however, so did the need for laborers and the opportunity for anonymity. By the early 1700s the immigration restrictions were breaking down, and many places were openly encouraging immigration.

Public relief efforts were increasingly supplemented by those of private agencies. Organizations such as the Scots Charitable Society in Boston and New York, the Carpenters' Company in Philadelphia, and the Fellowship Society in Charleston, plus churches and wealthy individuals, all made substantial contributions to alleviate poverty. Still, as time passed, population growth and the disruptions of the colonial wars continued to produce larger numbers of urban poor. The proportion of a city's population assisted by public or private money at any one time is difficult to discern; but it seems certain that for every relief recipient, several more lived at the subsistence level and received no aid and that poverty plagued American cities from the very beginning.

The attempts by the colonial cities to solve their problems highlight a curious, but also typical, intertwining of private interest and public welfare. On the one hand, the problems were common to all cities; they were predicaments of urban life, of many people living close together, and they required community regulation of formerly private activities. As one historian has written, "In the country a man might construct his home, build his fire, dig his well, erect his privy, and dispose of his rubbish without thought for the well-being of his neighbors, but in town these became objects of community concern and gradually of civic ordinance. In the country a man might be little affected by the poverty or wrong-doing of others, but the towns soon discovered their civic duty in the combatting and control of these social evils." Many of the problems of health, fire, water, and communications were insoluble at the time, and colonial urban dwellers simply tried collectively to minimize them and then to adjust as technological and scientific developments offered better means of solution. Social problems like disorder and poverty remained ever-baffling.

On the other hand, although people were tied together by a sense of community which usually linked private interests to public welfare, the knot could easily unravel under the strains of growth and diversity. Economic self-interest could allow Americans to avoid and oppose community obligations just as it could make them evade and condemn British mercantilist regulations. Thus they could refuse public duties—in

1743 twelve of seventeen "gentlemen" chosen for the Boston constabulary would not serve—, resist taxes for projects, such as paving, that did not benefit them directly, and tolerate the persistence of poverty. Nevertheless, the occasions during which the incompatibility between public and private interest became pronounced seem to have been relatively infrequent. A kind of public unity plus an inheritance of a European tradition of public endeavor enabled colonial cities to meet their problems and to set precedents for future urban generations.

THE SOCIAL MOSAIC

By the end of the seventeenth century the towns of colonial America were not only experiencing similar problems, but they also were developing similar social mosaics that set them apart from the surrounding countryside. Racial, cultural, and religious diversity jumbled urban society while economic distinctions sliced through it. With the exception of the New England towns immigration restriction seldom worked; the English composition of most cities was quickly diluted by other groups. By the early 1700s blacks were almost as numerous as whites in Charleston, and there were substantial numbers of blacks in cities all the way up the coast to Boston. Scotch-Irish and Germans comprised important segments of the populations of Philadelphia and New York where they met the growing need for laborers, but they also raised fears among some English residents. In addition to a greater social variety than could be found in rural areas, the cities also contained more institutions for the entertainment, edification, and refreshment of their residents. Moreover, increasing populations provided the cities with human and economic resources for the creation of educational facilities and information dissemination from the outside world.

Most colonists migrated or descended from European society where a definite hierarchy of status prevailed, and they accepted the existence of social distinctions in America. In fact, in New England a stratified society was justified as sanctioned by God. From the beginning an ordered social structure crystalized in the cities and in the rural settlements. Yet the structure operated differently in the cities than in the country. In the towns social diversity and economic expansion stretched the order so that the gaps between ranks widened over time; but this process also created a fluidity within the system which enabled people to move downward and, particularly, upward more readily than in most rural areas.

Although the lines between groups were often blurred, colonial urban society consisted of four principal status groups. In the top rank were the wealthy merchants and investors, plus an occasional clergyman or government official. These generally were the men who had collected wealth from overseas and inland commerce or had accumulated enough capital to use in lucrative money-lending or land rental businesses. In Charleston this group also included large planters who kept homes in the city. These men controlled most of the local wealth (property) and filled the higher positions in local government. As time passed they seem to have pulled farther away from those in the lower ranks by procuring proportionately more of the wealth. According to James Henretta, in 1687 the wealthiest 15 percent of Boston's population controlled 52 percent of the taxable wealth; by 1771 the top 15 percent owned two-thirds and just 5 percent owned 44 percent. In the latter year the wealthiest 10 percent in Philadelphia are believed to have owned an even larger proportion than their counterparts in Boston. Nevertheless, in Boston and Philadelphia, as well as in other cities, this upper order was neither a closed aristocracy nor a monolithic social class. Its membership was both large and diverse, including men who had advantages of birth and position as well as those who had emigrated from abroad or had risen from a lower rank. Throughout the colonial period wealth, more than birth, was the principle criterion for admission to this upper group.

Although the wealthy capitalists wielded considerable power, the life patterns of the lower ranks more typically described the nature of colonial urban life. Beneath the merchants and their allies was a large, fluctuating population of craftsmen, retailers, minor jobbers, and innkeepers that comprised the middle class. These groups carried on local manufacturing and merchandising in the preindustrial city, running the one-man shops that predominated in every town, often aided by an apprentice, indentured servant, or wife. Shopkeepers and craftsmen generally lived and worked in the same house. Their standard of living varied widely, but most were able to exist in relative comfort and to afford occasional luxuries. In every city the average artisan or shopkeeper usually owned enough property to vote and often filled a minor political office.

The expansiveness of the economy and the opportunity to rise socially through the acquisition of wealth attuned colonial urban society to bourgeois standards, but they also made the middle class vulnerable to dislocation resulting from rapid change. The middle class's position on the social scale rose and fell over time, depending on economic developments. As James Henretta has suggested for Boston, the early years of urban growth offered lucrative opportunities for small-scale investors and entrepreneurs. As the city grew, so did the size and specialization of its economic operations. By the middle of the eighteenth century economies of scale had set in and had squeezed small investors out of the high-return areas, such as commercial shipping. Between 1687 and 1771 the proportion of taxable wealth owned by Boston's middle class declined from 22 percent to 12.5 percent, while the percentage owned by the upper segment rose. Although Boston suffered an economic unsteadiness from the 1740s onward that did not affect other colonial cities as severely, the evidence indicates that the fortunes of urban middle-class groups in most cities became restricted until westward expansion and the dawn of industrialization in the early 1800s opened new avenues for advancement.

The third economic group consisted of a growing number of unskilled laborers, mariners, and some artisans. These people owned little or no property. Many were transients, earning a living on the docks and at sea or moving from town to town in search of work. They often lived at bare levels of subsistence, but in labor-scarce cities some could command high wages and acquire property. Geographical mobility and chances for improvement precluded the development of a permanent proletariat in the colonial cities. The entrance to any craft remained open, and local restrictions on newcomers failed to prevent lower-class families from migrating. Still the cities housed much higher proportions of poor and propertyless people than did the rural areas. By the close of the colonial period the poor comprised from 20 to 30 percent of many a city's population—though their numbers were somewhat smaller in southern towns where large numbers of slaves reduced the proportions of white laborers. The fortunes of the urban lower classes were especially sensitive to economic fluctuations. If the local economy was expanding, they could subsist and even improve their lot. But when periods of uncertainty and decline brought sacrifice and deprivation to the middle and upper classes, the lower classes suffered real struggles for survival.

The situation of a rising standard of living and mobility up and down the social scale, however limited, applied to about four-fifths of the colonial urban dwellers—a sizable majority. But the remainder, consisting of Negroes and Indians, slave and free, formed a permanent, inescapable lowest class. Indian slaves could be found in several northern towns, but blacks were more common everywhere, except Philadelphia where Quaker precepts repudiated slavery. In Charleston, Baltimore, New York, and Boston, blacks did much of the heavy manual work and provided most of the domestic servants. A few managed to enter skilled occupations, such as the construction trades, but even in skilled work free blacks earned less than whites. Slaves, whose owners hired them out, had to return all or most of their earnings to their masters. Urban life, with its varied activities and social contacts, was less regimented for a slave than servitude in the country, but it remained restrictive. By the early 1700s most towns had passed a number of ordinances, such as curfews and prohibitions on certain purchases, limiting the private activities of all blacks, slave and free. Even in northern cities white society manifested the same racist anxiety that would continue to haunt the South one hundred years later. In New York in 1712 and in 1741 rumors and acts of black insurgency provoked whites to react with vengeful terror. In both instances over a score of slaves were executed.

Thus colonial urban society may be paradoxically characterized as fluid and open while maintaining stratification and features of a caste system. The openness resulted from two kinds of mobility, vertical and horizontal. As Jackson Turner Main has indicated, except for the frontier where cheap land still remained, the chances for economic mobility in the towns were greater than in the country. The majority of urban dwellers, even some of the lower classes, were able to buy a little property and could live in relative comfort. Debt, which was very common, often clouded a family's prospects, but the evidence suggests that debts rarely became overly burdensome. Although the cities contained more indigents than the rural areas, and the urban middle classes found it more difficult to break into the upper class in some cities during the latter colonial years, status in urban society was based on talent and wealth; no social or legal impediments restricted opportunities to acquire both requisites. Thus many a man could live at a higher position than that of his father.

Second, an individual or family that was dissatisfied in one place could always pack up and move elsewhere. Colonial urban society was in constant flux as steady streams of people moved in and out. Migration, rather than natural increase (excess of births over deaths), accounted for most of the population growth in the towns, and the vast majority of the in-migrants had traveled relatively short distances. As early as the 1640s most of Boston's population increase consisted of immigrants from the surrounding towns and country, often people without land seeking a chance for improvement in the city. The attraction of cities remained strong throughout the colonial era for people from nearby districts and abroad. There were also large numbers flowing out from the cities. These included the "floating proletariat," unskilled workers who drifted from place to place without improving their condition, and laborers, artisans, and others who both moved and improved by entering a craft or opening a shop.

An equally important, but neglected, consequence of geographical mobility was an improvement in quality of life, a type of upward mobility not always related to acquisition of a better job or increased property holdings. A change in a family's residence often involved a shift to a better home. To be sure, most colonial houses were small, poorly lit, and poorly heated. People often ate, relaxed, and slept in the same room. By moving, families could obtain more living space, a larger fireplace, and sounder construction.

These opportunities could be found in the cities, but although most residents had access to them, an important segment of the population did not. Men and women lacking white skins were relegated to the "permanent proletariat" and given no chance to rise. Their status as bondsmen bridled them legally, but white society's prejudice and fear imposed equally strict constraints on their behavior and life chances. Thus blacks and Indians, free as well as slave, occupied the lowest rung in a permanent caste.

Significantly, the position of women in colonial urban society was anomalous when compared with male groups. Although their roles and work took them more frequently beyond the limits of household chores than would be the case in later years, their functions remained circumscribed. This apparent paradox resulted from divergent effects of necessity, tradition, and the urban economy.

On the one hand, women, particularly those of the emerging middle class, participated in a wide variety of activities. As Elizabeth Dexter has suggested, in an economy where most businesses and crafts were located at home, many women probably aided their husbands in their work. In this way wives and mothers served as apprentices and became trained in a large number of fields. When their husbands died, they were prepared to carry on the business to support themselves. Every colonial city contained a large number of widows who, mostly out of necessity, operated taverns, inns, specialty shops, groceries, and bookstores. Usually these women assumed their business from a deceased husband, but occasionally they opened a shop of their own. Women also became prominent in several trades such as millinery, laundering, and soap and candle making. Printing had an important female component, which included Ann Franklin in Newport, Margaret Draper in Boston, Cornelia Bradford and Ann Zenger in New York, and Sarah Goddard in Providence. Women (wives, as well as widows and spinsters) also made important contributions to education, particularly in the common schools, as schoolmistresses and to obstetrics as midwives and wet nurses. Urban society placed no social stigma upon a woman forced to support herself and her family. Unlike British women, American women could buy, sell, sue, be sued, act as administrators and executors, and have power of attorney.

Yet the participation of women in the urban economy was only an extension of their domestic duties rather than a manifestation of economic and social independence. With few exceptions most women who worked in business did so only to help their husbands and sons or because as widows or spinsters necessity forced them. Their basic function remained the nurture of the family, even though the physical limits of domestic activities reached beyond the household. The colonials adopted European assumptions of the inferiority and subordination of woman. American women were excluded from politics and higher education and defined in terms of the men in their lives—as wives and daughters, not as individuals. Moreover, by the Revolution several factors constricted women's roles in the larger society. Urban capitalism and commercial agriculture created a male-dominated elite that reinforced the traditional "division of spheres" between sexes. Women's functions began to be considered as enhancing rather than sustaining, ornamental rather than complementary. The ideal woman (or "lady") was to possess humility, gentility, and piety, for these qualities would enable her to impress her husband's associates favorably and to raise her children properly. The adoption of this ideal by the upper classes plus the beginning separation of work from domicile in the cities were preparatory to the celebration of woman's "place" in the home that was to pervade nineteenth-century America.

The varied nature of the colonial urban populations fostered new social institutions and modified old ones. An institution that particularly felt the impact of urbanization was the church. The initial period of growth of American towns was one in which religion pervaded every aspect of human life. Churches influenced political and economic affairs and absorbed social life as well. Whether in the Puritan North, the Anglican South, or the more divided middle colonies, the clergy were held in high esteem and exerted power over family life, education, and government. Religion defined and enforced social discipline.

As time passed two developments peculiar to urban growth threatened the supremacy of organized religion in the colonial cities. First, population growth and diversity spurred the multiplication of rival sects that broke down religious unity. Baptists, Presbyterians, and Anglicans contested Quaker preeminence in Philadelphia and Congregational hegemony in the New England cities. Particularly in New England, ministers could no longer command communal deference, since many families imitated the British aristocracy and joined the Church of England. Second, cosmopolitanism and economic opportunity provided townsmen with several alternatives to church attendance. Secular activities and amusements increasingly lured people away from the church and provoked Cotton Mather to lament with characteristic alarm "the peculiar Spirit and Error of the Time to be *Indifference* to *Religion.*" Thus although church membership grew absolutely in nearly every city, it rose at a relatively slow rate, continually widening the gap between a town's total population and its total church members.

A Colonial Tavern

This trade card advertises the reopening of a prominent tavern in Newburyport, Massachusetts. Such establishments performed vital, but often overlooked, functions for colonial urban dwellers. *Courtesy of The American Antiquarian Society.*

One institution that competed with the church was the tavern. Open to all men, these public houses were the most egalitarian of all colonial establishments. All classes came here to drink, eat, talk, and hear the news of the day. But the taverns served more than mere social functions; they provided centers for the discussion of politics, transaction of business, distribution of broadsides and pamphlets, and delivery of mail from visiting ships. As the number of establishments multiplied and members of various social groups began seeking out people of their own sort, many taverns acquired a reputation for catering to one class or another; but in most cities formal distinctions between places did not exist. Of course the services provided were open only to men; it was highly improper for a respectable woman to be seen tipping a glass of grog. Malt could justify God's ways to man, but woman had to look elsewhere.

By the end of the seventeenth century taverns and groggeries had become the most flourishing centers of urban life. However, their informality and profusion of rum and other alcoholic beverages also made them natural locations for disorder and vice. In response to rising complaints most towns attempted to exert control by adopting the English policy of licensing establishments. This did not diminish the number of public houses—by the 1720s there were over a hundred licensed taverns in Boston, and in the peak year of 1752 New York authorities issued 334 licenses—but it did give the town governments some measure of control, although licensing resulted in the rise of many illicit "speak-easies." Coffee houses and inns also became important centers for social, political, and commercial activity. In New York, for example, the Tontine Coffee House served as the merchant's exchange, and the Exchange Coffee House was the clearing house for many real estate transfers.

In addition to all of the activities of the public houses, the cities offered the vast majority of the educational and cultural opportunities. Following the lead of Boston, every city had a commitment to the support of some type of public school by the 1720s, and they all could boast several private schools for the wealthy as well as religious and charity schools for the poor. Even Indians and blacks could obtain learning, however limited, from English missionary efforts like those of the Anglican-based Society for the Propagation of the Gospel in Foreign Parts. At the same time, scores of bookstores appeared in the larger cities, and the colonial bookseller became instrumental in the spread of literary culture. Private libraries could be found in the towns and country; but cities, notably Boston and Philadelphia, pioneered the establishment of public libraries. Not only did the cities house and distribute written works, but they also printed them. By 1700 Boston, Philadelphia, and New York had print shops which were producing secular and religious prose and poetry books and pamphlets. More important, the printers supplied almanacs, blank forms, and newspapers, all vital to urban functions. And because the cities housed almost all of the museums, scientific associations, concerts, theaters, and artists, they dominated science and the arts as well as literary production. John Smibert, the noted eighteenth-century American portrait painter, worked in Newport and Boston; plays and dance exhibitions were particularly popular in New York and Charleston; and writers from all five colonial cities contributed scientific papers to the *Philosophical Transactions* of the Royal Society.

CITIES IN THE AMERICAN REVOLUTION

While colonial cities were generating common internal problems and complex social structures, they remained appendages of the British empire, founded and governed as cogs in a larger administrative and economic network. For over a century American urban dwellers lived outwardly at peace with the Mother Country, but beneath the relatively calm surface two forces, involving a type of self-interest, were gnawing away at the foundations of British mercantile control. First, in order to meet immediate problems of organization and services, the colonial towns had developed their own institutions that exercised considerable authority over local ordinances, taxes and finances because the Crown and Parliament were uninterested or unable to devote attention to every detail of management. This situation was particularly true in Boston where the town meeting influenced so many local matters, but also every one of the dozen or so other towns had achieved some degree of governmental independence by 1750 that they jealously protected. Second, colonial merchants had managed to coexist with the restrictive Navigation Acts by arranging with sympathetic customs collectors to pay only a fraction of the required duties or by evading the law altogether and engaging in illicit trade. Thus much of the trading community acquired and expected profits outside of the mercantilist system. Perhaps more important, many colonial townsmen translated their self-government and commercial independence into an ideology that enabled them to view their situation as the most natural and just and to consider any interference with their system illegal and tyrannical.

The Peace of Paris, ending the French and Indian (Seven Years') War in 1763, signaled a new era during which new British policies agitated these forces and converted them into the sparks for American independence. At the end of the war Great Britain faced the tasks of organizing her newly enlarged empire abroad and relieving economic pressure at home caused by soaring costs of colonial defense and administration. Thus in 1764 Parliament, under the leadership of George Grenville, passed the Molasses Act, attempting for the first time to raise revenue in America. This measure clamped down on smuggling and provided for stricter enforcement of a new, though reduced, molasses duty. Since 1733, the duty had been 6d per gallon; now it was to be 3d. The Stamp Act followed in 1765, the first direct internal tax ever to be laid on the colonies. It required revenue stamps, costing from a half-penny to upwards of twenty shillings, to be attached to all newspapers, almanacs, broadsides, pamphlets, advertisements, licenses, commercial notes, bonds, leases, and numerous other legal documents and commercial papers.

These acts hit cities hardest, directly affecting merchants, lawyers, and printers and indirectly affecting artisans, shopkeepers, tradesmen, and laborers. The repeal of the Stamp Act in 1766 did not lighten the burden, for in 1767 Parliament passed the Townshend Acts, adding import duties to glass, lead, paper, paint, and tea.

It is not surprising, then, that cities provided the arenas for much of the resistance to new British policies. The earliest and most organized activity came from the merchants. For them the Peace of Paris brought not only restrictive legislation but also the demise of wartime prosperity that had been largely derived from trade with England's enemies. The merchant's first reaction was to try to recapture evaporating profits by encouraging more inter- and intra-colonial trade. In April, 1764, some Boston merchants organized the Society for Encouraging Trade and Commerce Within the Province of Massachusetts Bay, and in the following months New York and Philadelphia merchants formed similar associations. The same year several prominent New Yorkers founded the Society for the Promotion of Arts, Agriculture, and Oeconomy to encourage more local manufacturing to offset the Navigation Acts and high price of imported goods. Leaders of other cities also followed this example. None of the efforts worked; they failed to change not only Parliament's policies but also the skewed balance of trade that drained the colonies of hard money, the only medium accepted by Royal tax collectors and London creditors. Therefore in 1765 merchants, particularly in the northern cities, adopted new tactics—boycott and nonimportation of British goods—and they formed associations to petition Parliament and the Crown for relief, to enforce nonimportation agreements, and to communicate ideas and activities to other colonies. It was this community of interests, activated in the 1760s but dating back to the seventeenth century, that coordinated resistance against the British and tied the first knots of American union.

These early protest activities were basically conservative. They included no notions of American independence. The merchants mainly wished to revive the conditions that had existed before 1763 and that had brought prosperity to traders in every city except Boston (see below). To be sure, the merchant community was not united; there were some, such as Thomas Hutchinson and Andrew Oliver of Boston, who aspired to the British aristocracy and who favored more, rather than less, British presence in America. Many merchants, however, had won wealth and position from smuggling and other types of illicit trade, certainly without any help from the Mother Country; and they cared little about the English social hierarchy. In fact as their protest to the economic restrictions mounted, they became increasingly antimonarchical. Still, until the 1770s most merchants were concerned for more about profits than independence.

The advent of hard times, high prices, and scarce money also aroused artisans, shopkeepers, and smaller merchants. These groups encountered the additional challenge of upper-class resistance to their ambitions of entering local power structures. Nevertheless, most craftsmen qualified for the franchise, and by using leverage at the polls, they wedged their way into both legal and extralegal agencies. By the 1770s they were filling half or more of the vacancies in local offices in Philadelphia, and in 1769 they assumed one-third of the positions on a Charleston Committee of Enforcement of a boycott against the Townshend Acts. Relations between merchants and skilled workers were often acrimonious; but in the end both sought to advance their own self-interests while preserving the existing social and (pre-1763) economic system, and both sought to achieve the same objective—relief from British oppression.

But in addition to the merchants and middle classes there existed another disaffected group, more numerous and perhaps more resolute, with its own grievances and its own brand of resistance. This was the urban lower class—people whose station in the social structure had accustomed them to disorder, not only as a means of letting off steam but also as a vehicle of political expression. The economic sag of the 1760s fell upon this group by bringing on high prices and unemployment. Thousands who had lived at or near the subsistence level faced real calamity. Jobs were even more scarce in cities such as New York and, later, Boston where British troops were stationed, for many soldiers bolstered their meager pay by underbidding local laborers for menial employment. Moreover, the British navy continued to find recruits by impressing American seamen and laborers, arbitrarily carrying off any able-bodied breadwinner, and angering and frightening whole communities. Jesse Lemisch has estimated that one night in 1757 a British gang operating in New York pressed some eight hundred men, about one-fourth of the city's adult male population. Several hundred men were subsequently released, but the scope of the raid reveals the impact that mass impressment could have on a city.

The lower classes had good reason to react against the British, and they did so with the one method they knew best—violence. Naval officers and their press gangs were threatened and attacked; customs collectors were manhandled and intimidated. Occasionally incidents grew into full-scale riots, such as the three-day uprising over impressment in Boston in 1747 or the clash between New Yorkers and British soldiers in the 1770 Liberty Hill Riot. Violence, much of it irrational and leaderless, had always been a part of lower class life, but by the mid-eighteenth century it had become increasingly a method of political protest against what many thought to be unjust conditions. And, as Gordon Wood has theorized, this violence was minimized not by its own restraint but rather by its success in intimidating the British so that they were reluctant to respond with force that would have provoked greater fury among the Americans.

One city—Boston—epitomized all the elements that were pulling the American colonies away from the Mother Country. Boston, alone among American cities, did not experience economic and population growth after 1740. Not only did Philadelphia and New York undercut Boston's commercial dominance, but also nearby rivals such as Providence, Portland, Salem, Gloucester, and Lynn raided her regional hinterland, already too small to support the magnitude of interior trade which blessed cities to the south. Boston's early progressivism now became a liability as expenses and taxes soared to care for mounting numbers of poor and to fulfill heavy commitments to municipal improvements. While costs rose and opportunities diminished, the city lost its attractiveness; and its population declined from 16,382 in 1743 to 15,631 in 1760. The economic maladies that brought discomfort to other cities in the 1760s only aggravated existing sores in Boston.

Friction between Bostonians and British authorities dated back to 1689 when a number of townsmen, including several prominent leaders, had actively resisted the usurpation of local prerogatives by Governor Edmund Andros. Over the years other clashes had occurred so that by 1765 the city had a reputation for direct action. That year frustration over the Stamp Tax culminated one August night when a mob invaded, looted, and damaged the homes of several government officials, including that of Lieutenant Governor Hutchinson. Similar protests occurred in other cities, but after the repeal of the Townshend Acts in 1768 the violence receded except in Boston. There the activities of the Sons of Liberty, particularly the harassment of customs officials, provoked the British into sending two regiments of troops. The presence of troops only deepened anxiety on both sides, and the tension burst on the night of March 5, 1770, when a line of soldiers fired into a jeering crowd in front of the Customs House, killing five and injuring six. Radicals like Sam Adams were quick to capitalize on this, the "Boston Massacre," by spreading word of all (and some extra) gory details throughout the colony and down the Atlantic Coast. Although not the first clash between troops and colonists, the Boston Massacre not only deepened anger and resentment in Boston but also raised fears in other cities that they next would bear the brunt of British brutality.

But it was Boston that became the center of action three years later in a confrontation over the Tea Act in which Parliament had granted a

virtual monopoly of the American tea trade to the British West India
Company. When the first ship carrying tea arrived at Boston Harbor in
December 1773, Sam Adams and his associates summoned an extralegal
mass meeting,—whose results are well known—the Boston Tea Party. As
the meeting adjourned on the night of December 16, a number of men
wearing Indian costumes boarded the ship and dumped its tea into the
bay. The reaction of the British to this threat to imperial authority was
an important catalyst in changing colonial resistance into rebellion. In
response to the tea party, Parliament closed the Boston port and asserted
its colonial prerogatives in a series of four "coercive" acts that limited
town meetings and elections in all Massachusetts, provided for the quar-
tering of troops in the colony's towns, removed the prerogative of the
towns to try British officials accused of crimes in America, and organized
a provincial government in Quebec without a representative legislature.

Only the Port Act punished Boston directly; the other measures reinforced the power of Parliament and the Crown along a broader spectrum.
But they all struck at the two most cherished urban life functions: self-
government and commerce. By choking off the city's economic blood-
stream and its organs of self-government, Parliament not only deepened
desperation in Boston, but also threatened the other cities. Bostonians
now faced certain ruin of the remainder of their commerce because the
closing of the port cut them off from the sea. Their town meetings and
local elections had been reduced to meaningless exercises. All their
attempts at reform and redress had failed. As G. B. Warden has observed, Sam Adams now "had little trouble in persuading his neighbors
and countrymen that England was 'making war' against every colonial
right and destroying every traditional means of security and self-
preservation." It was not difficult to raise fear that if the British could
tether the freedoms of Massachusetts colony and Boston, they could do
the same to other colonies and cities. When Adams and the Committee of
Correspondence sent an appeal to Philadelphia and New York asking all
Americans to join a boycott of all trade with Great Britain, New York
merchants responded by organizing the Continental Congress, which not
only conceived American independence but also nurtured American
union. Surely, to quote Richard C. Wade, "in this perspective, the American Revolution began on the cobblestones of Boston rather than on the
rolling greens of Lexington."

The predicaments of cities did not alone cause the American Revolution; the final break with England resulted from a number of forces that
had merged together at various moments in history. Yet cities were instrumental in the timing and the organization of the Revolution not only
because they bore the weight of British policy, but also because they
possessed the facilities and human resources to implement first resistance

and then rebellion. Their meeting houses provided forums for debate and protest, their printing shops helped spread news and propaganda, and their taverns and coffeehouses furnished workshops where logistics were planned.

Moreover, the separation of the thirteen colonies from Great Britain mirrored a process which had been occurring in the dozen or so American cities for nearly one hundred years. The residents of each town had developed a sense of community identification similar to that of traditional societies—an allegiance to a particular place where collective progress also meant individual enrichment. Motivated by public- and self-interest, merchants and mechanics could urge resistance to new British taxes. At the same time the urban dwellers had adopted ideals of the Enlightenment—a belief in the freedom and perfectability of man and a desire to shape their own destinies. By the 1770s commonality of interests and grievances, aided by increased intercolonial communication, had spread these concepts of community and the Enlightenment beyond individual cities to encompass all the colonies. Thus cities, with their characteristics of collectivism, opportunity, and diversity, not only kindled, but fed, the flames of American independence.

BIBLIOGRAPHY

The work of Carl Bridenbaugh, particularly *Cities in the Wilderness: Urban Life in America, 1625–1724* (New York: The Ronald Press, 1938) and *Cities in Revolt: Urban Life in America, 1743–1776* (New York: Capricorn Books, 1955), remains the most comprehensive, detailed analysis of colonial urban America, and it has contributed heavily to this chapter. Bridenbaugh's studies have been supplemented and extended by a number of recent books and articles. The city of Boston has received particular attention. Darret Rutman's *Winthrop's Boston: A Portrait of a Puritan Town, 1630–1649* (Chapel Hill: University of North Carolina Press, 1965) and G. B. Warden's *Boston: 1689–1776* (Boston: Little Brown, 1970) are among the more prominent books on the city's early social and political history. Aspects of colonial New York are included in Raymond A. Mohl, "Poverty in Early America, A Reappraisal: The Case of Eighteenth Century New York City," *New York History,* 50 (January 1969), 5–28, and James Richardson, *The New York Police, Colonial Times to 1901* (New York: Oxford University Press, 1970). Colonial and revolutionary social structure have been illuminated by Jackson Turner Main, *The Social Structure of Revolutionary America* (Princeton, N.J.: Princeton University Press, 1965); James Henretta, "Economic Development and Social Structure in Colonial Boston," *William and Mary Quarterly,* 22 (January 1965), 75–92; and Sam Bass Warner, Jr., *The Private City: Philadelphia in Three Periods of Its Growth* (Philadelphia: University of Pennsylvania Press, 1968), Part 1: "The Eighteenth Century Town." The situation of women in colonial urban America is best depicted by Elizabeth A. Dexter, *Colonial Women of Affairs: Women in Business and Professions in America before 1776* (Boston: Houghton Mifflin,

1931) and summarized in Gerda Lerner, "The Lady and the Mill Girl: Changes in the Status of Women in the Age of Jackson," *Mid-Continent American Studies Journal*, 10 (Spring 1969), 5–15.

Some books on the New England town, John Demos, *A Little Community: Family Life in Plymouth Colony* (New York: Oxford University Press, 1970); Philip T. Greven, Jr., *Four Generations: Population, Land, and Family in Colonial Andover, Massachusetts* (Ithaca, N.Y.: Cornell University Press, 1970); Kenneth A. Lockridge, *A New England Town: The First Hundred Years* (New York: Norton, 1970); and Michael Zuckerman, *Peaceable Kingdoms: New England Towns in the Eighteenth Century* (New York: Knopf, 1970) contain provocative implications for the urban context. Studies such as Jesse Lemisch, "Jack Tar in the Streets: Merchant Seamen in the Politics of Revolutionary America," *William and Mary Quarterly*, 25 (July 1968), 371–407; Charles S. Olton, "Philadelphia's Mechanics in the First Decade of the Revolution, 1765–1775," *Journal of American History*, 59 (September 1972), 311–26; and Pauline Maier, *From Resistance to Revolution: Colonial Radicalism and the Development of American Opposition to Britain, 1765–1776* (September 1972) provide analyses of urban middle- and lower-class activity in the years preceding the Revolution. See also Gordon S. Wood, "A Note on Mobs in the American Revolution," *William and Mary Quarterly*, 23 (October 1966), 635–42.

2

CITIES IN
THE NEW NATION

THE RISE OF A NATIONAL URBAN NETWORK

The process that generated urban growth continued long after the thirteen colonies merged into the American Union. Only now migration, economic change, and technological advance broadened the scale and quickened the pace. Whereas only five major and six or eight secondary cities constituted urban America in the colonial period, scores of towns sprouted and blossomed between the Revolution and the Civil War. When the first federal census was taken in 1790, there were only five cities with 10,000 or more inhabitants. In 1830 the number had risen to 23, and it had reached 101 by 1860. The number of people living in urban places mushroomed from 201,655 in 1790 to 6,216,518 in 1860. New cities filled much of our modern urban network, stretching from Buffalo to Seattle, from Mobile to San Francisco. By pulling the line of settlement across the continent, by steering the national economy, and by attracting the talent and leadership that tamed the West, these cities, like their predecessors on the Atlantic Coast, influenced the course of national development.

The established Eastern ports still dominated the urban scene as the young republic grappled with the problems of independence, although Baltimore superseded Newport as one of the top five cities. But in the 1780s new difficulties compounded those that had nagged urban dwellers since 1763. Merchants found themselves deprived of the economic advantages and protection they once had taken for granted as members of the British mercantile system. The middle and lower classes faced shortages of housing and consumer goods, accompanied by rises in prices, unemployment, and rents. During the winter of 1783–84 one-seventh of the population of Philadelphia received public charity. A genuine economic depression deepened the predicaments of all classes between 1785 and 1787. Since hard money and precious metals remained as scarce as before the Revolution, the states began to issue paper money of varying value. The lack of uniform standards of this paper money and its uncertain worth tangled commercial exchange. Additionally, contests over the content and quality of money in circulation occasionally sparked conflicts between capitalists who wanted a stable currency and debtors who wanted more paper money. The most acute struggle occurred in Massachusetts in 1786–87 where a band of interior farmers led by Daniel Shays disrupted county governments and threatened the General Assembly in Boston. They dispersed only after eastern merchants hired and armed a militia to hunt them down.

These conditions prompted many Americans to consider replacing the Articles of Confederation with a stronger central government. This is what the Constitutional Convention in Philadelphia in 1787 set out to do. Significantly, urban classes, intent upon protecting commerce and economic stability, played a leading role in the formation and adoption of the Constitution. Although only 5 percent of all Americans lived in cities, twenty of the fifty-five delegates to the Convention were urban dwellers; and another twenty, mostly lawyers and merchants, had urban contacts. When the Constitution was sent to the state ratifying conventions, urban interests in every state lined up on the side favoring adoption. Cities, towns, and their tributary regions in every state voted for delegates who supported the Constitution, while the areas dominated by small, subsistence farms chose delegates who opposed. In New Hampshire the seacoast and Connecticut River towns, commercially linked to Boston, helped swing the state in favor of ratification—and New Hampshire was the ninth and deciding state to accept the Constitution. New York City and its surrounding counties threatened to secede from the state if it did not ratify. Even in Virginia, the eastern tidewater regions, including Norfolk, were joined in support of ratification by areas of what became West Virginia that were developing commercial outlets to the Ohio River.

Economic and political conditions improved in the 1790s, and the urbanization of America began to gather momentum as the nineteenth century dawned. The promise of urban civilization was already appearing in towns along the Ohio Valley and surrounding Lake Erie, in the new national capital of Washington, D.C., and as far south and west as New Orleans, newly acquired with the Louisiana Purchase. The creation

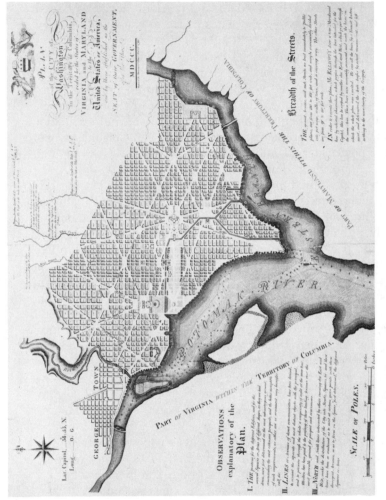

L'Enfant's Plan of Washington, D.C.

Most of this plan was incorporated into the actual construction of the capital. Note the imposition of wide, diagonal avenues on the gridiron layout. Although a few new towns adopted variations of this plan, most developers in the nineteenth century preferred a strict gridiron street system because it was easier to construct and made lot sizes more uniform. *The John Carter Brown Library, Brown University.*

and growth of cities were important, but it must be remembered that urbanization is an economic and social process that occurs in a society as a whole, not just in its cities. The existence of abundant open land in America enabled agricultural settlement to keep pace with the growth of urban populations. Until 1820 the nation's farm population grew at about the same rate as its city population, so that significant urbanization did not take place; although subsistence agriculture in this country seldom existed to the same extent as in Europe. Most American farmers sought commercial markets and thereby linked their interests to a major function of cities—the centralization and distribution of goods and services. Thus cities were salutary to inhabitants of surrounding hinterlands, as well as to their own residents. Not only were they the vanguards of the frontier, but cities also fostered economic expansion and commercialization of the nation's interior. They helped to weld local exchange into a national economy.

Nowhere is this influence more clearly shown than in the growth of western cities. As Richard C. Wade has demonstrated, Frederick Jackson Turner's depiction of a frontier (rural and sparsely-populated) edging ever westward was inaccurate. Instead cities accompanied and even preceded the frontier, acting as commercial outposts and depots from which settlement radiated. Along the Ohio and Mississippi river valleys the towns of Pittsburgh, Cincinnati, Louisville, Lexington, and St. Louis formed a new urban frontier, planted before the surrounding soil was broken for cultivation. Like their colonial predecessors, these cities were founded as commercial centers by commercial-minded men. Lexington alone was not located on a major waterway, and when the steamboat began chugging around inland rivers and lakes after 1815, Lexington failed to receive the benefits of increased trade and population. A generation later the process repeated itself in the Great Lakes region. Buffalo, Cleveland, Detroit, Chicago, and Milwaukee had emerged by 1840 as important western cities and had fostered settlement in the Old Northwest. As large-scale and mechanized production of finished goods began to permeate interior America, these cities developed industrial bases to complement their commercial functions. Pittsburgh produced glass, Louisville textiles, Cleveland iron products, and Chicago meat and agricultural implements. The South also had its own urban influence, although its major cities were located only around its perimeter. Baltimore, Charleston, Savannah, Mobile, New Orleans, Memphis, St. Louis, and Louisville ringed the South, and no comparable interior towns grew until after the Civil War. Still each city had a hinterland and commercial relations that stretched inward along the South's abundant navigable waterways.

This common pattern of commercial foundations and good transportation connections characterized city origins in the United States in the colonial era and the early nineteenth century. But in the latter period a new feature was added—land speculation. Although historians have directed much attention to the speculation in western farm land, they have often neglected the urban dimension of this activity. The nineteenth century witnessed a virtual mania of city building in this country, as enterprising (and often shifty) investors bought and plotted land for new towns and then sold it for hefty profit to other eager speculators who hoped their property would appreciate even more. It was this kind of expectation that produced spectacular land booms, such as the one in Chicago during the 1830s. Here a choice 80-by-100- foot lot that sold for $100 in 1832 brought $3,000 by 1834, soaring to $15,000 the following year. As one observer remarked, "Every man who owned a garden patch stood on his land and imagined himself a millionaire." But this kind of process could also have adverse affects. For every urban venture that succeeded, several did not. As early as the 1820s, according to Professor Wade, "the West was littered with ambitious towns that never grew." Some failed for lack of leadership, some for lack of money, some for excess of floodwaters. Many an optimistic urban speculator from the East came West holding a deed only to find his property in the midst of a mosquito-infested swamp. Still, both the successes and the failures reveal that western speculation was as much urban as rural.

The new cities of the West not only resembled those of the colonial era in origin and function, but they copied their approach to municipal organization as well. The cities of the Ohio Valley and the Great Lakes adopted the same collective approach to problems of streets, fire, health, markets, order, and buildings common in Boston, New York, Philadelphia, and Baltimore. The effort was conscious and even institutionalized. The government of Lexington sent a leading citizen to Philadelphia to inspect the street lighting system, and Pittsburgh sent a committee to Philadelphia, Baltimore, and New York on the same mission. The City Council of Cincinnati ordered its Board of Health to consult officials in Boston, New York, Philadelphia, and Baltimore for recommendations on construction of a sewer system. Charters of western towns intentionally included the same regulatory and taxing powers as those in the East.

The replication of these forms and functions, coupled with ties of commerce and culture, bound eastern and western cities into a national urban network where sectional differences were of little importance. Chicago, Baltimore, and Philadelphia resembled each other more closely than they resembled their surrounding countryside. But commonality of interest did not necessarily breed cooperation. Trade had accounted for the growth of almost all early American cities. Each successful urban center established an economic domain in its immediate vicinity in the first half of the nineteenth century, but commercial expansion was an ever-hungry process that pushed cities to reach out for more markets. Inevitably such forays led to collisions between cities that laid claims to overlapping hinterlands. The resulting rivalry, aptly dubbed "urban imperialism" by Professor Wade, would characterize an important dimension of urban interaction from the early 1800s to the present.

The urge for growth was connected with a concern for preservation, and the two made early nineteenth-century urbanization an aggressive, dynamic phenomenon. The belief was that a city had to keep growing in order to prevent economic stagnation. Increased immigration, markets, and transportation connections all fed upon each other to produce a "multiplier effect," an endless spiral that spun off greater and greater profits. In the 1820s, for example, the young towns of Cleveland and Sandusky vied for the northern terminus of a canal between the Ohio River and Lake Erie. Although Sandusky had more natural advantages, the Ohio legislature chose Cleveland, primarily because that city's businessmen were able to exercise more political leverage, within and beyond the bounds of fair play. This victory set in motion a chain reaction that accelerated the city's growth. The canal enabled Cleveland to attract more businesses, consequently providing employment opportunities and spurring population growth. Because of these factors, the city provided a natural transfer point when railroads began to crisscross the Midwest. New transportation links fostered *more* business, *more* population growth, *more* markets, and so on. Contests similar to the one between Cleveland and Sandusky were repeated hundreds of times in the West and South, as upstart towns fought for such prizes as the location of a county seat, railroad or canal terminus, college, or land office.

Eventually rivalries crossed political and geographical boundaries as larger cities clashed over hinterland markets. Here is where urban imperialism had national impact, for competing cities contributed to the construction of a national transportation network that rearranged axes of trade and politics. The construction of the Erie Canal, which linked the Hudson River to the Great Lakes, between 1817 and 1825 not only tied a large portion of the growing western markets to New York, but also provoked Philadelphia, Baltimore, and, to a lesser extent, Boston into constructing their own transportation lines into the West. The results included a maze of turnpikes, canals, and, ultimately, the Baltimore and Ohio and the Pennsylvania railroads. When Chicago businessmen obtained railroad connections to the region beyond the Mississippi River while their rivals in St. Louis remained committed to river transportation, a shift in the direction of western trade resulted. Instead of following water routes to St. Louis and then to the port of New Orleans, by the

1860s products of the West increasingly moved over rails to Chicago and from there often as far east as New York. The competition between larger cities did not leave any one contestant completely vanquished; nevertheless feelings of urgency and fears for survival enveloped every rivalry. As one Philadelphia businessman remarked when the state chose to construct a water and land transportation route between Philadelphia and Pittsburgh, the premium was on speed "before the commerce has acquired the correspondence and habitude that are so difficult to break."

Urban rivalry was one instance where public and private interests merged almost completely. The struggle for primacy created a local loyalty among businessmen and laborers alike and produced a personification of cities. A railroad or canal served not only the interests of residents in Baltimore, Philadelphia, or Chicago but also "Baltimore," "Philadelphia," and "Chicago" as entities themselves. Private capital was scarce, so that many projects were financed with state and local funds, making them genuinely public ventures. The public nature of urban conflict enabled residents of one city to relate personally to those of another. Thus an observer wrote in 1819, "I observed two ruling passions in Cincinnati, enmity against Pittsburgh and jealousy of Louisville"; and the Irish traveler Captain Marryat noted in 1838 the "great jealousy existing between the inhabitants of different cities" in America.

This kind of urban identification combined with the speculative nature of urban growth in the West to produce "boosterism," the optimistic —indeed pompous—promotion of a city in heroic language. The cities of the American West were new; they lacked anchors of identification, such as palaces, cathedrals, and monuments, that gave residents of European cities continuity with their past. Moreover, as Daniel Boorstin has observed, in mobile America the existence of a town "depended on the ability to attract free and vagrant people." Boosters solved the needs for identification and advertisement by means of rhetorical metaphor—they projected continuity from the present into the future and spoke of dreams as reality. It was this spirit that led a booster of St. Louis to predict that "we have but commenced to tell the wonders of a city destined in the future to equal London in its population, Athens in its philosophy, art, and culture, Rome in its hotels, cathedrals, and grandeur, and to be the central commercial metropolis of a continent." The boosters themselves were enthusiastic, enterprising community builders—men like Dr. Daniel Drake, whose writing and work brought fame to Cincinnati, and William B. Ogden, whose leadership and investments helped build Chicago from a village of a few thousand people when he arrived in 1835 to a metropolis of nearly half a million when he died in 1877.

Boosters were profit minded as well as public minded. Ogden's investments in land and railroads made him a multimillionaire, and Drake also planned and invested in railroads, as well as canals. But boosterism was more than greedy self-interest. It was a process by which businessmen hitched their private fortunes to the quick development of their city—the more the city grew, the better for individual profit making.

The consequences of this union were mixed. The premium on growth contributed to the unplanned expansion of American cities. Pressures for speed resulted in the hasty construction of railroads with little concern for future operability or safety. The bombast and fantasy of booster rhetoric could be used by con artists interested more in a fast buck than in city building. Yet boosterism did breed public spirit in some resourceful men and made them dynamic leaders as well as crafty businessmen. Ogden and Drake participated in practically every public enterprise undertaken by their respective cities—bridges, sewers, parks, hospitals, libraries, and medical colleges. They, and others like them, had faith in an urban future.

Boosterism was derived from the commercial expansion and urban land speculation that pervaded early nineteenth-century America. But beneath this surface bubbled the beginnings of industrialization that would later alter the country and its cities so drastically. Before the 1840s most manufacturing in American cities was confined to two types of products: (1) consumer items, such as refined sugar, leather goods, and distilled products, that merchants could exchange for meat, grain, and cotton in the West and South; (2) commerce-serving items, such as ships, sails, paper, and barrels. However, alongside some New England rivers and streams mechanized textile mills were beginning to establish genuine factory organization, and communities were emerging around them. Many of these mill towns in Connecticut, Massachusetts, and Rhode Island never grew beyond a few hundred people, most of them landless agrarians or families who split their time and personnel between millwork and farming. A few places did achieve more sizeable dimensions. Chicopee and Holyoke, both founded by an organization of investors called the Boston Associates, ranked among the larger factory towns. Even more well known was Francis Cabot Lowell's social and economic experiment at Lowell, Massachusetts, where he recruited New England farm girls to work and live in a tightly regulated—and paternalistic—mill community.

Until the Civil War, America's major cities remained primarily mercantile in function. But by the 1840s technological and economic changes were beginning to occur that launched the cities and the nation into an age of industrialization. For one thing regional railroad systems began to reach proportions that facilitated cheap and speedy delivery of raw materials and distribution of finished products. The 2,800 miles of rail track in 1840 grew into 30,600 miles by 1860, most of it linking urban centers. Expanded use of steam engines and replacement of wood fuels by coal enabled factories to locate inside larger cities and away from sources of water power. Production of interchangeable parts and development of the machine tool industry aided the creation of mechanized factory production. The onset of mass immigration from Europe provided a large labor pool supplying factory owners with unskilled, inexpensive workers. The immigrants and the imperialistic activities of commercial cities also helped increase the size and number of domestic markets. And lastly, the Jacksonian urge for opportunity and equality loosened traditional restraints on incorporation and popularized the formation of joint stock and limited liability corporations.

SERVICING THE CITY

Population increase and economic change heightened many of the old internal problems of American cities. Efforts to alleviate these pressures not only transformed cities themselves but swept urban dwellers into a whirlwind of complex social and political issues. Take, for example, the problem of securing adequate and pure water supplies. By the beginning of the nineteenth century, fear of fire and epidemics had induced city officials to think more seriously about providing water for their citizens. In the 1790s yellow fever ravaged the Northeast—striking Philadelphia particularly fiercely—and creating a passion for cleanliness in several cities as the only way to prevent or minimize disease. This need for sanitation meant a more liberal use of water. Most urbanites drew their water from public or private pumps, but springs that fed the wells simply could not supply tens of thousands of people and were often polluted with seepage from privies and graves. Attention focused on nearby rivers and streams as sources for larger, cleaner supplies of water. Who should undertake projects to tap these sources—the municipality or private corporations?

Under the pressures raised by yellow fever scourges, Philadelphia constructed the first major public waterworks in this country. In 1798 the City Council hired engineer and architect Benjamin Latrobe. He devised a system to pump water from the Schuylkill River to a high-ground reservoir called Centre Square, from where it could be pumped through wooden pipes to various parts of the city. Although it operated at a deficit—largely because people could not readily accept the idea of paying for water, and because the steam pumps often broke down—the Centre Square waterworks won national admiration. The system eventually accustomed Philadelphians to consider water as a public utility. When the city outgrew the system, it constructed a larger public waterworks in 1811, raising water from the Schuylkill to reservoirs atop Fair-mount Hill and distributing it through iron pipes.

But Philadelphia was the exception in these early years. Other large cities received water from private companies. The quality of service ranged from adequate in Baltimore, where the Baltimore Water Company was conscientious about its function, to intolerable in New York, where the Manhattan Company devoted most of its attention and capital to banking privileges granted by its charter. Private corporations were concerned about profits; few were willing to commit huge outlays of capital to construct and maintain an elaborate water system. In addition they catered to paying customers and balked at extending service to lower-class districts that would furnish little revenue. Looking to the example set by Philadelphia, leaders of other cities began to press for public waterworks. In 1835 New York voters solidly approved a project to bring water to the city over an aqueduct from the Croton River. In 1845 Bostonians accepted an act passed by the General Assembly enabling the city to construct its own water system. In 1857 the city of Baltimore purchased its private waterworks and began constructing an additional reservoir. By 1860 the country's sixteen largest cities had reasonably efficient water systems, only four of which were still privately owned.

Yet leaders who congratulated themselves for providing their cities with adequate water often became complacent. Abundance of water and higher standards of public health created new habits of consumption. Indoor plumbing, with its tub and toilet, now became a facility of city life, at least for the wealthy. Industrial use also rose. But as the pace of population growth and industrialization quickened, the ability of public and private water works to meet local demand faltered. The obstacle was one of leadership more than of technology. As Sam Bass Warner, Jr., has noted, Philadelphia's Fairmount works made running water available for middle-class houses and street pumps, but public leaders were reluctant to require and offer running water where it was needed most—in the homes of the poor. Industrialists in every city tapped water from public supplies because it was the cheapest and handiest coolant and waste-carrying agent; they had little concern for pollution or future shortages. Thus short-sightedness and the elevation of private needs over public welfare began to block the potential of public water systems.

Somewhat different issues were involved in the establishment of police forces. Most cities retained the colonial agencies of law enforcement—constables, sheriffs, and night watchmen—well into the nineteenth century. This system proved inadequate for large, diverse populations, because it provided only for a response to specific complaints rather than the prevention and detection of crime. Since early police forces were recruited from the general population for limited terms of service, they tended to be untrained, underpaid, and disrupted by personnel turnover. Yet many urban dwellers would probably have continued with this system had it not been for their fear of increased crime and disorder. Mob violence had characterized American cities since colonial days, but by the 1830s and 1840s ethnic, racial, political, and social conflicts were beginning to stir upper and middle classes to support the creation of stronger, more efficient police forces to preserve life and property. As the racial and ethnic populations of cities grew more complex, riots became alarming in their size and frequency. Between 1830 and 1855 there were major race riots in Philadelphia, Providence, and Cincinnati; antiabolition riots in New York and Boston; anti-Catholic and anti-Irish riots in Philadelphia, Boston Baltimore, St. Louis, and Louisville; and bread riots in New York.

As a consequence cities established permanent, professional bodies of police. In 1838 the Massachusetts General Assembly enabled the City of Boston to appoint salaried policemen. New York obtained similar authority in 1844, Philadelphia in 1850, and Baltimore in 1857. Residents of these and other cities soon discovered, however, that the creation of a strong police failed to solve old problems of law enforcement and even raised new ones. There were never enough policemen to preserve order. Between 1845 and 1855 New York's population grew from 250,000 to 630,000, while its police force was increased from 800 to less than 1200. Other cities suffered from similar shortages. In addition police forces could become embroiled in heated political conflicts. In an effort to lift police appointments in New York City out of local corruption and party politics, the New York General Assembly in 1857 created a state-controlled Metropolitan Police. Mayor Fernando Wood resisted this imposition of state power over his Democratic regime and refused to disband the local police with the result that the city was patrolled by two competing police forces. The U.S. Court of Appeals forced Wood to back down, and the Metropolitan Police remained in operation until the 1870s, even though it failed to improve law enforcement in the city. Yet the New York example sparked the subsequent creation of state-controlled municipal police in over a dozen large cities from Baltimore to San Francisco, Detroit to New Orleans.

More importantly the police as agents of law enforcement were buffeted between conflicting urban groups who held different notions of what the law was and how it should be enforced. There were, for example, people who demanded strict enforcement of vice, temperance, and fugitive slave laws. Yet police action in these areas could antagonize others who saw no harm in a little gambling, whose cultural background included the use of wine or beer, and whose moral values condoned the protection of fugitive slaves. Furthermore, according to Roger Lane, in earlier years police activity had been directed at individual offenders or at "a voiceless class of unfortunates," such as vagrants or drunks. With the establishment of more formal police, however, law enforcement could affect a much broader population—including those who considered themselves law-abiding. In the late 1840s vigorous police activity in Boston resulted in the arrest of hundreds of people for failing to clear ice off their sidewalks and for keeping unlicensed dogs. Clearly a gap existed between society's idealistic intentions for criminal law, particularly the moral aspects, and peoples' actual desires for individual freedom of action. The police were buffers between these pressures, fulfilling the felt need for law enforcement on the one hand, and easing the impact of the law by their action or inaction on the other. The achievement of the proper balance has always stymied urban Americans, because changes in living standards, ethnic and racial mix, technology, and moral attitudes occurred faster than government institutions could react. Urban dwellers of the mid-nineteenth century were just beginning to feel the forces and frustrations that perplex the modern age.

Apprehensions about disorder derived from more than crime and violence. Poverty, delinquency, mental illness, disease, and moral decay combined with criminality to raise fears among civic leaders that American society was falling apart. The police could deter, prevent, and arrest, but what could be done with the people already afflicted with some social ailment or degradation—the poor, criminals, insane, prostitutes, and delinquents? In colonial times the answer had been easy. A town simply excluded any suspected deviants by refusing to allow them to settle in the community. Criminals convicted within town borders were fined and whipped; paupers and orphans were farmed out to relatives and other townsmen. These methods became unfeasible in the nineteenth century. Cities grew too large for officials to keep track of all newcomers, and old forms of punishment and relief failed to eliminate crime, sin, and poverty. Moreover, a constant and awesome population migration churned the social composition of all cities (see below), increasing anonymity and aggravating fears about a breakdown of social control. As David Rothman has observed, community spokesmen believed that society was losing its stability. Their response was to try to control those whose behavior disturbed them. Their methods included attempts to infuse the poor and depraved with Christian morality and the establishment of institutions such as penitentiaries, asylums, and public schools to instill these classes with values of deference, order, and prudence.

American tradition considered poverty to be the result of individual moral failure. In a land of opportunity, according to the theory, only a person's laziness or intemperance could make him or her poor. In the eighteenth century urban Americans accepted poverty as inevitable, a necessary component of a social hierarchy sanctioned by God's will. In the early nineteenth century, however, growth of urban populations and increasing scale of geographical movement revised social attitudes. The expansionism of the age led many to fear the poor as subversive to an ordered society, while simultaneously an optimism presumed the poor to be objects of rehabilitation. A number of agencies now began to direct their efforts toward pulling people out of the throes of poverty. In the 1820s the evangelism of the Second Great Awakening prompted the establishment of missions in eastern urban centers, and the city missionaries became increasingly concerned with the poor. The deeply religious members of organizations, such as the New York Tract Society, believed that the greatest service they could render to the downtrodden was to endow them with the Grace of God. But they also offered more mundane assistance: lodging houses for vagrants, summer camps for slum children, and medical assistance for indigents. Other religious groups undertook similar projects. For example, Catholic eleemosynary agencies established orphanages, hospitals, and direct aid to the sick and aged poor.

Because they stressed moral and religious regeneration as necessary to individual improvement, the missionaries attempted not only to spread Christian truths to the poor but to abolish sinful activities, such as drinking, gambling, and prostitution. This moralism also reflected secular attitudes that derived from the prevalent attitude that there was a distinction between poverty and pauperism. Poverty was defined as the loss or deprivation of the means of self-subsistence and a consequential dependence upon charitable assistance. It entailed no necessary stigma of depravity. In contrast pauperism implied a preference for support by alms rather than by personal labor. Because they assumed poverty to be a moral problem, and because they defined pauperism as a vice in itself, moral reformers devoted most of their energies to trying to guarantee the virtue of charity recipients. They often opposed secular relief projects. According to Boston's Unitarian minister Joseph Tuckerman, general public charities "set aside the charity of religion and substitute for it something which is not charity. . . . (This is) an encroachment which law has made upon moral rights and moral duties."

Yet a number of people who were concerned about the effects of rapid change and who observed the predicaments of the poor most closely came to believe that social and economic conditions, not individual failure, were responsible for poverty. These reformers asserted that society had failed to provide all of its members with opportunities to avoid indigence and thus had an obligation to care for those who lost or lacked means of subsistence. Their solution was to replace *outdoor*, direct grants of aid with *indoor*, institutional relief. Housed together away from the evils of the outside world, the poor could be rehabilitated by a controlled environment that would teach them values of orderliness and industry. Between 1820 and 1840 scores of cities and towns opened almshouses and workhouses to handle poor relief. These institutions won support as much because they removed the poor from the streets and were more economical than outdoor assistance as they did for their reformatory functions. Nevertheless, these institutions did signal a new approach to relief.

The belief that deviant behavior was the product of social, rather than individual, failure was also applied to the criminal, the insane, and the delinquent. Penitentiaries, asylums, and houses of correction were constructed to serve the same functions for these groups as the almshouses served for the poor—reform induced by regimented control. The sentiment behind these institutions subsequently took two paths. On the one hand, the sense of community responsibility for the alleviation of social problems foreshadowed the spread of the Social Gospel across the urban scene later in the nineteenth century. On the other hand, as Professor Rothman has shown, the ideal of confining deviants and dependents in order to reform them could easily slip into an objective of incarcerating these groups simply to keep them away from the rest of society.

Almshouses, penitentiaries, and asylums could neither hold nor reform all the poor, however. A more inclusive institution was needed to destroy the growing cycle of poverty, a process whereby succeeding generations of the same families failed to escape indigence and became increasingly dependent upon public support. Thus beginning in the 1820s urban leaders began to rally to the public school as the instrument to break the chains of destitution while restoring social stability in the same fashion as other institutional reform. Politicians, humanitarians, and educators alike boosted the common school as insurance against social upheaval. Schooling, they said, would instill discipline and civic responsibility in the lower classes and lift them from poverty by preparing them for economic advancement. It would assimilate the immigrants and teach all children to shun the moral temptations of modern life. As cities grew and problems mounted, the public education movement gained momentum. Boston established free elementary schools in 1818; New York followed suit in 1832, and Philadelphia in 1836. On the eve of the Civil War, the majority of cities and states in the North and West had some kind of public education, largely due to the efforts of urban leaders. Horace Mann, a Boston lawyer, Henry Barnard, a leading citizen of Hartford, Connecticut, and Calvin Stowe, professor of biblical literature at Cincinnati's Lane Theological Seminary, were among the most influential contributors to this early era of school reform.

By mid-century, however, reformers aiming to school all classes were feeling the thorns of several problems, some of them self-inflicted. In many cities population increased faster than new schools could be built. As immigration accelerated in the 1840s, illiteracy rose instead of declined. At the same time, social reformers, attempting to bring all children into the schools, contended with officials and taxpayers determined to hold down public expenditures. More and more children were squeezed into existing schools, overtaxing facilities and diluting the quality of education. By 1850 Boston's schools could provide only one teacher for every fifty-five students. Moreover, even among the liberal-minded educators, social insurance could easily become social control. Recently historians have suggested that early crusades for educational reform often involved centralization of curriculum planning and bureaucratization of administration, with the objective of imposing the middle-class values of community leaders on the rest of society. And, according to Michael Katz, the development of a professionalized bureaucracy by the 1860s was sapping educational reform of its enthusiasm and warmth. Thus many of the dilemmas which haunt urban schools today stretch back well over a century.

A sometimes-neglected service activity, but one involving important consequences, was the development of urban parks. Since their earliest days American cities had been arenas for conflict between those who wished to preserve open space for public enjoyment and those who coveted unoccupied land for private development. The latter force had usually prevailed. Even in places such as Philadelphia and Savannah, where provisions for public squares had been explicit, open land within the city limits had not been able to withstand encroachment by private building projects for very long. Acreage devoted to public open space in New York decreased by 50 percent between 1800 and 1850, while population and the city's area increased several hundred percent. Because buildings were multiplying so rapidly, and because notions of public health considered fresh air and greenery requisites to physical and moral well-being, a number of leaders became concerned about the disappearance of open land in their cities. The plan of Washington, D.C. and the construction of Philadelphia's Fairmount waterworks had created sizeable urban parks. By the 1840s proponents in other cities were urging the preservation and design of green areas large enough to resist piecemeal destruction.

The most important development occurred in New York. Here public figures, such as architect Andrew Jackson Downing and poet William Cullen Bryant, succeeded in convincing the state legislature to reserve over 600 acres for a public park on Manhattan Island. A state-appointed commission opened competition to determine the best design for the park and awarded the prize to a young landscaper and journalist, Fred-

erick Law Olmsted, destined to become one of the most influential figures
in American urban and landscape design.

As superintendent of the project, Central Park, Olmsted attempted to
bring what he believed to be the physical and social enjoyment of rural
beauty to urban dwellers. This objective involved Olmsted and his
associate, Calvert Vaux, in two kinds of designing. First, they tried to
create an idealistic, pastoral effect by improving upon nature in different
ways to suit different people. Thus their design included a series of distinct vistas, some rough in terrain, others more formal. They also built
sunken roadways to conceal city traffic and planted trees strategically to
screen out abutting buildings. Second, they inserted special features to
meet different needs. They laid 114 miles of pipe to feed and drain
ponds for boating and skating, provided trails for riding and hiking, and
designed a mall for social gatherings and concerts. The park was an
instant success, attracting 25,000 visitors a day even before it was completed. Although plagued by political squabbles over park control and
declining public commitment to its maintenance, Olmsted remained as
superintendent until 1878 and constantly studied the park's use and
misuse in order to improve it.

Central Park and Olmsted's design inspired similar efforts throughout
urban America—many of them designed by Olmsted and Vaux or by
their equally influential contemporary, H. W. S. Cleveland. Yet Olmsted's importance reaches beyond the landscaping of parks: his concern
for preserving and improving urban space spawned broader projects of
city planning. Urban development in early nineteenth-century America
had followed the dictates of speculators and private landowners. The
result was the spread of the grid layout across the country. This system,
with its rectangular blocks, right-angle streets, and uniform lots, enabled developers to maximize land use and to sell property conveniently.
However, it ignored topography and left rigid limitations on house size
and open space. A plan for the expansion of Manhattan Island according to the grid system, implemented in 1811, not only influenced the layout of countless cities in succeeding years but also planted the seeds of
New York's future congestion. The plan, drafted by a trio of state-
appointed commissioners, divided the city's blocks into 25-by-100-foot
lots, almost eliminating space between dwellings (accounting for the
commonality of row houses) and making possible the construction of two,
or even three, structures in tandem on the same lot.

Although they were unable to undo the past, Olmsted, Cleveland, and
a few others revolted against what they called "the tyranny of the gridiron" in the years after the Civil War. When they were hired in 1868 by a
development company to design Chicago's suburb of Riverside, Olmsted
and Vaux transferred their ideas about park planning to community de-

sign, and in so doing, influenced the course of American suburban development. In Riverside, as in Central Park, Olmsted and Vaux tried to preserve what they believed to be "rural attractiveness." They planted trees at irregular intervals to convey a sense of spontaneity, required houses to be constructed back from the streets, created unfenced parks and playgrounds, separated business from other traffic, and wound roadways around natural features—the first time that American urban streets were intentionally curved. Of course Riverside could be inhabited only by the wealthy; its lavish use of open space made land too expensive even for middle-income families. Yet it was an important symbol—it set the pattern for future attempts to preserve and improve upon natural topography in modern urban design.

The park movement of the middle and late nineteenth century was thus an important antecedent to city planning at the end of the century, because it prodded landscapers, architects, and public officials to pay more attention to the aesthetics and efficient use of urban land. It is significant that the climax of Olmsted's career was his contribution to the planning of the World's Columbian Exposition in Chicago in 1893, the epitome of the "City Beautiful." Yet, ironically, parks had a consequence not foreseen by landscapers and planners. Instead of unifying people of the city by offering havens for relaxation and socializing, parks often became battlegrounds and no man's lands between conflicting groups who inhabited bordering neighborhoods. Parks and boulevards, optimistically designed to protect a city's social and physical health, could become boundaries separating ethnic and racial antagonists.

The urban problems discussed above—disease, disorder, poverty, crowding—repelled the country's early intellectual leaders. Ralph Waldo Emerson scorned the materialism and artificiality of urban life, and Nathaniel Hawthorne half-seriously proposed that "all towns should be made capable of purification by fire, or of decay, within each half century." Yet most social critics, except for those like Henry David Thoreau who shunned society completely, felt a strong attraction for the city, whether it was Boston, New York, Cincinnati, Chicago, or some other place. Although reluctant to admit it, they recognized that cities brought together all kinds of people and resources and therefore offered potential for the good life as well as the bad. Only urban populations could support a multiplicity of theaters, museums, concerts, libraries, and other cultural activities. The attitude that cities had positive, as well as negative, potential became quite explicit in popular and religious writing of the mid-nineteenth century. Writers of both moral essays and adventure novels involving city life expressed faith that with a little effort, American cities could become zeniths of world civilization. Such sentiments could be found in works as divergent as Joseph Tuckerman's treatise,

On Elevation of the Poor and Edward Zane Carroll Judson's—pen name
Ned Buntline—lurid novel, *The Mysteries and Miseries of New York.*
Thus in spite of their problems, cities retained the promise of opportunity
as Americans entered the modern age.

THE SOCIAL IMPACT OF URBANIZATION

Just exactly how much opportunity and for whom have become questions
of considerable historical interest. Data on property ownership have suggested that by the time of the Revolution, American urban society had
become graded, with wide gaps between ranks. As new land in the West
opened, as new cities sprouted, and as older cities expanded in the
decades that followed independence, it would seem that increased opportunity could have loosened the social rigidity and enabled larger
numbers of people to improve their conditions. Belief that such conditions existed led the French intellectual, Alexis de Toqueville, to reflect
upon their consequences. He wrote in *Democracy in America* that "In a
democracy like that of the United States, fortunes are scanty . . .
[because] . . . the equality of conditions [that] give some resources to
all the members of the community . . . also prevent any of them from
having resources of great extent." Other observers, foreign and native,
similarly noted American egalitarianism.

Recently historians have begun to dismiss such characterization as
an "egalitarian myth." Analysis of urban social structure in the middle
third of the nineteenth century has revealed that small numbers of people were accumulating large proportions of the available wealth, and
the chances of a person improving his or her economic station remained
small. In Boston where 5 percent of the population had owned 44 percent of the taxable property in 1771, the richest 4 percent owned 59 percent of the wealth in 1833 and 64 percent by 1848. In New York the
upper 4 percent controlled 49 percent of the wealth in 1828 and 66 percent in 1845. Similar concentrations could be found in Philadelphia,
Brooklyn, Baltimore, St. Louis, and New Orleans. Every city contained
families (in New York they numbered in the scores) whose fortunes
rivaled those of Europe's wealthiest. The vast majority of elites had not
followed a rags-to-riches path; they had maintained or increased the
wealth accumulated by their forebears. Among the middle and lower
classes there were opportunities for advancement by acquiring property
or by moving into proprietary or skilled craft occupations. But such
attainments were precarious. National economic panics and depressions,
which occurred almost regularly,—1819, 1837, 1857—and growing scale of
many businesses snuffed out the chances of many a small investor. Thus

even though upward economic and occupational mobility seems to have remained fairly stable in places, like Boston and Philadelphia, between 1830 and 1860 downward mobility increased.

It would appear, then, that at least for the cities, de Toqueville was mistaken. Egalitarianism was a myth. The rich were becoming richer, and the rest, though improving in an absolute sense (after all, total wealth was increasing and not all of the increase went to the wealthiest), were lagging behind. There were notable exceptions. In smaller cities such as Paterson, New Jersey, Providence, Rhode Island, and Springfield, Massachusetts, which were rapidly expanding on a heavy industrial base in the 1850s and '60s, a larger proportion of the business elite contained new blood—men of relatively recent arival in the community who had risen from lower social strata. In many places prejudice held immigrant Irish and blacks in the lower class while giving native whites, plus some English and German immigrants, better opportunities to rise. Moreover, whereas social and economic conditions might have choked off opportunities for upward occupational mobility, a family may have been able to achieve a somewhat higher status by saving money and acquiring property. Yet such mobility could often be obtained only by considerable sacrifice, and its meaning could be lost in the deprivation involved. As Stephan Thernstrom and a number of other historians have demonstrated, the parcel of success in terms of occupational or property mobility that a middle- or lower-class family could attain was a meager one —if it existed at all. Most people might have had middle-class aspirations or even considered themselves members of that social order, but there was a gap between hope and reality.

Yet there still might have been a way in which families and individuals could improve their life situations, not reflected by acquisitions of wealth or occupational change. The extent of geographical mobility in the nineteenth century was even more striking than in the colonial era. Americans have always been, and remain, a migratory people. Some moved because circumstances beyond their control—economic, personal, or natural misfortune—forced them. Most, however, seem to have exercised a kind of restlessness, a search for a better life in another place. The half century preceding the Civil War witnessed the beginning of three tides of migration: the influx of immigrants from abroad, the trek westward, and the shift from the country and small towns to the large urban centers. Each year millions of people were on the move, arriving at cities and leaving for somewhere else. Peter R. Knights has estimated that between 1830 and 1840 a total of 35,775 households moved into and out of Boston alone; there were 49,350 between 1840 and 1850; and 95,154 between 1850 and 1860. When multiplied by the average number of individuals per household, these figures become hundreds of thousands. Even a substantial error of overestimation would leave the numbers very large, especially in comparison with Boston's population, which was only 61,000 in 1830 and 134,000 in 1860. When we add in the people changing residence within the city, the totals involved in the process of residential change become awesome. Viewed in another way, only two in every five residents at one point in time were likely to be present in Boston a decade later. Evidence indicates that other cities underwent similarly extensive turnover. Between 1830 and 1860 only about a third of Philadelphia's residents remained in the city for as long as ten years. In the same period smaller cities like Waltham, Newburyport, Northhampton, and Poughkeepsie also experienced remarkable in- and out-migration.

All this geographical mobility affected the people as well as the cities. It brought individuals and families into contact with new environments and new opportunities. Not everyone was able to take advantage of new situations. Professor Thernstrom has identified a "floating proletariat" in nineteenth-century America, a mass of unskilled laborers who shifted from town to town without ever improving their condition. Yet movement did often mean improvement. And if the change was only marginal in a relative sense—that is, betterment among those at the top of the urban social scale was occurring faster than for those underneath—the change in an absolute sense remained meaningful and left inducement for further movement. The entrepreneurs who moved to Paterson and rose in the locomotive and other industries did not quite attain the Social Register, but they still acquired considerable affluence. Farmers and their wives, sons and daughters, pushed off the land by population pressures, natural disasters, or economic decline, could find jobs in the cities even if they were the least prestigious and lowest paying. Black slaves running away from the plantations or from urban compounds could taste a morsel of freedom, however tiny, in the bustle and anonymity of life in northern and southern cities. Workmen and shopkeepers from older cities of the East could find better jobs or more customers in Buffalo, Cincinnati, Chicago, St. Louis, New Orleans or San Francisco. Moreover, a move from farm to city, from one city to another, or from one residence to another within the same city could have brought an improvement in environmental amenities—more space, better facilities for light, heat, and ventilation, better accessibility to jobs, schools, and shopping. To be sure, increasing numbers of urban in-migrants were squeezed into cellars, lofts, and other unsuitable lodging places because housing did not keep pace with population growth. But the opportunity—and the desire—to move always existed.

Another consequence of geographical movement was the amplification of social complexity. Migration had always been central to American development, and cities had been heterogeneous from their inception. But by the 1850s population growth from migration gave many places unprecedented cosmopolitanism. Samples taken from Boston's 1850 and 1860 household heads revealed that only 10 percent had been born in that city; half were foreign-born. In 1860, 30 percent of all Philadelphians were foreign-born, and an even greater proportion had moved to the city from the surrounding countryside and towns. Western cities, such as Buffalo, Cleveland, Cincinnati, St. Louis, and Chicago, received not only substantial numbers of foreigners (mainly Irish and Germans) but also thousands of immigrants from Massachusetts, New York, Pennsylvania, and even Virginia. In each case the groups present one year could be completely reconstituted the next because as more people arrived, others moved on. A similar process transformed sections within cities as people moved from one neighborhood to another.

In many ways, population movement and urban expansion, coupled with industrialization and growth of the economic scale, promoted specialization and fragmentation. The result was the "breakdown of community" into interest-group associations. Sometimes these associations—be they labor or business organizations, ethnic or fraternal societies, religious or political clubs—overlapped; sometimes they conflicted with each other. Regardless of their interrelationships, they split the city into a series of exclusive cells, the sum of which no longer equaled the public interest. Urban society had always been structured, but now the complexities of modernization closed off the old openness and coexistence between groups and forced people to join clubs and associations in an attempt to recapture lost sense of community. With so many people on the move, membership in even the fragmented parts of society could be fleeting. Thus "community," defined in terms of commonality of interest between people and identity with a particular place, was subverted. The old social harmony that had given small town society its cohesiveness dissolved in the cities. Municipal institutions, such as the city government and schools, became increasingly responsive to the needs of private interests that no longer coincided with the public welfare.

Yet questions can be raised as to whether such a breakdown of community was new in the middle of the nineteenth century and how strongly the urban community ever existed in America. As early as the seventeenth century these same processes—migration, commercialization, diversification—were segmenting Boston economically, politically, and socially. In subsequent years other cities experienced these same effects of expansion. The rise of boosterism in eastern cities as well as in the West did allow individuals to blend their private concerns into those of a given city. But like people, boosterism was easily transferred. A dis-

The Walking City

This extraordinary daguerreotype is one of a series taken of Cincinnati in 1848. The view shows the concentration of settlement and business along the waterfront with substantial homes perched on the hills overlooking the city. *The Public Library of Cincinnati and Hamilton County.*

appointed promoter of one town could, and often did, relocate to another site and become just as ardently chauvinistic toward it as he had been toward his former city. The point is that the American city has always been a divided and divisive place. Times of upheaval, increasingly frequent in the early nineteenth century, bared these divisions. Disorder and violence growing out of social and racial diversity, economic conflict produced by expanding economic and technological scale, and political friction rising from a more broadly enfranchised electorate combined with the geographical instability of the population to give cities a very complicated texture. Attempts to reconstruct a well-ordered urban society collided with historical forces too strong to deflect. What was needed, but seldom perceived, was a toleration and coordination of the various networks of associations that had developed, rather than an inclusive community of interest within any single city.

Regardless of the existence of an urban community, migration and new forms of economic organization were changing urban society in the early nineteenth century. The transportation revolution, with its wagons, steamboats, and railroads; the commercial revolution, with its corporate enterprises and expanded marketing and credit techniques; and the industrial revolution with its factories and mass-produced goods worked to increase the size of economic activities and to undercut the one-man shop that had characterized the early urban economy. Yet the change was evolutionary, not abrupt. Take, for example, the growth of the working class and the decline of small artisan trades in industrializing cities.

To some extent the factory system, appearing in northeastern cities in the antebellum years, created a class of exploited, unskilled workers and inhibited mobility by destroying the handicraft trades. The numbers of unskilled laborers in urban populations increased steadily from the 1820s to the end of the century. But at the same time, large numbers of artisans and tradesmen survived for two fundamental reasons. First, changes in the modes of production during this period resulted less from mechanized factory organization than from what has been termed "merchant capitalism." The expansion of transportation and growth of interior cities in the 1830s and '40s created lucrative domestic markets and tempted eastern merchants to invest in native operations that produced goods for internal consumption. Instead of exchanging American raw materials for European manufactured items, merchants now began to use their advantages of capital, marketing skill, and organizational experience to muster large numbers of craftsmen together under one roof for the purpose of producing goods for sale in the West and South. This type of organization occurred most prominently in Philadelphia, where independent shoemakers were drawn into large enterprises, but it also spread to other industries such as clothing and jewelry. Thus in several areas a few large producers consolidated manufacturing without inducing mechanization. The urban artisan class was not eliminated by early industrialization. Rather it partially lost its independent status as some of its members were forced into the ranks of wage earners.

Second, the factory itself had two basic effects. It was (1) capital-intensive, centralizing investments to maximize efficiency and profitability; and (2) labor-saving, enabling more productivity per worker. This latter effect is very important because it meant that even in the most rapidly industrializing cities the laboring class (or proletariat) grew relatively slowly. Many of the most mechanized industries, as well as the merchant-capitalist firms, simply concentrated skilled workers into a single establishment—machinists or metal workers, for example. Moreover, the growth of urban populations from migration created a further demand for the products and services of many artisan crafts, so that the numbers involved in traditionally small-scale operations increased along with the factory workers. Thus in Providence, Rhode Island, where development of the textile, base metals, and precious metals industries was occurring at a rapid pace in the 1840s, the number of consumer-serving tradesmen such as smiths, bakers, cabinet makers, carpenters, carriage makers, engravers, and masons increased by almost 50 percent at the same time.

Table I illustrates the growth of the above artisan occupations in Providence between 1845 and 1850, but it also reveals the extent of in- and out-migration that the city experienced. Of the 365 tradesmen selected in 1850, 205, or 56 percent, had not been listed five years earlier. Some of these men may have been apprentices or children too young to have been listed in 1845, but undoubtedly most were newcomers to the city, for Providence's population increased by 30 percent between 1845 and 1850. The same pattern occurred with regard to the city's shops and consumer services such as confectionaries, groceries, drugs, and dry goods establishments. They increased in number by over 40 percent, and of those small merchants present in 1850, nearly two-thirds had arrived or entered their businesses since 1845.

It would appear, then, that industrialization did not necessarily stifle

TABLE 1

Growth of Artisan and Retail Services in Providence, Rhode Island, 1845–1850

Occupation	Number Listed in 1845	1850	New in 1850
Artisans and Services			
Bakers	11	16	11
Blacksmiths	33	55	20
Cabinet Makers	9	13	4
Carpenters	65	91	54
Carriage Makers	16	23	14
Engravers	9	17	11
House Painters	29	38	22
Masons	17	28	14
Printers	6	9	5
Shoemakers	52	72	45
Tinsmiths	17	25	15
Total	264	365	205
Retailers and Services			
Brokers	16	23	13
Coal Dealers	14	21	10
Commission Merchants	27	37	27
Confectioners	19	15	10
Druggists	8	13	7
Fancy Goods Dealers	8	14	9
Furniture Dealers	7	15	10
Jewelry & Leather Dealers	18	25	9
Lumber Dealers	20	21	13
Marketmen and Merchants	66	105	83
Milliners	29	40	26
Paint & Paper Dealers	12	13	4
Shoe Dealers	31	32	22
Stove Dealers	6	19	16
Total	281	393	259

certain traditional businesses and trades, nor did it exclusively account for the growth of urban populations in the 1840s and '50s. The expansion of transportation links, which made goods more accessible and which moved people from place to place, plus a broadening of credit, which enabled craftsmen or entrepreneurs to buy tools and merchandise and to open a shop, spurred urbanization as much, if not more, than the development of factories. The opportunities for migration and the expansion of markets also slowed the impact of industrialization on American cities. To be sure, in some places, particularly the mill towns of the Northeast, an industrial working class comprised a large proportion of the population. But in the larger, more diverse cities, the occupational distribution retained a preindustrial character.

Certainly the fluidity and economic diversity that characterized the early nineteenth-century city revised the nature of several social institutions. As Richard C. Wade has shown, the urban context gave the institution of slavery forms that differed considerably from those on the plantations. In the rural South field hands had unchanging, regimented tasks supervised by masters or overseers. In southern cities slaves took on a wide variety of jobs, ranging from domestic duties to artisan trades and industrial labor; and their masters frequently hired them out to other employers. On the plantation discipline was a matter between slave and owner. In the towns, because slaves often traveled about away from their owner's eyes, discipline became a public concern. City governments erected public whipping posts and passed ordinances regulating the behavior of slaves on city streets. Plantation bondsmen had limited social contact; they lived isolated in their own quarters and saw only their master's family and occasionally slaves from a nearby plantation. City slaves partook of a wider world. They had access (even when it was illegal) to the food, drink, entertainment, and common sociability of urban life. They had their own churches, and they often sneaked away to talk and drink with fellow slaves, free blacks, and lower-class whites in speak-easies and other clandestine places. Some even obtained permission to work *and* live away from their master's supervision. Their only obligation was to bring their owners a certain sum of money each week or month.

All evidence indicates that urban slavery was profitable for the owners, as well as for those who hired or rented slaves. But the contrast with rural slavery presented whites with a dilemma. All slavery thrived on absolute control by masters of their bondsmen. Yet the nature of urban life made it impossible for owners to supervise the activities of their chattel every minute of the day. The varied conditions of social and economic activities loosened the chains of discipline and gave urban slaves a narrow parcel of freedom—freedom that the prevailing racial order could not tolerate. The ultimate reaction was two-pronged: (1) Cities enacted more stringent laws to restrict the activities of all blacks, slave and free, resulting in formalized segregation—the exclusion of blacks from most public accommodations and the confinement of blacks to separate and unequal facilities. (2) Owners limited urban slave populations by either selling their blacks (particularly young males) to rural masters or failing to replace slaves who died or ran away. In 1840 the total slave population of the ten largest southern cities equaled 67,755; in 1860 it was 68,013. Meanwhile the total white population of the same cities ballooned from 233,000 to 690,000. Only in Richmond, Virginia, where black manpower was integral to the iron and tobacco industries, did a large proportion of slaves still exist by 1860. In New Orleans, on the other hand, the number of slaves dropped from 23,000 in 1840 to 13,000 in 1860. Among whites, racist fears overcame the profitability of the system. "Hence," observed Professor Wade, "the response of owners and officials was to tighten rather than adjust, to expel rather than emancipate, to segregate rather than liberate." Urbanization left most southern blacks deurbanized.

Another institution that felt the effects of changing conditions was the urban household. The growth of economic scale produced as a major consequence the separation of place of work from place of residence. This divorce, which had always existed in cities but had become increasingly prevalent by the nineteenth century, ended the family's function as an economic unit. The household now became fragmented as its members gravitated into specialized tasks—work or schooling outside the home, assigned domestic duties within it. Yet at the same time, conditions of migration and economic change seem to have increased human solidarity, at least in terms of the numbers of people living together. Evidence indicates that in both eastern and western cities large numbers of urban dwellings contained boarders as well as servants, apprentices, and laborers—outsiders who expanded households beyond ties of kinship. These outsiders consisted of single men who were employed or looking for jobs, working girls and domestics, and occasionally whole families. Often they were newcomers to the city, coming singly to seek work or as part of a chain leading from friends and relatives in the city back to a village on the rural countryside or across the ocean to England, Ireland, or the German states. Thus studies of individual cases from censuses have begun to reveal that although the vast majority of urban families remained nuclear in composition—that is, two generational, consisting of only parents and their children—large numbers of *households* were extended in nature, harboring more boarders and lodgers than in the past.

Regardless of whether they lived in their own houses or in someone else's, most men had access to all the opportunities of economic ex-

pansion, urbanization, technological advances, the transportation revolution, and geographical mobility. Women, for the most part, did not.
More than ever before, women were expected to remain at home in their
"proper sphere," subjects of a patriarchal order. The early nineteenth
century witnessed the rise of the "cult of domesticity," the institutional-
ization of woman as homemaker, queen of the house, tender of husband
and children. Gentility, submissiveness, nurture, and support—all exercised within the realm of the home—became the virtues and duties
of womanhood. It was almost as if the specialization of the era was
forcing society to define the tasks of women according to the laws of
Nature. Thus a critic in 1843 could accuse working women of violating
"the proper female sphere . . . for which God designed woman . . .
[and becoming] totally unfitted for the peculiar responsibilities and
duties of that station in life, that is and *should be* the object of the aspirations of every virtuous female."

The celebration of women's functions was an urban, middle-class
ideal. Periodicals designed for middle-class readership, such as *Godey's
Ladies Book,* helped to create and perpetuate the "cult" with their widespread circulation. But the requisites and opportunities of urban life
created situations that counteracted the ideal. While the cult of domesticity was gathering its idolators, thousands of women were moving into
the urban labor market, into jobs created by industrial and commercial
growth. In many cities female labor became important to the growth of
factories. This was particularly true in the textile industry. In 1831 women
outnumbered men in cotton mills by 33,506 to 18,059; in towns like
Lowell the ratio was over three to one. Most women who worked in factories did so as an extension of their domestic functions; that is, they
worked only to support, or help support, their families rather than to
achieve personal and economic independence. Yet such employment undoubtedly did give women a sense that their labor had some value beyond that of domestic contribution. Poet John Greenleaf Whittier, at one
time a resident of Lowell, wrote that factory work was providing women
with "the opportunity of taking the first and essential step of securing
. . . a comfortable competency." It gave a woman "a self-sustaining
power," a feeling "that she is something in and of herself," and it placed
her labor "essentially upon an equality with man." It did not place her
wages on an equality with man, however. Factory labor usually brought
women about $2 to $4 per week, while men often received twice as much
for similar work.

Thus factory jobs, however debilitating and exploitive, gave some
women an alternative to the home. But other sections of the urban
economy offered opportunities. Many women worked in middle-class
and proprietary pursuits, although the female proportions in these oc-

cupations were probably smaller than in the colonial years. Every city contained female shopkeepers who sold books, china, groceries, hosiery, or dry goods. There were also boardinghouse keepers, public house owners, and skilled artisans such as printers, milliners, and tailoresses. As had earlier been the case, most of these women were widows who had either assumed their husband's business or had begun their own establishment to support themselves. However they, as well as their male counterparts, occasionally employed single females as clerks and helpers.

In the professions there was both decline and expansion of female personnel. Growing formalization in the practice of medicine pushed most women out of their traditional monopoly on obstetrics. Barred from professional training, female midwives were replaced by male physicians in urban areas by the middle of the nineteenth century. At the same time, women increasingly populated other fields of education. As the public education movement spread from city to city, it generated scores of schoolmistresses. In 1840, 39 percent of the schoolteachers in Massachusetts were women; by 1865 the proportion had reached 65 percent. A major reason for this increase was that local governments could pay women much less than they could pay men. Thus two or three women could be hired for the salary of one man.

Another "profession" that became more noticeable was prostitution. As urban populations multiplied, the instances and opportunities for vice alarmed moralists, such as New York aristocrat George Templeton Strong, who complained that New York was infested with a "whorearchy." It is difficult to say whether or not such revulsion resulted from an actual increase in the proportion of prostitutes in the population or more indirectly from the growing tendency of middle-class males to divide women into categories: sex partners and wives-mothers. Nonetheless prostitution thrived on the bustle and anonymity of urban life. No doubt a few women were able to achieve as prostitutes a modicum of economic independence and success that otherwise would never have been possible. More likely most prostitutes remained beneath levels of self-sufficiency, trapped by male exploiters and by conditions of deprivation that had driven them into their calling. The early nineteenth century, then, was a paradoxical era for women in the cities. Urbanization and industrialization drew women into jobs outside the home in greater proportions than ever before. Yet prevailing social norms idealized, even demanded, women's place inside the home. Furthermore slicing through these general trends were the attempts by some educated and affluent women to assert their independence and to influence the course of events, efforts ranging from moral reform and abolition to women's rights and suffrage.

Migration, industrialization, and social change charged the first half of the nineteenth century with extraordinary activity, and all these movements fused in the cities. Although the United States was far from an urbanized nation on the eve of the Civil War (in 1860 one-fifth of the population lived in cities), the three decades before the war witnessed the most intense growth of cities this country would ever experience. Between 1830 and 1840, the total number of urban residents grew by 64 percent; between 1840 and 1850, by 92 percent; and between 1850 and 1860, by 75 percent. By 1860 twenty-one cities had more than 40,000 inhabitants. These places and the activities that they supported had

TABLE 2
Populations of Major Cities, 1830–1860

	1830	1840	1850	1860
New York	202,589	312,700	515,500	813,600
Philadelphia	161,271	220,400	340,000	565,529
Brooklyn	15,396	36,230	96,838	266,660
Baltimore	80,620	102,300	169,600	212,418
Boston	61,392	93,380	136,880	177,840
New Orleans	46,082	102,190	116,375	168,675
Cincinnati	24,831	46,338	115,435	161,044
St. Louis	5,852	14,470	77,860	160,773
Chicago		4,470	29,963	109,260
Buffalo	8,653	18,213	42,260	81,130
Newark	10,953	17,290	38,890	71,940
Louisville	10,340	21,210	43,194	68,033
Albany	24,209	33,721	50,763	62,367
Washington	18,826	23,364	40,001	61,122
San Francisco			34,776	56,802
Providence	16,833	23,171	41,573	50,666
Pittsburgh	15,369	21,115	46,601	49,221
Rochester	9,207	20,191	36,403	48,204
Detroit	2,222	9,012	21,019	45,619
Milwaukee		1,712	20,061	45,246
Cleveland	1,076	6,071	17,034	43,417
Total urban population	1,127,000	1,845,000	3,544,000	6,217,000
Percent of U.S. population that was urban	8.8	10.8	15.3	19.8
Percent increase in urban population		63.7	92.1	75.4

Sources: U.S. Censuses of 1850 and 1860; and Blake McKelvey, *American Urbanization: A Comparative History* (Glenview, Ill.: Scott, Foresman and Company, 1973), table 3, p. 37.

helped to bring the nation into a period of transition—one between pre-industrial and industrial economics, one of new opportunities and old frustrations.

CITIES AND THE CIVIL WAR

For the most part the Civil War intruded upon American urban development rather than placed it at a crossroad. The issues of slavery and secession heated some local political debates, and the war itself pumped life into some outfitting and manufacturing centers, particularly in the North. But the social, economic, and political patterns of most established cities already were evolving in their own ways before the onset of the crisis of union. Still the relationship of cities to the conflict is an important one, and some played a major role in influencing its outcome.

From an urban standpoint a dichotomy between an urban-industrial North and a rural-plantation South exaggerates actual conditions. The North was only primitively industrialized in the antebellum years. Heavy manufacturing and the factory system remained minor factors in the economies of most cities of the Northeast and Midwest into the 1860s. Nor was the South completely un- or antiurban. It had cities of its own and urban boosters, such as New Orleans editor J. D. B. DeBow. Southern cities resembled their northern counterparts in social complexity. In addition to their native whites and blacks, places such as New Orleans, Memphis, Mobile, and Savannah contained large numbers of foreign-born, comprising from fifteen to thirty percent of their total populations. There were, of course, instances where a conflict of civilizations manifested itself. Because the South was less urbanized, its economy depended heavily upon northern commercial centers. New York City particularly influenced southern affairs. By the 1850s New York merchants bought and shipped much of the South's cotton and tobacco, and they imported many of the goods demanded by the section's consumers. Southerners often accused northern merchants of taking unfair advantage of the South's dependence, by fixing prices and accumulating overly high profits. In this light it is no wonder that one of the first actions taken by the Confederate government after secession was to invalidate southern debts to the North, most of them owed to merchants and banks in New York and Boston.

In spite of this antagonism, however, commercial links between southern and northern cities remained advantageous for interests in both sections. Northern businessmen valued southern customers and fought to retain them. On the eve of the Civil War, the Boston *Post*, arguing for a conciliatory policy toward the South, said that southern markets were worth $60 million a year to Boston alone. Many mercantile leaders of the South recognized the importance of close ties with the North and opposed the secession movement as disruptive to trade. This stand provoked those favoring separation to accuse the cities of obstructing southern unity and independence. Thus as the crisis over slavery and states' rights heated up, the South found itself jostled by an internal urban-rural conflict. The New Orleans *Delta* of October 2, 1860 noted that "Three-fourths of the planters are of one party, and an equal proportion of merchants are the opposite." About the same time a reporter for the New York *Herald* observed, "While the merchants in the [southern] cities desire peace and Union, the planters desire protection in the Union, or independence under their own self reliance out of it."

As Ollinger Crenshaw demonstrated in a study published in 1941, voting patterns of the 1860 presidential election reflected this division and revealed a similarity of outlook between northern and southern cities. That election evoked the final issue of whether or not the South would remain in the Union, and it developed into a four-man contest. Senator Stephen A. Douglas of Illinois, the Democratic nominee, and Senator John Bell of Tennessee, the candidate of the Constitutional Union Party, represented policies of moderation, if not conciliation, between the conflicting sections. Southern rights Democrats who had seceded from the regular Democratic convention nominated Vice-President John C. Breckinridge of Kentucky and adopted a proslavery platform. The new Republican Party offered Abraham Lincoln of Illinois and wrote a strong antislavery plank into their platform. Thus Breckinridge and Lincoln, though at opposite poles, represented the extreme approaches to the issues.

In the actual balloting southern urban voters overwhelmingly rejected Breckinridge, while giving pluralities to Bell and preferring either Bell or Douglas by heavy majorities. The combined votes for Bell and Douglas in Louisville, Richmond, Petersburg, Memphis, Nashville, Augusta, Mobile, and New Orleans equaled 70 percent or more of the total vote in each city, while the share won by Breckinridge rarely rose above one-fourth. At the same time, the rural percentages for Breckinridge in Kentucky, Tennessee, Virginia, Alabama, Georgia, and Louisiana were substantially higher, often doubling those in the cities. Similarly, though to a lesser extent, northern cities also favored Bell and Douglas over Lincoln, the candidate at the other extreme. Boston, Cambridge, New Haven, New York City, Brooklyn, Buffalo, Albany, Troy, Jersey City, Philadelphia, Cincinnati, Detroit, and Milwaukee gave significantly fewer votes to Lincoln than did the rural areas of their states. There were notable northern exceptions: Providence, Rochester, Pittsburgh,

Cleveland, and Chicago; yet generally these voting figures imply a preference for moderation in northern and southern cities.

There were two important deviations from these patterns in the South. Savannah voters gave a two-thirds majority to Breckinridge, and in Charleston, Breckinridge's support was undoubtedly just as strong, although voting totals do not exist because there was no popular vote for presidential electors. Just as the situation in Boston had been central to the Revolutionary era, Charleston was an important factor in southern secession. Throughout the first half of the nineteenth century Charleston's colonial prominence evaporated, and its economy declined. As southern expansion, particularly the cotton culture, spread to new areas of the Southwest, the South Carolina port was superseded by cities closer to the new areas of economic activity—Mobile, Memphis, and New Orleans. New York and New Orleans captured Charleston's potential share of the import trade, and Savannah raided much of the commerce remaining along the South Atlantic coast. Efforts to develop manufacturing and new commercial contacts were too few and too late. As early as 1850 Charleston was a city of stagnation and frustration. Over the succeeding years a number of its citizens came to believe that only in a separate southern confederacy could their city renew its growth and prosperity; secession would make Charleston the New York of the South. A similar sentiment developed at Savannah. Though more aggressive than Charleston, the Georgia city faced the same kind of competition from western rivals and northern ports. A similar frustration bred the hope that Savannah also could prosper more outside the Union —away from the shadow of New York—than within it. Although the other southern cities were reluctant to commit themselves to secession, Charleston and Savannah were at the forefront in the move for separation. It is more than coincidence that just as the first incidents of the Revolutionary War occurred around the frustrated city of Boston, the opening volleys of the Civil War were fired in the Charleston harbor.

While the two South Atlantic ports pondered the merits of a separate South, diagonally across the continent two western cities were locked in a contest that not only affected the sectional struggle but also reset patterns of commerce after the Civil War was over. In the 1840s and '50s Chicago and St. Louis were among the fastest growing cities in the country, and businessmen from both cities sought to obtain profitable commercial relations with the newly settled regions around and beyond the upper Mississippi Valley. Located on the Mississippi River near its junctures with the Ohio and the Missouri, St. Louis lay at the heart of the great midwestern river network. Water traffic gave the city its sustenance. By the 1850s steamboats heading northward from New Orleans,

westward from Cincinnati and Louisville, southward from the upper
Mississippi, and eastward from the Missouri Valley converged at St.
Louis, giving it a booming economy.

To the north, St. Louis' rival was also prospering. A canal, completed
in 1848, enabled boats to travel from the Mississippi up the Illinois River
to the canal and on to Chicago and Lake Michigan. The route gave
Chicago jobbers and processors an opportunity to draw trade from interior Illinois away from St. Louis. But it was the railroad that fed Chicago's
commercial growth. By 1853 the highly successful Galena and Chicago
Union Railroad, saved from failure by William B. Ogden, had reached
Freeport, 121 miles to the northwest. Shortly thereafter the Illinois
Central, promoted by Senator Stephen A. Douglas and former mayor
"Long John" Wentworth, gave Chicago connections to Cairo at the
southern tip of the state, to the Ohio River, and ultimately to Mobile
and New Orleans. About the same time, the Rock Island was constructed
westward to the Mississippi River. This road diverted to Chicago much
of the traffic that formerly ran from the upper Mississippi Valley down
to St. Louis.

From the vantage point of historical hindsight we can see that St.
Louis' prosperity bred complacency. For several years business leaders
in St. Louis disregarded their upstart rival to the north. The rivers had
given St. Louis its boom, and there seemed no reason to fear the loss of
this trade. Meanwhile, Chicago investors—with help from the East—were
committing their fortunes to the railroads. By the late 1850s thousands
of miles of track could be reached from the city, and hundreds of trains
entered and departed daily. A bridge across the Mississippi at Rock
Island linked Chicago to the newest western areas and cut more deeply
into St. Louis' once-powerful commercial hegemony. The locomotive had
not quite supplanted the steamboat as the major vehicle of western trade,
but it helped prepare Chicago to overtake St. Louis as the most important western city in the years which followed the Civil War. Leaders of
St. Louis, such as Pierre Chouteau, John O'Fallon, Daniel Page, and
Henry Bacon, were prudent, conservative merchants and bankers who
were content with their city's growth and who lacked the expansionist
spirit necessary to attract new enterprises and entrepreneurs. They
hesitated to risk their fortunes on railroad projects and were cool to
outside investors. In contrast the aggressive boosterism of Ogden, Wentworth, and banker J. Young Scannon lured to Chicago others like them
—industrialist Cyrus McCormick, retailer Potter Palmer, and journalist
Joseph Medill, for example. Such leadership brought the city fame and
customers. By 1860 Chicago had not only rail connections to the North,
West, and South but also rail *and* water connections eastward to Toledo,
Detroit, and New York. That same year only 181 miles of track entered

St. Louis; lack of capital and enthusiasm had squelched all but a few railroad projects. St. Louis still had its waterways, but rivers could no longer control the commerce of their valleys.

As Wyatt Belcher has indicated, the economic rivalry between St. Louis and Chicago shifted the axes of trade in the West during the close of the antebellum period. Although St. Louis businessmen remained cautious and confident that the North-South flow of trade through their city was a permanent, natural condition, a sprawling network of railroads leading in and out of Chicago pulled the lines of commerce into an East-West direction. The agricultural products and raw materials of the trans-Mississippi West increasingly moved by rail into Chicago for processing. Then they were distributed regionally or were shipped to the East via rail or lake steamer. Between 1852 and 1856 receipts of wheat in Chicago rose from one million to nine million bushels corn, from three million to twelve million bushels. The footage of received lumber quadrupled, and the tonnage of coal doubled. Volume of trade at St. Louis increased also, but at a much slower rate. More and more farmers in the new western areas found transportation arrangements eastward to Chicago and beyond more convenient than those leading southward to St. Louis and New Orleans. As early as 1851 J. D. B. DeBow complained that northern canals and railroads had "rolled back the mighty tide of the Mississippi and its ten thousand tributary streams until its mouth, practically and commercially, is more at New York and Boston than at New Orleans."

The Civil War not only hastened the rearrangement of trade routes but also turned St. Louis' geographical advantage into a liability. When hostilities broke out, the Union Army closed the lower Mississippi to commercial traffic and imposed strict surveillance on all goods shipped out of St. Louis, even those heading northward. These conditions paralyzed business in the city and blessed that of Chicago by further diverting trade to an East-West flow. The result of Chicago's prewar expansion and the war's effects on St. Louis was that the West became the economic, as well as the political, ally of the North against the South. By the time St. Louis recovered, Chicago had surpassed it to become the principal commercial metropolis of the country's heartland.

BIBLIOGRAPHY

The historiography of urban America in the early national period branches into a number of topical areas. The growth of cities in the West is best examined by Richard C. Wade's The Urban Frontier: 1790–1830 (Cambridge: Harvard University Press, 1957) and by Bayard Still, "Patterns of Mid-Nineteenth Century Urbanization in the Middle West," Mississippi Valley Historical Review, 28 (September 1941), 187–206. Several works have probed the development of urban rivalries. Among the most notable are Julius Rubin, *Canal or Railroad? Imitation and Innovation in the Response to the Erie Canal in Philadelphia, Baltimore, and Boston* (Philadelphia: American Philosophical Society, 1961); Harry N. Scheiber, "Urban Rivalry and Internal Improvements in the Old Northwest, 1820–1860," *Ohio History*, 71 (October 1962), 227–39; and Wyatt W. Belcher, *The Economic Rivalry Between St. Louis and Chicago, 1850–1880* (New York: Columbia University Press, 1947). The boosters who often spurred these rivalries are described in Daniel J. Boorstin, *The Americans: The National Experience* (New York: Random House, 1965). The development of city services has received considerable attention in such works as Nelson Manfred Blake, *Water for the Cities: A History of the Urban Water Supply Problem in the United States* (Syracuse: Syracuse University Press, 1958); Roger Lane, *Policing the City: Boston, 1822–1885* (Cambridge: Harvard University Press, 1967); James F. Richardson, *The New York Police: Colonial Times to 1901* (New York: Oxford University Press, 1970); Charles E. Rosenberg, *The Cholera Years: The United States in 1832, 1849, and 1866* (Chicago: University of Chicago Press, 1962); Raymond A. Mohl, *Poverty in New York, 1783–1825* (New York: Oxford University Press, 1971); Carol Smith Rosenberg, *Religion and the Rise of the City: The New York City Mission Movement, 1812–1870* (Ithaca: Cornell University Press, 1971); David J. Rothman, *The Discovery of the Asylum: Social Order and Disorder in the New Republic* (Boston: Little, Brown and Company, 1971); Stanley K. Schultz, *The Culture Factory: Boston Public Schools, 1789–1860* (New York: Oxford University Press, 1973); and Michael Katz, *The Irony of Early School Reform: Educational Innovation in Mid-Nineteenth Century Massachusetts* (Cambridge: Harvard University Press, 1968). For the interplay between population and economic growth, the need for services, and the impact of change upon the urban community, see Sam Bass Warner, Jr., *The Private City: Philadelphia in Three Periods of Its Growth* (Philadelphia: University of Pennsylvania Press, 1968); and Michael Frisch, *Town Into City: Springfield, Massachusetts, and the Meaning of Community, 1840–1880* (Cambridge: Harvard University Press, 1972). Economic and geographical studies include, Allan R. Pred, *Urban Growth and the Circulation of Information: The United States System of Cities, 1790–1840* (Cambridge: Harvard University Press, 1973); David T. Gilchrist, ed., *The Growth of Seaport Cities, 1790–1825* (Charlottesville, Va.: University of Virginia Press, 1967); George R. Taylor, *The Transportation Revolution, 1815–1860* (New York: Rinehart, 1951); Robert G. Albion, *The Rise of the New York Port, 1815–1860* (New York: Scribner's Sons, 1939); and David Montgomery, "The Working Classes of the Pre-Industrial American City, 1780–1830," *Labor History*, 9 (Winter 1968), 5–22.

Recently, scholars have begun extended research into aspects of social history in the early nineteenth century. Many of the studies were spawned by Stephan Thernstrom's *Poverty and Progress: Social Mobility in a Nineteenth Century City* (Cambridge: Harvard University Press, 1964). Other works on social structure and mobility include Peter R. Knights, *The Plain People of Boston: A Study in City Growth* (New York: Oxford University Press, 1971); John Modell, "The Peopling of a Working Class Ward: Reading, Pennsylvania, 1850," *Journal of Social History*, 5 (Fall 1971), 71–96; Edward Pessen, "The Egalitarian Myth and the American Social Reality: Wealth, Mobility, and Equality in the 'Era of the common Man,'" *American Historical Review*, 76 (October 1971), 989–1034; and the articles by Clyde Griffen, Herbert Gutman, and Stuart Blumin in Stephan Thernstrom and Richard Sennett, eds., *Nineteenth Century Cities: Essays in the New Urban History* (New Haven: Yale University Press, 1969). Issues concerning women and family life have been probed by Gerda Lerner, "The Lady and the Mill Girl," *Mid-Continent American Studies Journal*, 10 (Spring 1969), 5–15; Barbara Welter, "The Cult of True Womanhood, 1820–1860," *American Quarterly*, 18 (Summer 1966), 151–74; and William Bridges, "Family Patterns and Special Values in America, 1825–1875," *American Quarterly*, 17 (Spring 1965), 3–11. The situation of blacks is examined in Richard C. Wade, *Slavery in the Cities: The South, 1820–1860* (New York: Oxford University Press, 1964); Leon Litwack, *North of Slavery: The Negro in the Free States, 1790–1860* (Chicago: University of Chicago Press, 1961); Constance McLaughlin Green, *The Secret City: A History of Race Relations in the Nation's Capital* (Princeton, N. J.: Princeton University Press, 1967); and Letitia Woods Brown, *Free Negroes in the District of Columbia, 1790–1846* (New York: Oxford University Press, 1972). Immigrants are examined by Oscar Handlin, *Boston's Immigrants: A Study in Acculturation* (Cambridge: Harvard University Press, revised edition, 1959); Earl F. Niehaus, *The Irish in New Orleans, 1800–1860* (Baton Rouge, La.: Louisiana State University Press, 1965); Robert Ernst, *Immigrant Life in New York City, 1825–1863* (New York: King's Crown Press, 1949); and Rowland Berthoff, *British Immigrants in Industrial America* (Cambridge: Harvard University Press, 1953).

3
THE BIRTH OF
THE MODERN CITY:
MASS TRANSIT AND
INDUSTRIAL GROWTH

THE WALKING CITY

In our historical memory dramatic episodes often obscure the importance of quieter, but equally consequential, developments. While the hardy pioneer and the bombastic booster were invading the West, and while southerners and northerners glared at each other with gathering rage, less explosive forces were transforming the physical, social, and economic configurations of American urban life. Although its birth remains undatable, the modern American city had arrived by the last third of the nineteenth century.

Until the 1850s almost all American cities could be characterized by their compactness. Located near harbors or river junctions, they focused their activities on the waterfront. Here wharves, warehouses, mercantile offices, and manufacturing establishments (usually processing operations of commerce-related industry like shipbuilding or ropewalks) were built, because access to water transportation was of principal importance. Public buildings, churches, hotels, and a few shops clustered nearby. The homes of the more prominent families often were interspersed among these structures or, as in Cincinnati, Providence, and St. Louis, were located on a nearby hill overlooking the port. Around these cores and in the valleys between hills were situated the residential areas of craftsmen, storekeepers, and laborers. In these districts two-and three-story buildings contained shops and workshops on the bottom floors; residential quarters were in the back or above. Certain businesses needing water supplies

—mills, tanneries, slaughterhouses, breweries—grouped along nearby streets. As the nineteenth century progressed, some heavy industry, particularly base metals, grew on the outskirts near railroad connections. Most business establishments, however, remained dispersed throughout the settled areas of town.

Wagons, carriages, horses, mules, and pedestrians jammed the central streets. Neither public officers nor mechanical signals regulated the speed and direction of traffic. People seldom observed any custom of keeping to one side of the street or the other, and right of way at intersections went to the boldest—or most reckless. Cobblestones or gravel paved only a fraction of urban thoroughfares; most retained their original dirt surfaces that nature and traffic turned into choking dust or slogging mud.

The heaviest users of streets were not wheels or hoofs, but human feet. In the premodern American city the vast majority of people walked to their destinations, and it was this form of transportation that determined the size and shape of the city. Studies of commuting and intracity traffic, from the early nineteenth century down to the present motor age, indicate that few people travel more than thirty or forty minutes to work, shop, or visit. Until the 1850s the settled areas of even the largest cities like New York, Boston, and Philadelphia rarely extended beyond two miles from the city center—the average distance a person can walk in half an hour. Thus historians have labeled this early configuration the *walking city* because of its size and major mode of conveyance. No specific policies or legislation limited the area of any city; it was simply more convenient for people to locate businesses and residences on available sites that had easy access to most business and social activities.

The limitations of walking largely contributed to the compactness of the premodern city, a compactness with several important features. First, land use was mixed—commercial, storage, residential, and industrial buildings mingled together. There were few distinct districts; even waterfront property had several types of use. As cities grew their business districts became more defined, but here too, residences and primitive factories remained interspersed with the stores, banks, and offices.

Second, mixed and intensive land use meant that urban dwellers were relatively integrated. Short distances separated poor from rich, immigrant from native, black from white. There was very little segregation among immigrants and occupational groups in mid-nineteenth century Philadelphia, Boston, and other cities inhabited by heterogeneous populations. In southern cities the highest and lowest ranks of society lived together because black slaves inhabited compounds behind their masters' houses. As time passed and populations increased, enclaves of certain groups did form. In Boston the newly arrived Irish filled the North End and the neighborhood along the wharves. In Philadelphia blacks clustered in the southern wards of the city. In the South residential districts of free blacks and living-out slaves grew on or outside the edges of places like Charleston and Richmond. Still, however, the relatively small areas of all cities left all groups of people physically close together. Moreover, people not only lived near to each other, they also lived near, or at, their places of work. Those who worked away from their residences walked to and from their jobs. It has been difficult to uncover exactly why urban dwellers lived where they did, but it seems likely that proximity to place of work was *not* a primary consideration because most places of employment were accessible by foot from any part of town.

The restraints of walking confined the horizontal expansion of premodern cities, but in addition, technological limitations prevented vertical expansion. Only after the 1850s did the invention of the elevator and the use of iron, rather than masonry, for structural support enable the construction of buildings more than a few stories in height. The skyscraper, with its steel frame and electric elevators, did not begin to appear until the 1880s. Until then the major type of physical development occurred when builders covered remaining empty property within the walking city or reclaimed land by leveling hills, draining marshes, or filling in coves and bays. As cities filled up and vacant lots disappeared, the value of land soared, especially in comparison with costs of construction. Now more than just speculation and boosterism inflated urban land values; rising demand and diminishing supply became ever-important. In Chicago, for example, the total valuation for land within a one-mile radius of the central business district increased from $810,000 in 1842 to $50,750,000 in 1856, a 6,000 percent gain.

Meanwhile many cities were practically bursting at their seams. It has been common for Americans to consider urban crowding a consequence of industrialization and mass immigration, occuring during the late nineteenth and early twentieth centuries. Yet at no time in the country's history were total urban densities as high as they were in the mid-nineteenth century. Chapter 2 noted that these years witnessed the greatest proportionate growth of urban populations this country has ever experienced. An almost annual excess of new arrivals over those departing doubled and tripled populations of St. Louis, Pittsburgh, and Cincinnati between 1840 and 1850. Densities in settled areas swelled. By 1850 there were 135.6 persons per acre in New York, 82.7 in Boston, 80.0 in Philadelphia, and 68.4 in Pittsburgh. In Providence, Rhode Island, at mid-century, an average of two families occupied every dwelling, a much larger figure than those for similar-sized towns in Europe, or even in fast-growing regions of England. Slum wards of most big cities would become even more densely populated in the latter half of the century, but because areas at midcentury were smaller, crowding spread to a larger proportion of urban districts.

Beginning in the 1820s and 1830s bridges and ferries were built across nearby bodies of water in increasing numbers, opening up new areas for development. Suburbs—that is, smaller towns adjacent to, and often dependent upon, a major city—had existed since colonial days, but now many more neighboring regions became accessible. Areas opened for suburban settlement included the Jersey shore across the Hudson River from Manhattan, Brooklyn across the East River; South Boston, Roxbury, Cambridge, and Charlestown near Boston; and land across the Schuylkill River at Philadelphia, across the Allegheny and Monongahela at Pittsburgh, the Cuyahoga at Cleveland, and the New Buffalo Creek at Buffalo. Populations in these places doubled and tripled in a single decade. By 1860 Brooklyn, the ultimate nineteenth-century suburb, contained more people than Boston and was the third most populous urban area in the country. Most suburbs had their own local economies and retained their political independence, preferring only to purchase services like water and gas from the nearby city. Few as yet served as residential areas for large numbers of commuters who left in the morning and returned at night. Nevertheless these suburban areas did act as satellites. The bridges and ferries gave big-city merchants links to new local markets and enabled some of the wealthiest families to escape the crowded walking city and to live in more attractive surroundings.

THE GROWTH OF MASS TRANSIT

By the middle of the nineteenth century three accelerating forces were breaking apart the walking city. The rise and spread of mass transportation, the application of technological and economic innovations to industrial production, and the flows of foreign and internal population migration refashioned the contour and character of urban America and created the city as we know it today. The three developments are closely interrelated, but for the sake of simplicity, migration and immigration have been relegated to the next chapter. The remainder of this chapter will focus on mass transit and industrialization and their consequences.

Professor Richard C. Wade has written, "No incendiary ever looked so poorly suited to the task of creating such far-reaching change as [the] awkward object moving down Broadway in 1829." This object was an omnibus, a large, horse-drawn coach designed to transport the urban public over fixed routes for fixed fares. The omnibus combined the functions of two traditional types of public transportation: the hackney, an early version of the taxicab, which carried passengers where they wished; and the stagecoach, which operated over long-distance routes at scheduled times. The idea originated in France and first appeared in this country in 1827 when Abraham Brower ran a stagecoach up and down Broadway in downtown Manhattan, picking up and discharging passengers at their request for a flat fee of one shilling (12½ cents) per ride. In 1829 Brower added another vehicle to the route. This coach contained seats running lengthwise, instead of across the breadth, and an entrance at the top of an iron stairway at the rear. About the same time Ephraim Dodge initiated mass transportation in Boston by driving a hack on a regular schedule between Boston and South Boston. The schemes of Brower and Dodge spread quickly. By 1833 some eighty omnibuses operated on the streets of New York, and by the middle of the decade similar companies had appeared in Boston, Philadelphia, New Orleans, Washington, D.C., and Brooklyn.

An omnibus drawn by two horses normally seated twelve people, but when traffic was heavy, several more riders could be packed inside. In the winter some operators replaced their wheels with runners for easier conveyance over the snow. At first a boy was employed to collect fares at the rear, but eventually his job was eliminated by a fare box located next to the driver's platform. Since the driver could not see inside the coach, an arrangement was needed to signal him when to start and stop. The mechanism, according to John Anderson Miller, consisted of "a strap running from the rear door to the driver's leg. A pull on the strap indicated that the door was being opened by someone who wanted to get off or on. A slack strap indicated that the door was closed." Needless to say, such an arrangement must have offered irresistible temptations to pranksters and short-changed riders. Most omnibuses were individually owned, often by men who had previously engaged in some aspect of horse-drawn transportation: carriage-making, blacksmithing, or hauling. The owners were entrepreneurs—small businessmen whose objective was to make as much money as they could. Seldom, if at all, did they consider their operation as a public service. Thus they ran their vehicles only on those streets which promised the most riders. Almost all stretched their routes between two important centers of activity—usually a wharf, railroad depot, or suburb at one end, and a focal point of the business district at the other.

Although there was often keen competition between operators for favorable routes, the rapid proliferation of omnibus companies and vehicles attests to their success. New York City alone granted licenses to 108 omnibuses in 1837, 260 in 1847, 425 in 1850, and 683 in 1853. One observer claimed that one coach coming from each direction crossed a particular intersection on lower Broadway every fifteen seconds. By mid-century the omnibus had multiplied and become essential to transportation in other cities as well: Boston, Philadelphia, Washington, Baltimore, Pittsburgh, and St. Louis. In several areas coach traffic became so heavy that it clogged thoroughfares and endangered human life. Congestion and reckless driving provoked local governments to require the relocation of some omnibus routes and to impose fines on drivers who failed to operate their vehicles safely. In spite of increasing regulations the citizenry constantly complained that drivers intentionally ran down pedestrians and private carriages.

Inside a crowded coach the situation was no better than outside. The seats were usually primitive benches, and construction was such that there was never enough ventilation in summer and always too much in winter. A bumpy, noisy journey of twenty people in a space intended for twelve strained the bonds of human solidarity. The New York *Herald* described the situation vividly, if a bit over dramatically, in 1864:

Modern martyrdom may be succinctly defined as riding in a New York omnibus. The discomforts, inconveniences, and annoyances of a trip on one of these vehicles are almost intolerable. From the beginning to the end of the journey a constant quarrel is progressing. The driver quarrels with the passengers, and the passengers quarrel with the driver. There are quarrels about getting out and quarrels about getting in. There are quarrels about change and quarrels about the ticket swindle. The driver swears at the passengers and the passengers harangue the driver through the strap hole—a position in which even Demosthenes could not be eloquent. Respectable clergymen in white chokers are obliged to listen to loud oaths. Ladies are disgusted, frightened, and insulted. Children are alarmed and lift up their voices and weep. Indignant gentlemen rise to remonstrate with the irate Jehu and are suddenly bumped back into their seats, twice as indignant as before, besides being involved in supplementary quarrels with those other passengers upon whose corns they have accidentally trodden. Thus the omnibus rolls along, a perfect Bedlam on Wheels.

Such mayhem did not discourage people from riding, however. An 1853 New York guidebook advertised that some 120,000 passengers rode the city's omnibuses daily. Yet in spite of its wide use, mass transportation remained a luxury. Early urban transit never met the expectations of those who believed omnibuses would erase class lines by bringing all types of people together. In 1841 an optimistic writer for *Godey's Ladies Journal* had proclaimed, "The statesman and politician . . . the greasy citizen who votes against him and the zealots of different sectaries, dismounted of their several doxies, are compelled to ride cheek by jowl, with one another. Such is the levelling and democratic Omnibus." But the realities of economics prevented most "greasy citizens" from riding vehicles of mass transit. In the 1840s, '50s, and '60s the ordinary wage earner received little more than a dollar a day and rarely more than two. The fares on most omnibus lines ranged from six to twelve and a half cents per ride. Very few laborers could afford outlays of twelve to twenty-five cents a day for transportation.

Although it was mainly used by middle and upper classes, the omnibus altered urban life styles in several important ways. It not only made wheeled transportation available to more people than did hackneys and carriages, but it also carried people over a set route for a standard price on a reasonably predictable schedule. It facilitated intracity communications in an age when economic specialization was making such communications increasingly necessary. Probably most importantly the omnibus made possible the commuter—enabling the affluent to escape the crowded walking city and live in outlying regions. And, as Professor Glen Holt has suggested, the omnibus's rapid expansion and growing numbers of customers helped urban dwellers develop a "riding habit," a disposition few had ever had before.

The omnibuses were not the only new transportation means. While these vehicles began rumbling down city streets, steam-powered trains were beginning to travel between cities. Although originally promoted to carry freight and passengers over long distances, several early railroads also engaged in short distance commuter services. By mid-century nearly all the trains leaving Boston made commuter stops within fifteen miles of the city, and railroads based in New York and Philadelphia ran several trains daily to and from nearby towns. Over the next decade such service spread into the Midwest. A person living outside the city could now take the train into town and then ride an omnibus, which stopped at the railroad depot, to his or her ultimate destination.

The commuter railroad, even more than the omnibus, was a convenience for the wealthy. A one-way ticket cost fifteen to twenty-five cents, too high for most workingmen. Cheaper rides could be obtained by purchasing season tickets, but few people could afford single outlays of ten to thirty dollars for three- or six-month passes. But like the omnibus, the commuter railroad opened outlying areas for settlement. In 1854, for example, the Chicago and Milwaukee Railroad (later renamed the Chicago and Northwestern) built a depot in Evanston, Illinois, and helped populate—and popularize—that northern suburb of Chicago. By 1859 forty trains were running daily between Philadelphia and Germantown, almost all their passenger traffic consisting of commuters.

The New York and Harlem Railroad pioneered the next major development in urban mass transportation. In 1832 John Mason, one of the New York and Harlem's promoters, decided to combine the technologies of the omnibus and the railroad. By running horsedrawn coaches over rails instead of cobblestones, he could offer faster, smoother rides and enable the horses to pull larger, heavier cars. Over the next two years Mason laid four miles of track in lower Manhattan and thus began the first street, or horse, railway. By 1860 street railway companies were operating in at least eight other major cities, and there were 142 miles of track in New York and 155 miles in Philadelphia. The cars held two or three times as many passengers as omnibuses and could travel faster, while utilizing the same number of horses. In addition because horse cars moved on rails only down the middle of the street, they interfered less with other traffic than did the omnibuses.

Horse railways and, particularly, their tracks created several new social and political situations. Rails made mass transit routes completely fixed and predictable. This certainty combined with the new, ordered structure of time, a product of incipient industrialization, to give people more regimented lives, with daily routes and routines dictated by working hours and transit schedules. And because the equipment and construction costs of horse railways were so much more expensive than they were for omnibuses, company owners had to be even more concerned with laying track and running cars along the most profitable routes. Although horse railways spread people into outlying areas, they also provided limited service, often operating along the same streets that omnibuses traveled. Because transit owners built track only where it appeared that settlement would be most dense, and because subdividers and builders located their real estate projects near mass transit lines, outward expansion proceeded unevenly. In St. Louis, for example, mass transportation stretched the built-up area far to the northwest, while land to the southwest remained long underdeveloped because it lacked transit service. And in Boston the early street railways extended real estate development in the same directions as omnibus lines; only slowly did they fill in the vacant districts between existing fingers of settlement.

Finally, the issue of control became more pressing. Early omnibuses had evoked few public regulations. Local governments established little more than licensing taxes, vehicle inspection, and speeding restrictions. But the laying of track and the capitalization of horse railway companies complicated the relations between mass transit companies and public authority. Incorporation of the company required a charter from the state, and construction of track on city streets necessitated permission from the local government. Beginning in the 1850s such permission was usually obtained in the form of a franchise that enabled a company to operate over a specific route for a limited, though renewable, period of time. Most early franchises granted monopolistic or semimonopolistic privileges, often for terms of fifty to one hundred years. Although the contracts generally stipulated maximum fares, usually five cents, the privilege of an exclusive franchise, plus almost certain population growth

—and therefore increasing passengers—assured recipients of high profits.

With several street railway and omnibus companies contesting for such grants, mass transportation inevitably became involved in local politics. The problem was that city councils seldom granted franchises on the basis of purely objective decisions. Other utilities besides mass transit, such as street lighting and water, were also provided by private companies who sought franchises. In some instances local officials were so intent upon securing these services for their community that they paid little heed to the consequences of generous franchises. In their anxiety they gave transit and other companies long-term, exclusive contracts that included low tax rates on their property and revenues, low fees paid to the city, no responsibility to repair torn-up streets, and other advantageous provisions. More often these favors were obtained by political manipulation and corruption. The granting of public franchises in scores of cities in the latter half of the nineteenth century lured city officials and businessmen into illicit collusions that included bribes, kickbacks, illegal transfers of stock, and other influence-buying activities. The use of public land by private companies, of which horse railways and mechanically powered mass transit were major participants, helped to create the unsavory connections between business and politics—connections that would become objects of municipal reform in succeeding generations.

The next major breakthrough in urban mass transportation occurred in the last quarter of the nineteenth century when innovators applied mechanical power to their vehicles. Aspiring entrepreneurs tried a variety of devices of propulsion, including steam engines and large springs—the latter method was akin to running a streetcar with a rubber band—but the first successful effort was the cable car. Cleaner and faster than horses, the cable car was introduced in San Francisco by Andrew S. Hallidie in 1873. Hallidie, a wire manufacturer, had known that English miners hauled coal cars along large cables, and he decided to try the idea on San Francisco's steep hills, where horsecars could not operate. His system utilized an endless, underground wire rope driven by a steam engine. Each cable car ran along track and had a gripping clamp that extended through a slot in the pavement. The clamp attached to, or detached from, the cable at the will of the vehicle's operator. Brakes, similar to those on horsecars, could halt the vehicle after the grip had been released from the cable. The scheme was so impressive that a company headed by California railroad magnates Leland Stanford, Mark Hopkins, and Collis P. Huntington applied for one of the first franchises.

Although the cable car has remained a historic relic of San Francisco, its widest use occurred in Chicago. Here cable car lines spread rapidly in the 1880s, particularly to the city's South Side; and by 1894 Chicago had 86 miles of cable track and over 1,500 grip and trailer cars. Initial costs of construction and equipment were very high, but cable cars were generally more economical to operate than were horsecars, mainly because horses required higher maintenance costs. Cable cars had their drawbacks, however. A break in the cable halted all traffic, the intricate mechanical equipment suffered frequent breakdowns, and operating a car required considerable skill. Nevertheless cable lines existed for varying periods of time in Washington, D.C., Baltimore, Philadelphia, New York, Providence, Cleveland, St. Louis, Kansas City, Omaha, Denver, Oakland, and Seattle.

The era of the cable car lasted for less than two decades. By the beginning of the twentieth century electric trolleys had almost completely replaced horse railways and cable cars as the major means of urban transportation. Since the 1830s inventors in Europe and America had been experimenting with electricity as a source of power for vehicles, but it was not until 1886 that someone harnessed electric energy to propel a city-wide system of transportation. The previous year James Gaboury, one of the leading promoters of mass transit in the South, had hired Charles J. Van Doeple, a Belgian sculptor and engineer, to construct an electric railway in Montgomery, Alabama. Service began in spring, 1886, using vehicles resembling those pulled by horses but containing a motor on the front platform. A chain running from the motor to the wheels powered the vehicle, and a cable from an overhead wire to the motor transmitted electrical power. During the same time a young electrician, Frank Sprague, built a similar system in Richmond, Virgina, utilizing a four-wheeled device pulled along the overhead wires to transfer electricity to the vehicle. This device was called a *troller* due to the manner in which it was pulled. According to John Anderson Miller, a corruption of the word produced *trolley*, the term used for electric streetcars. In 1888 Sprague allayed all doubts about electrified mass transit when he successfully demonstrated that his cars could conquer the steep grades of Richmond and that electrical generators could provide enough power to operate several cars concentrated on a short stretch of track.

Soon electric railways became well established across the country. In fact, during the 1880s and 1890s nearly every large city in the country granted franchises to trolley companies. In 1890 when the federal government first surveyed the nation's street railways, it found about 5,700 miles of track for vehicles operated by animal power, 500 miles of track for cable cars, and 1,260 miles of electrified track. By 1902 the total of electrified track had swelled to 22,000 miles while that of horse railway had dwindled to 250 miles.

At the turn of the century companies in some of the largest, most congested cities raised part of their track onto stilts, giving their vehicles unrestricted right of way, free from the interference of pedestrians and animal-powered vehicles. These were the electric elevated railways—the *els,*—and they became most prominent in New York, Chicago, Boston, Philadelphia, Brooklyn, and Kansas City. Although New York had had a successful steam-powered elevated since the 1870s, the noise, vibration, dirt, and danger to traffic below made other cities unwilling to risk an el. Thus it appeared in only a few places, even after Frank Sprague had designed a control mechanism that enabled steam elevateds to be electrified.

Sprague's device, a master control that operated the motor and control on each car of the train, could be used for railways below, as well as above, ground. The subway originated in London in the 1860s when coal-burning locomotives began pulling mass transit cars through tunnels beneath the city. Promoters raised the idea in America, particularly in New York, but fears of smoke and tunnel cave-ins, plus heavy opposition from street railway companies prevented construction. Electrification and the success of the London experiment removed some of the objections, and in Boston Henry M. Whitney, who had consolidated most of the city's transit lines under his ownership, obtained permission to construct tunnels for his trains. At a cost of $4,350,000, he built a subway one and two-thirds miles in length underneath Tremont Street. In 1897, its first year of operation, the subway handled more than 50 million passengers, running as many as 400 cars in each direction at peak periods while still reducing travel time in the downtown area. This success prompted the revival of interest in New York, and in 1904 that city's first subway opened. The extraordinary costs of construction and its disruption to above ground activity limited subway expansion, however. With the exception of a combined el-subway, which appeared in Philadelphia in 1908, no additional underground projects occurred until the 1930s when work began in Chicago.

Subways and elevateds were the only means of *rapid* transit that American urban dwellers were to have, and only in a very few cities did schemes, which were many, materialize. Mass transportation was almost always considered a private business, not a public utility, so that profitability was the chief criterion for the construction of any system. At first omnibus and street railway companies made huge profits from a population eager for urban expansion and anxious to cut down traveling time—or at least to travel farther in the same amount of time. There were other benefactors too. Land values along streetcar lines soared, and real estate developers scrambled to buy up property along projected routes. The screeching wheels and unnerving vibration of els eventually drove the wealthy classes away, but land adjacent to elevated track remained lucrative for tenement and commercial investment. Technological advances made mass transit more efficient and convenient, but they also raised costs of construction and maintenance. Because electric elevateds, subways, and street railways required heavy outlays of capital, mass transportation in many cities quickly became the domain of just one or two large-scale operations. As early as the 1880s shrewd businessmen were consolidating independent companies under their aegis. Colorful personalities such as Henry M. Whitney of Boston and Charles Tyson Yerkes of Chicago deftly and ruthlessly established city-wide railway systems and huge personal fortunes.

Systems such as those of Whitney and Yerkes brought several benefits to their riders. The increased scale of operations enabled companies to preserve the five cent fare, while the constant quest for new riders pushed the construction of track into new districts. Equally important, the merger of several lines produced free transfers from one route to another, enabling passengers to travel farther for a single fare. Yet also the combined functions of public service and private profitability loaded transit companies with nagging predicaments. The limits of a five cent fare, whether self-imposed or legislated by government, forced traction companies to seek higher revenues by increasing their passengers. But if they laid track into newer districts, they risked overextension and fewer riders than anticipated. If they restricted operations to densely settled areas, they faced public charges of inadequate and discriminatory service. In addition the huge capitalization necessary to construct elevateds, subways, or trolley lines often invited stock watering and nonlocal investors. The result was that managers, intent on profits rather than on public service, directed company policies wholly toward producing dividends for anxious stockholders.

The riding public understandably had little sympathy. According to Professor Holt the traction companies too often cited their financial plights as an excuse for failure to improve service, and they used their positions of indispensibility to force local governments to grant additional privileges, such as renewed franchises or lighter taxes. Moreover as reformers sought new legislation to regulate public transportation, they encountered growing collusion between traction interests and local politicians, an alliance that, as noted earlier, included graft and boodling for the sake of personal gain. Indignation at such activities often pulled reformers together, and they translated their revulsion into a move for governmental reform, including municipal ownership of mass transit. New York in the early 1890s and Chicago in 1907 established municipal authority to build or buy public transit systems. As scores of companies fell into bankruptcy during and after World War I, public ownership became the only way to sustain mass transit in a number of cities. But public assumption of mass transportation responsibilities occurred just at the time when the private automobile was becoming the idol of mobile America and was replacing the streetcar as the major mode of conveyance. The American hunger for speed and convenience had outgrown mass transit, but not until the omnibus and all its descendents had made their mark on urban life.

THE BEGINNING OF URBAN SPRAWL

Mass transportation revised the social and economic fabric of the American city in three fundamental ways. It catalyzed physical expansion, it sorted out people and land uses, and it accelerated the inherent instability of urban life. By opening vast areas of unoccupied land for residential expansion, the omnibuses, horse railways, commuter trains, and electric trolleys pulled settled regions outward two, three, and four times more distant from city centers than they were in the premodern era. In 1850, for example, the borders of Boston lay scarcely two miles from the old business district; by the turn of the century the radius extended ten miles. Now those who could afford it could live far removed from the old walking city and still commute there for work, shopping, and entertainment. The new accessibility of land around the periphery of almost every major city sparked an explosion of real estate development and fueled what we now know as urban sprawl. Between 1890 and 1920, for example, some 250,000 new residential lots were recorded within the borders of Chicago, most of them located in outlying areas. Over the same period another 550,000 were plotted outside the city limits but within the metropolitan area. Anxious to take advantage of the possibilities of commuting, real estate developers added 800,000 potential building sites to the Chicago region in just thirty years—lots that could have housed five to six million people.

Of course, many were never occupied; there was always a huge surplus of subdivided, but vacant, land around Chicago and other cities. These excesses underscore a feature of residential expansion related to the growth of mass transportation: urban sprawl was essentially unplanned. It was carried out by thousands of small investors who paid little heed to coordinated land use or to future land users. Those who purchased and prepared land for residential purposes, particularly land near or outside city borders where transit lines and middle-class inhabitants were anticipated, did so to create demand as much, if not more, than to respond to it. Chicago is a prime example of this process. Real

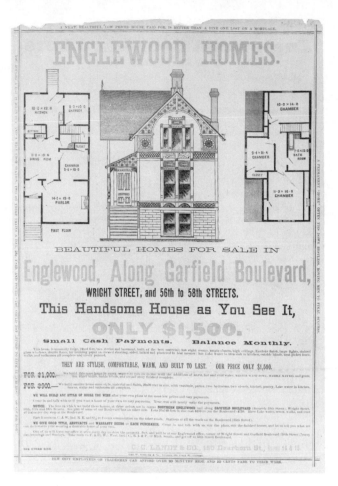

The Suburban Dream

During the construction boom of the 1880s, city newspapers were filled with ads like this one for middle-class houses built in the periphery and suburbs. *Courtesy Chicago Historical Society.*

estate subdivision there proceeded much faster than population growth. The addition of new lots reflected the booster spirit that had characterized the city's history. It was the transformation of anticipation into reality. This belief led the Chicago *Times* to decree:

> Chicago, as most people are aware, is situated on an open prairie, skirted on the east by the lake. In the latter direction, therefore, the enterprising real estate developer meets with some difficulty in disposing of water lots, but westward there is an unlimited space, bounded only by the swamps of the Calumet, the Mississippi, the British Provinces and the imagination. Some day the Queen's dominions will be annexed, and then there will be no limit to Chicago's enterprise.

A Secondary Business Center
The intersection of Milwaukee Avenue and Chicago Avenue in Chicago became one of many nodes of retail activity that grew around intersections of important arteries and streetcar routes. *Courtesy Chicago Historical Society.*

One of the most significant side effects of residential sprawl was the decentralization of economic functions. The increased concentration of people living around the city periphery and traveling on lines of mass transit turned outlying transfer points, such as streetcar intersections and elevated railway stations, into natural business centers. The result was a multinucleated development of commercial districts. That is, as consumers moved outward, businesses followed them. Groceries, drug stores, specialty shops, and saloons developed along traffic centers in newer regions of settlement. There they were joined by chain stores, banks, and theaters that had branched out from the main business district. These secondary business centers quickly became important focuses for neighborhood life.

Mass transit also helped to create finer distinctions between social and economic districts. Not all were able to afford mass transportation; fares were too high for working class families who lived at, or below, barest levels of subsistence. Yet, as Sam Bass Warner, Jr., has noted, probably half or more of American urban dwellers could be ranked within or above the middle class. For these people the streetcars offered the opportunity to escape the crowding, dirt, noise, and crime of the central city. They could afford homes (if not to build or to buy, then to rent) in the city's periphery or the suburbs, as well as the fares to commute to and from work every day. So they moved into the rings of residential areas that were forming outside the old urban cores. Here they could fulfill the rural ideals of private life in a single-family dwelling and security in a small community setting. The outskirts became places of detached houses, private yards, and tree-lined streets. People living in these areas now divided their lives between a city of work and a city of homes. Various regions in the outskirts and in the suburbs acquired

A Streetcar Subdivision

This 1883 newspaper advertisement heralds a new suburban tract just north of Chicago (it was annexed to the city in 1889). Note how transit plays a central role in the ad. *Courtesy Chicago Historical Society.*

The Birth of the Modern City
State Street in downtown Chicago around 1870 was beginning to become a major business center, but it was still unpaved and its sidewalks were wooden. After the Great Chicago Fire in 1871, it was rebuilt and became one of the most famous streets of urban America. *Courtesy Chicago Historical Society.*

differentiating characteristics, determined not as much by the nationality or occupation of their residents as by architectural style, lot area, and dwelling size.

What had once been the entire walking city now became the zone of work, crammed with offices, stores, warehouses, and factories and girded by row houses and tenements. As middle-class residents departed, immigrants took their places, doubling and tripling up in old houses or filling tenements built after single-family structures had been razed (see Chapter 4). Frequently, commercial buildings replaced residential structures, creating genuine central business districts, such as the Loop in Chicago and Lower Manhattan in New York. Even smaller cities had a distinct downtown section. More than ever before these districts contained an extraordinary concentration of economic and cultural functions. Chicago's Loop represented the ultimate central business district. As one official described it in 1910:

Within an area of less than a square mile there are found the railway terminals and business offices, the big retail stores, the wholesale and jobbing

businesses, the financial center, the main offices of the chief firms of the
city, a considerable proportion of the medical and dental professions, the
legal profession, the city and county governments, the post office, the courts,
the leading social and political clubs, the hotels, theaters, Art Institute, principal libraries, labor headquarters, and a great number of lesser factors of
city life.

Thus by pushing city borders outward and creating separate social
and economic districts, mass transit generated forces that were simultaneously centripetal and centrifugal. On the one hand, most of the
city's important economic activities remained centralized within the old
core, and commuters streamed inward each day on the trolleys and els to
work and to shop. "Downtown" acquired a clear image: a place where
stores and offices formed canyon walls surrounding streets clogged with
human and vehicular traffic. On the other hand, the streetcars launched
people (or the half of the population that could afford it), into the urban
periphery, and the people dragged with them many economic institutions
that began small-scale operations in the outskirts. Transportation also
enabled new industrial plants, shut out from the crowded core, to build
on vacant land outside the city. The growth of industry in these areas

A Nineteenth-Century Traffic Jam
This congestion of people, animals, and vehicles on a Philadelphia cobblestone
street in 1897 combines nearly all early forms of urban transport—pedestrians,
horse-drawn wagons and carriages, and an electric trolley car. *U.S. Bureau of
Public Roads. The National Archives.*

pumped life into many suburbs and created new boom towns such as Cambridge and South Boston near Boston and Cicero, Aurora, and Elgin near Chicago. Freight and commuter railroads carried goods and people between these places and the big city nearby. The expansion of transportation spread companies and people into regions far removed from the old walking city, while also drawing new areas into the city's orbit.

But there were social costs involved in the outward sprawl and sorting out of people and districts. As Professor Warner and others have noted, the new residential areas were open to all who could pay the price. Ethnic origins seldom mattered, as long as middle-class values were the most distinguishing traits. But nearly half of the urban population could not afford the new way of living. Families whose breadwinners earned only a dollar or two a day and whose children worked in mills and sweatshops to help feed their brothers and sisters, could dream of escaping their crowded quarters and filthy street; but for many the goal was elusive. The exodus of the middle class intensified the problem that urban population growth had always bred. Those with resources fled and left the discomforts, disease, and decay to those least endowed to cope with them.

Eventually (often within the span of one generation) some lower income families could and did escape, usually first to the *zone of emergence*—the ring between the slums and the areas of new houses—and then to the outer neighborhoods. But in many cases their outward migration destroyed the ideal that suburban and peripheral development had sought to achieve. As Warner has shown, a tacit consensus had encouraged each suburban builder to erect a house similar in size and style to those that surrounded his. High down payments and short-term mortgages, however, made home ownership difficult, even for the middle-class families who first occupied these dwellings. When lower income groups sought homes in neighborhoods beyond the slums, they could afford only modest payments for mortgages or rents. Moreover, most were young families who needed four- and five-room cottages, not the six- and eight-room houses that had been built for larger, more affluent households. Thus some newcomers had to double up in dwellings originally built to house one family. Even when a family could afford to live alone in a house, it seldom had enough money to maintain the structure at the standards of repair that were originally intended. Those who moved from cramped flats and tenements into single and divided houses of the outer neighborhoods undoubtedly improved their living conditions; but they also brought with them the accompaniments of more intensive land use, not just more *people* per acre, but more businesses, more traffic, more garbage, more noise. The unplanned nature of outward growth, which had ignored future land uses and architectural needs, very quickly began to haunt the modern city. Those who had enough money, or who scraped together enough, kept moving farther away—a flight that has continued unabated to the present—but the specter of decay was always close behind.

A third consequence of mass transportation was its effect upon population mobility. Trains and trolleys enabled people to travel farther and faster. Speed and punctuality became urban habits. The new urban sprawl, made possible by mass transit, reinforced the migratory tendency that had always marked American life. The numbers of people moving from one home to another throughout the nineteenth, and into the twentieth, century clearly reveal that there is nothing new about our present transient society, and residential mobility has been one of the most dynamic and pervasive features of American history. There are three kinds of population movement that affect cities: in-migration, out-migration, and intraurban migration. The first two are part of the process to be discussed in the next chapter. The third type, change of residence within the same city, is no less important because it was (and is) one of the most constant characteristics of city life. It affected practically every family, every neighborhood. It made the ideal of a stable community a fantasy, and it became an available path for those who sought a way to higher socioeconomic status.

Today social analysts note with wonder that one in five Americans changes residence each year. Yet evidence suggests that decades ago, residential mobility was as frequent—if not more frequent—as it is presently. A study of Omaha, Nebraska, at the end of the nineteenth century and beginning of the twentieth has revealed that less than twenty-five percent of the city's young and middle-aged families lived in one place for five years; only three percent failed to move in twenty years. Of those who remained in the city for as long as fourteen years, over half had lived in three or more places over the time span; and of those who remained for twenty years, one-third had occupied four or more dwellings. Not every group shifted with the same frequency: foreign-born moved less often than native-born, white-collar workers moved less often than blue-collar. However, the differences between groups were slight; more important was the entire population's remarkable impermanence, an impermanence that characterized almost every city.

Certainly some of those who skipped from one home to another within a city never improved their condition; they were fleeing delinquent rent payments or were seeking new quarters because their old residences were to be torn down. So they moved to a house or tenement down the street or around the corner. Yet it appears that many more people did better themselves by changing residence. In Boston, Philadelphia, Omaha, and a host of other cities, thousands of families followed the streetcar lines into the newer neighborhoods where housing was roomier and yards were greener. A family's most common residential pattern involved a series of moves, all radiating outward from the center of the city toward the periphery or suburbs. The frequency of movement often frustrated reformers who sought to order society by creating stable communities. "I want to arouse neighborhood interest and neighborhood pride," pleaded Jacob Riis in 1901, "to link the neighbor to one spot that will hold them [sic] long enough to take root and stop them from moving. Something of the kind must be done or we perish." Such a goal ran counter to the dynamics of urban life. Quests for more space, more convenience, better facilities uprooted families and overturned neighborhoods. In the half century after the Civil War, these urges were as strong as before the war. Only now the new forces of urban growth and opportunity—outward sprawl, real estate boom, and mass transit construction—spread people into new and more numerous directions.

THE QUICKENING PACE OF INDUSTRIALIZATION

The rise of streetcars and els furnishes but one example of the interrelationship between urban growth and technological advance. While mass transit was changing the face, pace, and space of American cities, the larger force of industrialization was increasingly guiding the course of urbanization. If we define industrialization as the coordinated development of economic specialization, mass mechanized production, mass consumption, and mass distribution of goods and services, it is important to repeat that this phenomenon did not occur on a large scale until the last third of the nineteenth century. The construction of railroads and canals, the increased use of water power and steam engines, and the introduction of the factory system in the Northeast by 1850 had laid the foundations for industrial growth. But the real burst came after the Civil War when transcontinental transportation links and the proliferation of urban sites created a mass, national market for goods and services and when new applications of science and invention radically altered business, employment, and living styles.

During the 1860s and '70s four transcontinental railroads pushed westward to the Pacific, triggering urban growth at many points along their routes. Indeed the railroads helped to complete the national urban network whose framework was laid in the first half of the century. Between 1860 and 1910, the number of cities with populations of over 100,000 swelled from 9 to 50; the number with 25,000 to 100,000 grew from 26 to 178, and those with 10,000 to 25,000 rose from 58 to 369. A list of the most prominent new cities boosted by the railroads contains nearly the

A Product of Geographical Mobility
Budding frontier towns such as Helena, Montana—photographed above in 1870—
sprouted all over the West as migrants sought their fortunes in urban as well as
rural communities. *Geological Survey, The National Archives.*

entire urban West: Albuquerque, Butte, Cheyenne, Dallas, El Paso, Fort
Worth, Kansas City, Los Angeles, Minneapolis, Oklahoma City, Omaha,
Portland, Reno, St. Paul, Salt Lake City, San Antonio, San Diego, San
Francisco, Santa Fe, Seattle, Spokane, and Tacoma. Railroads brought
urban growth to the South as well, fostering cities such as Atlanta,
Birmingham, Memphis, and Nashville.

Most of the towns that the railroads helped boost to cities had become
centers of commerce before any track had been laid. Omaha, for example, was an important outfitting center for settlers crossing the Missouri
River, and Seattle served as a lumber port and intermediary transfer
point between San Francisco and northwestern Canada. These places
became natural locations for terminals once the railroads began construction. However, the iron horse could turn a regional trading post into
a boom town, and competition for railroad connections amplified the
urban aggressiveness (dubbed imperialism in Chapter 2) that was so
characteristic of American economic expansion. Omaha subscribed
money to build a bridge across the Missouri; leaders of Kansas City
offered generous subsidies and land grants; and literally the whole population of Seattle laid its own stretch of track—all to lure the railroads to
their front doors. Cities, therefore, built railroads as much as railroads
built cities.

Meanwhile the major components of industrialization were converging —new sources of raw materials and energy, new machines and modes of production, new supplies of labor and skills. During the 1860s inventors in France and America developed methods of producing high-quality steel from iron and carbon—providing the basic staple of industry. Over the next generation technicians harnessed electrical energy to furnish almost unlimited power for operating huge machines or for lighting streets and buildings. At the same time discoveries such as the refinement of petroleum, the production of high explosives, and the creation of new alloys (such as aluminum) opened new possibilities for the application of physics and chemistry to industrial concerns. The development of successful new products and processes heartened would-be inventors who deluged the U.S. Patent Office with ideas, prompted academic institutions to expand programs for training scientists and engineers, and inspired large businesses to establish their own laboratories or to subsidize research in technological colleges. The demands for capital made by expanding industry encouraged widespread adoption of corporate organization with its stocks, bonds, limited stockholder liability for company debts, and bureaucratic management of operations. Increased scales of production, the use of more mechanically-powered devices, and the adoption of interchangeable parts as a means of standardizing products paved the way for assembly line production and created a huge demand for labor—unskilled workers to man the machines, specialized and supervisory personnel to tend the machines and oversee the workers, and clerical and managerial employees to fill the white-collar needs of business bureaucracy. These developments generated a *pull* factor of employment opportunities that attracted people from Europe to America and from one place to another inside U.S. borders. (See Chapter 4).

As the place that centralized resources, labor, transportation, and communications, the city became the chief arena of industrial growth. By the end of the nineteenth century urban factories were responsible for nine-tenths of America's industrial output. As Blake McKelvey has noted, however, the types of industrial cities responsible for this production were quite varied. Some cities utilized unskilled immigrant labor and new, easier techniques of production to furnish goods for mass consumption. Thus the shoe industry became prominent in Rochester and Philadelphia, clothing in New York, and textiles in Lawrence, Lowell, and Fall River. Other cities exploited and processed the products of their agricultural hinterlands: flour in Minneapolis, cotton seed oil in Memphis, meat and butter in Omaha, beer in Milwaukee. Others grew by extracting and utilizing other kinds of nearby resources: minerals in Denver; fish and lumber in Portland and Seattle; coal and iron in Cleveland,

Industrialization

Silk warping and skein winding to spools at the Royal Weaving Company, Pawtucket, Rhode Island, about 1910. Machines and female operatives extend almost endlessly into the background. *The Rhode Island Historical Society.*

Pittsburgh, and Birmingham; oil in Dallas, Houston, Los Angeles, and Oklahoma City.

There were other variants, other industries—technological advances such as Detroit's automobiles, Akron's tires, or Dayton's cash registers—but in each case industrialization involved several common requisites. First, the cities needed the traditional ingredients of economic growth: land, labor, entrepreneurship, transportation, market demand (a population of consumers), and specialization (some principal product or function that could be exported for profit). These elements had existed in American cities in one degree or another since the late seventeenth century. But by the late nineteenth century large amounts of available capital and increasing technological innovation appeared and mixed with the old factors to feed the process of industrial change. That is, industrialization proceeded most strongly in those cities where successful commercial activities produced capital for industrial investment. All the western cities and most of the eastern were founded on a speculative and commercial base. Their commercial functions—attracting and distributing raw materials, wholesaling and retailing goods and services—remained integral to their industrial development and their economic viability, because they created capital for investment, and because they generated the "multiplier effect" of spiraling growth. Only when their economies filled out with a complete range of business and consumer services could one-industry towns reach the stage of maturity that qualified them as genuine regional metropolises—nodes connecting and controlling a large, surrounding area. To be sure, in the closing decades of the nineteenth century manufacturing, rather than trade, provided the major impetus to urban growth, but still no city could exist without its commerce.

In sum, urbanization and industrialization were not the same process. Cities had grown long before modern manufacturing was possible, and factories could and did develop outside of urban areas. But by the onset of the Civil War, urban and industrial growth were bound tightly together. The commercial cities and transportation revolution of the early nineteenth century bred the manufacturing cities and industrial revolution of the late nineteenth century. The twin forces of urbanization and industrialization now fed upon each other; each reinforced and modified the course of the other. Together they induced unprecedented economic change and freed the United States from reliance upon European products and capital. Imports and forign investments still flowed into the country, but increasingly cities and their factories transformed the United States from an agricultural, debtor nation into a manufacturing and financial power.

BIBLIOGRAPHY

Some valuable perspectives on the premodern American city (the walking city) can be found in Sam Bass Warner, Jr., *The Urban Wilderness: A History of the American City* (New York: Harper & Row, 1972); Warner, *The Private City: Philadelphia in Three Periods of Its Growth* (Philadelphia: University of Pennsylvania Press, 1968); Richard C. Wade, "Urbanization" in C. Vann Woodward, ed., *The Comparative Approach to American History* (New York: Basic Books, 1968); and Allan R. Pred, *Urban Growth and the Circulation of Information: The United States System of Cities, 1800–1840* (Cambridge: Harvard University Press, 1973). The best studies of the development and consequences of mass transportation include George R. Taylor, "The Beginnings of Mass Transportation in Urban America," *The Smithsonian Journal of History,* 1 (Summer and Autumn 1966), 35–50 and 31–54; Glen E. Holt, "The Changing Perception of Urban Pathology: An Essay on the Development of Mass Transit in the United States," in Kenneth T. Jackson and Stanley K. Schultz, eds., *Cities in American History* (New York: Knopf, 1972), pp. 324–43; Joel A. Tarr, "From City to Suburb: The 'Moral' Influence of Transportation Technology," in Alexander B. Callow, Jr., ed., *American Urban History: An Interpretive Reader with Commentaries* (New York: Oxford University Press, 2nd ed., 1973), pp. 202–12; George M. Smerk, "The Streetcar: Shaper of American Cities," *Traffic Quarterly,* 21 (1967), 569–84; and Sam Bass Warner, Jr., *Streetcar Suburbs: The Process of Growth in Boston, 1870–1900* (Cambridge: Harvard University Press and M.I.T. Press, 1962). John Anderson Miller's *Fares Please! From Horsecars to Streamliners*

(New York: Appleton-Century-Crofts, 1941) is a lively, popular account of the growth of mass transit.

Other types of urban land use and real estate trends have been examined in Homer Hoyt, *One Hundred Years of Land Values in Chicago* (Chicago: University of Chicago Press, 1933); Helen Corbin Monchow, *Seventy Years of Real Estate Subdividing in the Region of Chicago*, Northwestern University Studies in the Social Sciences, No. 3 (Evanston and Chicago: Northwestern University, 1939); and Walter Firey, *Land Use In Central Boston* (Cambridge: Harvard University Press, 1947). Aspects of geographical mobility are analyzed in Stephan Thernstrom and Peter R. Knights, "Men in Motion: Some Data and Speculations about Urban Population Mobility in Nineteenth Century America," in Tamara K. Hareven, ed., *Anonymous Americans: Exploration in Nineteenth-Century Social History* (Englewood Cliffs, N.J.: Prentice-Hall, 1971), pp. 17–47; Howard P. Chudacoff, *Mobile Americans: Residential and Social Mobility in Omaha, 1880–1920* (New York: Oxford University Press, 1972); and George W. Pierson, *The Moving American* (New York: Knopf, 1973). Works on urbanization in the industrial age include Blake McKelvey, *The Urbanization of America, 1865–1920* (New Brunswick, N. J.: Rutgers University Press, 1963); Constance McLaughlin Green, *American Cities in the Growth of the Nation* (London: The Athlone Press, 1957); Charles N. Glaab, *Kansas City and the Railroads* (Madison: State Historical Society of Wisconsin, 1962); Frederick C. Jaher, ed., *The Age of Industrialism in America* (New York: The Free Press, 1968); and Ralph Turner, "The Industrial City. Center of Cultural Change," in Carolin F. Ware, ed., *The Cultural Approach to History* (New York: Columbia University Press, 1940), pp. 228–42. On technology and architecture, see Leo Marx, *The Machine in the Garden: Technology and the Pastoral Ideal in America* (New York: Oxford University Press, 1964); Christopher Tunnard and Henry Hope Reed, *American Skyline* (Boston: Little, Brown and Company, 1961); John Coolidge, *Mill and Mansion: A Study of Architecture and Society in Lowell, Massachusetts* (New York: Columbia University Press, 1942); and Siegfried Giedion, *Mechanization Takes Command: A Contribution to Anonymous History* (New York: W. W. Norton, 1948).

4
NEWCOMERS AND THE URBAN CORE, 1850-1920

Today the American metropolis is a dichotomy, a population center separated into inner and outer parts. The division is a legacy from the social, economic, and technological changes that advanced from the middle of the nineteenth century onward, setting in motion centrifugal waves of settlement. But while the middle classes accompanied the trolley lines into the periphery and suburbs, working class immigrants squeezed into the older districts and transformed the walking city into the urban core. To those on the outside the residential rings that surrounded business and manufacturing districts embodied the worst of American urban life because of the problems they bred—slums, crime, disease. Yet for those who lived there, the inner city served necessary functions. It provided shelter and jobs. It created opportunities for social contact and group activity. It eased uprooted peasants into a new, urban-industrial world. And it blended millions of foreigners into pluralistic, American society.

Between 1860 and 1920 the total number of people living in American cities of 8,000 or more inhabitants mushroomed from 6.2 million to 54.3 million. Although an excess of births over deaths accounted for some of the population growth, the bulk of the increase consisted of newcomers—people who arrived from native rural areas, a foreign country, or another town or city. This migration resulted from two factors: a *push* and a *pull.* A variety of pressures drove young people and whole families from their farms in America and from their villages in Europe: declining prices for crops, rising prices for provisions, high taxes and rents, drought, hard winters, insect plagues, and overpopulation. But they left because there was somewhere else to go. European peasants thought the United States offered freedom and opportunity. Its cities, with their promises of money and jobs, beckoned to rural Americans and to Europeans. Here is where national economic forces bore down upon the city to produce the dynamics of urbanization. The commercial revolution of the eighteenth and early nineteenth centuries, the transition through merchant capitalism of the early and middle nineteenth century, and then the industrial revolution created the jobs and other opportunities that charged cities with magnetism. Moreover, the cities themselves generated labor opportunities. In the second half of the nineteenth century and first decades of the twentieth, practically every major city constructed or enlarged its basic facilities, all with the help of unskilled immigrant labor and most with public funds. Streets, bridges, water and gas systems, sewers, schools, and government buildings were built by and for the new urban dwellers.

TABLE 3
Population Compositions of Major Cities, 1910

	Total	Foreign Born White Number	%	Native Born of Foreign or Mixed Parentage Number	%	Black Number	%
New York	4,766,883	1,927,703	40.4	1,820,141	38.2	91,709	1.9
Chicago	2,185,283	781,217	35.7	912,701	41.8	44,103	2.0
Philadelphia	1,549,008	382,578	24.7	496,785	32.1	84,459	5.5
St. Louis	687,029	125,706	18.3	246,946	40.0	43,960	6.4
Boston	670,535	240,722	35.9	257,104	38.3	13,564	2.0
Cleveland	560,663	195,703	34.9	223,908	39.9	8,448	1.5
Baltimore	558,485	77,043	13.8	134,870	24.1	84,749	15.2
Pittsburgh	533,905	140,436	26.3	191,483	35.9	25,623	4.8
Detroit	465,766	156,565	33.6	188,255	40.4	5,741	1.2
Buffalo	423,715	118,444	30.0	183,673	40.4	1,773	0.4
San Francisco	416,912	130,874	31.4	153,781	36.9	1,642	0.4
Milwaukee	373,857	111,456	29.8	182,530	48.8	980	0.3
Cincinnati	363,591	56,792	15.6	132,190	36.4	19,639	5.4
Newark	347,469	110,655	31.8	132,350	38.1	9,475	2.7
New Orleans	339,075	27,686	8.2	74,244	21.9	89,262	26.3
Washington	331,069	24,351	7.4	45,066	13.6	94,446	28.5

Source: Derived from 1910 U.S. Census.

Who were these newcomers? Exactly where did they come from? Many came from the American countryside. Although the number of farms in this country almost tripled between 1860 and 1900, productivity increased even more rapidly, driving down prices and forcing farmers to work harder for equal or diminished returns. Poverty and isolation began to take their toll. Hamlin Garland, who portrayed rural despair in his moving short stories, expressed a common sentiment through one of his female characters: "I'm sick of farm life. . . . It's nothing but fret, fret, and work the whole time, never going any place, never seeing anybody but a lot of neighbors just as big fools as you are. I spend my time fighting flies and washing dishes and churning. I'm sick of it all."

Thousands of families drifted off the farms toward the manufacturing cities of the Northeast and Midwest. Rural areas of several states, including New Hampshire, Vermont, New York, Maryland, Ohio, and Illinois, suffered absolute as well as relative declines in population in the 1880s. (Natural increase had always compensated for any loss of residents due to migration, but now the exodus surpassed the birth rate.) Ironically, however, the movement off the farms into the cities helped to relieve the loneliness and isolation of rural districts, particularly in the Old Northwest—Ohio, Indiana, Illinois, Michigan, and Wisconsin. In the last half of the nineteenth century, migration boosted the growth of not only Detroit, Cleveland, Chicago, and Milwaukee, but also a host of secondary cities that shortened distances between markets and social centers. Dayton, Toledo, Indianapolis, Fort Wayne, South Bend, Grand Rapids, Kalamazoo, Peoria, Rockford, LaCrosse, Oshkosh, and many more brought the amenities of modern life closer to the farmers. The growth of these towns plus the spread of specialized farming, railroad construction, and big city mail-order department stores soothed much of the rural discontent in the Old Northwest by the 1890s, leaving behind the Populist unrest of the Plains and South where urbanization had proceeded more slowly.

A more significant source of immigration was the European countryside. Foreign migrants, to a greater degree than native migrants, shaped the American urban environment and were shaped by it. Ethnicity and religious identification, key components of our modern urban culture, have derived from the immigrant experience in American cities during the past 150 years. Certainly in the half century that followed the Civil War foreign immigrants living in the urban cores provided the focuses of most social and political issues.

Foreign immigration to the United States is traditionally split into two major waves: one beginning in the 1840s, peaking in the 1880s, and ebbing thereafter; and the other beginning in the 1880s, peaking between 1900 and 1910, and declining in the 1920s—when federal legislation closed the doors to unrestricted influx. The first wave of immigrants consisted of five main groups: Irish Catholics; German Catholics and Protestants; English Protestants, and Scandinavian Protestants. Most entered through one of the large eastern ports. Settled newcomers built chains of migration, across which traveled relatives and friends from the Old World to the New.

Often these immigrants were too poor to go farther, or they found ready use for whatever skills they had, so they remained in the eastern cities; or they ventured only a short distance away to growing secondary towns like Providence, Paterson, Newark, or Reading. Others almost immediately plunged into the hinterland. From the 1850s onward, Germans, Swedes, and Norwegians took up farming in the states of the Old Northwest and the Plains. English, Welsh, and Scottish immigrants traveled inland to work in the coal mines of Pennsylvania, West Virginia, Ohio, and Illinois. Many followed the rivers and railroads into the new, growing cities of the West, settling in ports along the Ohio River or around the Great Lakes. Some moved on even farther, adding a foreign flavor to newer places like Minneapolis, Des Moines, Omaha, Denver, and Kansas City. Often their funds ran out in one of these cities, and the immigrants suffered the pangs of poverty as much in the West as in the East. But the western towns offered opportunities for men with skills, and many immigrants achieved nominal success—Scandinavians in construction trades, Germans in brewing, English and Irish in jobbing and retailing. In fact the commercial elites of many western cities often included foreign-born members.

These "old" immigrants, as they came to be called, brought with them new and different traits that modified the American urban environment—dialects, dress, culinary and drinking habits (wine, ale, and beer now competed with traditional American rum and whiskey), and social agencies. The most consequential of the new features was religion. Between 1840 and 1890 seven and a half million Irish and German immigrants arrived in America; of these, five and a half million were Catholics. These groups transformed the United States from a Protestant to a Protestant-Catholic nation. By 1870, 40 percent of all churchgoers in this country were Catholics. Although American Catholicism lacked internal unity because of its ethnic diversity and the semiautonomous nature of local parishes, external forces imposed a kind of unity upon Catholics by emphasizing their divergence from Protestantism. A latent fear of "popery," transferred from England in colonial times, surfaced and joined with a growing nativist sentiment in the 1830s, '40, and '50s to intensify criticism, prejudice, and violence. Anti-Catholic sermons and pamphlets plus the nativist Know-Nothing party spread into several cities, raising emotions to a fevered pitch. As one fearful editor wrote,

> Have we not reason to believe that now while popery is losing ground in Europe, that this land presents to the Pope a fine field of operations, and that he is endeavoring by every means in his power, to establish his falling throne, and that he is now sending out his minions to accomplish his fiend-like purpose, to prepare the way before him, that he may make a grand a triumphant entree [sic] into this country when he shall be hurled from his tyrannous and polluted throne in Europe.

Occasionally, bloody clashes erupted. In 1834 a mob burned and sacked an Ursuline convent near Boston. In 1844 Protestants and Irish Catholics fought in Philadelphia, and thirteen were killed. In 1855 twenty died in a battle between Germans and nativists in Louisville. In other cities churches were burned, and homes were looted. Other foreign religious groups would make their own mark, though less emphatically —Jews from Germany and Lutherans from Denmark, Sweden, and Germany. But the native-Protestant/foreign-Catholic dichotomy, fashioned primarily in the cities during the first period of mass immigration, would remain as one of the most decisive factors in determining issues of party politics, educational debates, and family organization to this day.

The second wave of immigration resembled and contrasted with the first. Like their predecessors, most of the newer immigrants were poor and of peasant origins. But the numbers of the more recent arrivals were much greater. Between 1840 and 1880 the average influx per decade was about 2.4 million, and 2.8 million emigrated to the United States in the 1870s. In the 1880s, over 5.2 million immigrants arrived; 8.8 million came between 1900 and 1910. Although the English, Irish, Germans, and Scandinavians continued to come in large contingents, they were far outnumbered by four new groups: Catholics from eastern Europe; Catholics from Italy; Jews from Russia and eastern Europe; and Catholics from Canada. Other smaller sources included Greece, Syria, and Mexico. A larger percentage of the new immigrants settled in cities than did the old. The Dillingham Commission of 1907–1911, which in large part was responsible for perpetuating artificial distinctions between "new" immigrants and "old," reported that in 1920, 78.6 percent of those born in eastern and southern Europe lived in urban areas, compared with 68.3 percent of those born in northern Europe and the British Isles. Less skilled than the old immigrants, those arriving from new areas brought only their willingness to work. As immigrant authoress Mary Antin described her Russian-immigrant father, "His history . . . is the history of thousands who came to America, like him, with pockets empty, hands untrained to the use of tools, minds cramped by centuries

The Plight of Newcomers
A group of immigrants, newly arrived and impoverished, scavenges in a refuse dump in Providence, Rhode Island, around 1900. Such activities scandalized strait-laced moralists, frustrated public health reformers, and stirred settlement house workers and other social reformers to find some means of helping the poor. *Courtesy Rhode Island Historical Society.*

of repression in their native land." These newcomers manned the sweatshops and factories of larger cities and the mills, slaughterhouses, construction gangs, and dock crews of most cities outside the South. Although these groups concentrated in eastern centers (particularly New York), they also spread across the continent quite rapidly. By 1920 Poles were the largest foreign-born group in Detroit and Toledo, Russians in Denver, Czechs in Omaha, Italians in Youngstown, and Hungarians in Akron.

The arrival of millions from Italy, Russia, Hungary, Romania, and what later became Czechoslovakia, Yugoslavia, and Poland completed the formation of America's white religio-cultural mosaic. Newly arrived Catholics moved into industrial centers along the Northeast coast and often comprised half or more of a city's population. As they moved westward, they joined the Irish and Germans to raise Catholic proportions in Buffalo, Cleveland, Chicago, and Milwaukee to 40 or 50 percent. As before, the Church lacked uniformity, primarily as a result of its very catholicism. Traditionally the hierarchy centralized the Church, and geography determined parish boundaries. This system was derived from

Europe where most parishes contained only one nationality. But in American cities, Catholics of very different ethnic origins were in close contact with each other, and friction was inevitable. In several cities Italian, Polish, and French Canadian Catholics clashed with Irish and German bishops over demands for priests of the same nationality as the parish. Newer immigrants struggled to retain, for themselves and their children, their sense of ethnic and religious unity in their new environment. However, the younger generation, descendants of earlier Catholic immigrants, disavowed this kind of protection. They tried to Americanize the Church, because they believed that as long as there existed doubts about their own and their fellow Catholics' loyalties, the Church would never be accepted in America. A group of Catholics led by Cardinal James Gibbons of Baltimore, Archbishop John Ireland of St. Paul, and Bishop John L. Spalding of Peoria worked to minimize points of conflict, such as languages and parochial education, between Catholics and other Americans. The task proved difficult, however. Prejudice and bigotry continued to confront Catholics, particularly during hard times, when social tensions were most acute. Moreover, increasing Catholic immigration after the turn of the century only sharpened the dialogue between *retentionists* and *accommodationists*.

Jews also wrestled to retain their consciousness while adjusting to American urban life. They were probably the most urbanized of all immigrant groups—in 1910 close to 85 percent of Russian Jews lived in cities. New York City alone contained a million and a half Jews. Unlike their European ancestors Jews in the United States no longer lived in forced isolation: the law gave them religious freedom, civic equality, and political privileges. Yet like other immigrants, they sought self-identification. Like the Catholics, children of earlier Jewish immigrants developed an accommodationist sentiment. Many of them adopted Reform Judaism, a movement originated in the 1840s by German intellectuals who wished to conciliate Judaism with middle-class society. To many liberal Jews in America, the Reform Movement seemed ideally suited to ease problems of cultural difference that occurred when Jews attempted to find their place in diversified urban society. Leaders such as Rabbi Isaac Mayer Wise of Cincinnati, reformed the prayer book, Anglicized the service, and loosened the rigors of ritual in an attempt to use religion as an Americanizing instrument. The movement reached full flower in Pittsburgh in 1885 with the adoption of a platform that rejected the national character of Judaism and stressed the position of Jews as a religious group which should adapt itself to the modern world.

At this time, however, disruption of the eastern European land system and brutal pogroms broke apart Jewish communities and sent waves of immigrants to America from Romania and Russia. These Jews, poverty-stricken and often illiterate, crowded into the cities where they soon outnumbered their co-religionists whose ancestors had arrived earlier. Like their Catholic counterparts, these newcomers tried to anchor their lives with religious ways of the past. They recoiled from Reform Judaism, seeking instead to recreate the orthodox, ritualistic Judaism of eastern Europe. Although forms of religious expression continued to split the two major Jewish groups, a philanthropic concern for the plights of their co-religionists at home and abroad gradually bound the two together. As the second generation of eastern European immigrants matured, some of them tried to adjust to the diversified urban environment through a new branch of Judaism, the Conservative movement. Led by Rabbi Sabato Morais of Philadelphia and founder of the Jewish Theological Seminary in New York, and later led by Solomon Schechter, Rabbi Morais' successor, this group retained much of the old ritual as well as Hebrew prayers and readings, but it dropped outmoded customs —such as segregating women from men in the synagogue—and eased English into the service. Like Reformism, Conservatism grew out of the junction between the immigration experience and the urban environment.

Despite differences in origin, skills, and religion, most of the foreigners who came to American cities between 1840 and 1920 shared several characteristics. First, they were a long way from home. Although the immigrants brought some of their "cultural baggage" with them, the journey across land and sea left behind old ways of life—village communalism and activities directed by the changing seasons. Meanwhile, their new urban surroundings confounded their lives with polyglot streets, a regulated work day, the uncertainties of housing and employment. Their own disorientation plus external pressures, including native disdain and bigotry, forced the immigrants back upon themselves into a search for self-identity. The search inevitably led them to their origins. That is, the American experience helped create national identifications out of local loyalties. People from County Galway and County Cork became Irishmen; those from Mecklenburg and Wurtenburg became Germans; and those from Campania and Calabria became Italians. Regional rivalries persisted, but all Germans could read the same foreign language newspapers, and Italians could take their communion together. Moreover, native Americans nearly always grouped immigrants by their nationality (or, in the case of Jews, by their culture)—a tendency resulting from innocent classification and vicious stereotyping. These conditions evoked not only national identification but also nostalgia among the immigrants. Oscar Handlin has written, "As the passing years widened the distance, the land the immigrants had left acquired charm and beauty. Present problems blurred those they had left unsolved behind; and in the haze of memory it seemed to these people they had formerly been free of present dissatisfactions."

Second, nearly all who came to America during the years of mass immigration were lured by the promise of economic opportunity. The dream of land propelled many, but more were attracted by the hope of jobs in the growing cities, for jobs meant money, and money meant security, something rare to the European peasant. Many immigrants came to this country with no intention of remaining. Once here, however, the vast majority never realized their schemes of working for a while and returning home in affluence. Still there was an often-ignored current of migration that ran out of the eastern ports back to Europe. Although government statistics were not kept until after 1908, there is some evidence to indicate that many foreigners re-migrated, especially during hard times. Some even shuttled back and forth across the Atlantic to take advantage of seasonal wage differences. Return migration became especially possible from the 1870s onward, when steamships made ocean passage safer and faster and made more European ports accessible to America. It has been estimated that for every 100 aliens who entered the United States between 1820 and 1870, 10 to 20 left the country. The figures for 1870 to 1900 and 1900 to 1914 are 24 per 100 and 33 to 40 per 100, respectively.

A third characteristic common to both sets of immigrants was their propensity to live initially in the older, inner districts of a city. The Irish and Germans began to arrive just as the transportation and industrial revolutions were creating the modern city with its expanded residential area and segregation of social groups. The transformation left almost all cheap housing in the urban cores. Unable to afford any but the meanest quarters, the early immigrants and those who followed in succeeding decades pushed into these districts. Heavy concentrations of foreigners appeared in cities across the continent, in New York's Lower East Side, Boston's North End, Chicago's West Side, and the inner wards of Pittsburgh, Cincinnati, St. Louis, Buffalo, and San Francisco.

At the end of the nineteenth century a third type of population movement began. The migration of blacks from rural South to urban North and West involved people who were native born, but their impact upon cities became just as important as the flood of foreign immigration. As of 1890 well over 90 percent of blacks lived in the South. But that year the slow pace of migration to the North accelerated. Like other migrants, blacks moved in search of better employment, and they followed rail and water routes into expanding commercial and industrial centers. Once they had reached their destinations, they too encouraged relatives and friends to join them. In 1900 there were 32 cities with more than 10,000 black inhabitants, and of all blacks who lived in the North and West,

70 percent could be found in urban areas. In 1910 Washington, D.C., had the largest black population of any city in the country. New York was close behind, Philadelphia fifth, and Chicago eighth. By 1920 New York, Philadelphia, and Chicago ranked first, second and fourth. Moreover, newer cities like Denver, Oklahoma City, and Los Angeles experienced phenomenal increases in their black populations. Blacks moved to southern cities also. Between 1880 and 1900 the black population of Memphis tripled, and that of Chattanooga grew by 600 percent.

Although blacks resembled foreign migrants in their peasant backgrounds, their urban destinations, and their economic motivations, several factors distinguished them from foreign imigrants. While foreign groups tended to contain overrepresentations of young males, black women outnumbered men in New York, Philadelphia, southern cities, and border cities around the rim of the South. Apparently most of these women were attracted by a high demand for domestic service. Also a much larger proportion of black women than white held jobs. In 1900 although only one-fourth of all women in the eleven largest cities of the North worked, 46.3 percent of the black women were classified as wage earners. In New York the proportion reached 55 percent. Of all male and female blacks employed in the cities, two-thirds were engaged in what was classified as "domestic and personal service." Studies by social reformers of conditions in turn-of-the-century Boston, New York, Philadelphia, and Chicago identified all the characteristics so common to the black urban experience: higher infant mortality than whites, higher rents for inferior quarters, lower wages for the lowest jobs.

Poverty and bigotry pushed blacks together into ghettos—areas of forced residence from which escape is extremely difficult—more than any other migrant group. These teeming, decaying residential districts became the womb of black urban culture. Within the ghetto, black Protestantism assumed its distinctive character. Each city had a few large black congregations of Methodists and Baptists; but the numerous, informal storefront churches, outgrowths of the southern experience, sprouted everywhere and became fixtures of ghetto life. In several cities an indigenous black elite arose, consisting of clergymen, small businessmen, educators, lower public officials, doctors, and vice operators. These people, all men, had achieved minor success and were torn between hopes of raising their community within the larger white society and the reality of rigid segregation imposed by that white society. Though there were strong differences, in some ways this ambivalence resembled the struggle between self-identification and accommodation that occurred among immigrant Catholics and Jews.

More important than its religious institutions or the leadership it developed was the way in which the ghetto became the cultural center for all blacks. Its streets shook with violence and despair, but they also offered social and physical outlets with their informal comraderie and impromptu athletic events. Its saloons offered escape into vice, alcohol, and drugs, but they also nurtured the musical expression of the black soul.

The cityward migrations of native whites, foreign whites, and native blacks were not one-way movements. While millions streamed into the cities, an almost equal tide flowed out. Each year countless families and individuals moved away, often to a nearby town or suburb, probably more often to a place tens or hundreds of miles away. The exodus occurred in every city, whatever its size or location. Table 4 reveals the magnitude and scope of the process by listing the proportion of adult males who left a city within ten years. Thus of a sample of adult males living in Atlanta in 1870, over half were gone by 1880. Some of the disappearance may be attributed to death, but certainly out-migration accounted for most of the loss.

With the number of out-migrants so great, the extent of in-migration to any city must have been very high to replace those who had left and to increase the total population. Also the sum of people on the move—in-migrating and out-migrating—must have been extraordinary. The case of Boston, one city where the magnitude of these phenomena has been studied, proves to be revealing. Between 1880 and 1890 Boston's population grew from 363,000 to 448,000, an increase of about 85,000. Natural increase accounted for about 20,000 of the additional people, leaving a net growth due to migration of 65,000. But this latter number gives only a tiny glimpse of what happened to Boston during these ten years. Histor-

TABLE 4
Percent of Original Residents at Beginning of Decade
Who Had Left by End of Decade

Decade	City	Percent Who Had Left
1870–1880	Atlanta	56
	Poughkeepsie	50
	San Francisco	52
1880–1890	Boston	36
	Mobile	62
	Omaha	60
	San Francisco	50
1900–1910	Omaha	59
1910–1920	Boston	59
	Norristown	41

ians Stephan Thernstrom and Peter Knights have investigated in- and out-migration patterns and have estimated that over just one decade 158,000 families moved into Boston while 138,000 moved out. The two figures produce a sum of 296,000 families involved in either in- or out-migration (probably some participated in both). The average family contained four or five members, so the total figure of individuals involved (296,000 multiplied by four or five) would push well beyond a million. Thus an increase of 65,000 due to migration in just one city involved the movements of over one million people. When such analysis is extended to include other cities, many of which experienced in- and out-migration rates much higher than those of Boston during the same period; and when the extraordinary amount of intraurban mobility is included, the number of people on the move at any one time becomes astronomical.

HOUSING AND HEALTH

Where to live? All migrants face this predicament, but only recently has the dilemma become a concern of public policy makers. The requisites of housing had evaded public control since this country's beginning. Thus the cities had made no provisions for housing the millions of newcomers who arrived in the decades that followed the Civil War. Peripheral and suburban growth was siphoning many of the middle and upper classes away from the central city, but the half of the population—the majority of the immigrants—that worked at low-paying jobs was confined to the inner core because mass transit and single-family suburban homes were beyond their budgets. Housing for this group had to be near employment, whether that employment was real or potential. This meant that the working-class family had to live close to downtown.

As native and foreign migrants streamed into the inner regions of northern cities, they pressed private housing markets beyond their capacities. In the late nineteenth century three out of every four urban dwellers lived in rented quarters; in working class districts the proportion was much higher. Increases in population and rising land values drove up rents and tempted landlords to squeeze every penny from their tenants. Thus inner city rents became very high, given the amount of services and space a family received for its money. The middle and upper classes could avoid this plight by expending capital to buy or build houses in the outskirts where land was cheaper. Lower class families had to find a different solution. They frequently lacked the resources to reduce costs per area. But they could reduce cost per capita by sharing their space—and their rents—with others. Countless families took in lodgers, and often two or three families occupied a single three- or four-room flat.

Builders and property owners developed several types of multiple-family structures from city to city, and the extent of crowding varied. But everywhere the private market fit supply to demand on a makeshift basis, with no assistance and little direction from public authority. Since the eighteenth century row houses had been the most common form of housing in central Philadelphia, and after the Civil War builders continued to erect these dwellings, making them smaller and packing more people into them. The new style row house was only sixteen feet wide, but a two-story building held four to six familes. The same pattern appeared in Baltimore. In New England the predominant style was the three-decker; a long, narrow, frame building, consisting of three stories and a loft. Pleasant-looking, substantial three-deckers housed one family to a floor, and often appeared in middle-class neighborhoods. But because they were among the least expensive types of housing to construct, three-deckers more frequently were located in working-class districts of Boston, Providence, Worcester, and other industrial cities. Here they housed two and three families to a floor and one each in the loft and cellar. In Chicago and St. Louis two- and three-story wooden buildings, and later brick tenements, squeezed against each other. In Detroit, Milwaukee, Omaha, and Seattle—as well as in the larger cities —lower-class immigrants crowded into converted warehouses and into single-family dwellings split up for multiple-family occupancy.

The case of New York City shows the most acute crowding and the most degenerate housing. In this sense it is unique. But the development of mass housing there is important because it influenced construction patterns in other cities and kindled the first concerted effort for housing reform. The city plan of 1811 set standard lot size over most of Manhattan Island at 25-by-100 feet. Thereafter these measurements rigidly determined the exchange of land and the size of buildings. In the early 1800s one of these lots might have contained a single row house or cottage inhabited by one or two families. Because the lot was so narrow, the house may have abutted adjacent buildings, leaving no room for side windows; but there was light in front and rear and enough space to accommodate four to six people. As population increased, by the middle of the century, demand may have encouraged the house's owner to convert it into a four-family unit, with two or three families living on the ground floor and one each in the attic and cellar. Since the house occupied only forty or fifty feet of the length of the lot, there would have been room to build another house in the back yard. This dwelling could hold four families in a fashion similar to the one in the front. By the 1860s the 25-by-100 foot lot, originally plotted to hold one family, now housed eight. As this process of tranformation spread across the city, the growth of slums accelerated.

But the crowding had only begun to approach its limits. Property owners met population pressure from immigration in the 1860s and '70s by razing the old houses and replacing them with four- and six-story tenements. These buildings were usually eighty feet long and contained four apartments to a floor. Each building could hold a minimum of sixteen to twenty-four families. Usually, however, tenants shared or sublet rooms within their apartments, so that a single building would often house nearly 150 people. A 200-by-1,000-foot block filled with these buildings might contain 2,500 families. Inside the structures living conditions were abominable. Rooms were miniscule, some barely eight feet wide. Only those few rooms facing the front or rear had direct light and ventilation. Indoor plumbing was almost nonexistent; privies were located in cellars or along the alleys. There were no kitchens and no heat. A wood-burning stove was the only appliance, and it was usually provided by the tenants.

These were the conditions that evoked the first concerted efforts at housing reform. Certainly not all inner neighborhoods were so squalid, and certainly New Yorkers had been concerned about slums well before the mid-nineteenth century; but the crowding, disease, vice, and crime of the slums that seemed to multiply as immigration increased wounded the middle class urge for propriety, and clouded visions of a well-ordered, conflict-free society. In 1876, for example, the New York Times reported that ". . . young girls are found sleeping on the floor in rooms where are crowded men, women, youths, and children. Delicacy is never known, purity is lost before its meaning is understood." Beginning in the 1850s, a mixed sense of alarm and optimism prodded humanitarians to seek ways of controlling the threat posed by slums. Their alarm led reformers to investigate the facts of slum life and to support measures that would regulate the practices of builders and landlords. Their optimism led them to expect that better conditions would result from heightened public consciousness and enlightened capitalism.

The character of housing reform developed in New York and spread to other cities. In 1864 the Council of Hygiene of the New York Citizen's Association launched a campaign to create a new health department for the city. When the Tammany machine of Boss Tweed stymied its efforts, the Council undertook an investigation of the city's housing and sanitary conditions to alert the public to the dangers of crowding and filth. Directed by Dr. Stephen Smith, a prominent physician who was a leading figure in the nation's public health movemoent for six decades, the Council's investigation produced an indictment of slum housing. The report raised enough publicity, so that when a cholera epidemic threatened in 1866, the New York General Assembly created a Metropolitan Board of Health and gave it authority to regulate housing and sanitary conditions through provisions of the Tenement House Law of 1867. This law required landlords to furnish minimum facilities for fire escape, for ventilation to interior rooms, and for indoor plumbing. The provisions were very weak (one privy per twenty inhabitants and one water tap per building satisfied the legal requirements), and enforcement was difficult. But the law had symbolic value. It imposed public regulation on a landlord's property rights, and it established a precedent for stronger codes in the future.

Before the Council of Hygiene had begun its activities, other reformers were trying to reconcile housing improvement with the aims of capitalism. Beginning in the 1850s the New York Association for Improving the Conditions of the Poor (AICP) advanced the idea of a model tenement, a type of housing in which private investors would accept lower profits for the sake of safer, healthier facilities and philanthropic service to the poor. To set an example the AICP constructed its own model tenement in 1854. Although the project failed completely, the idea continued to dominate housing reform attitudes for the rest of the century because it left the provision of housing to private builders.

In fact the model tenement idea was responsible for the notorious *dumbbell* tenement that spread across New York after 1879. The dumbbell, named for its shape rather than its designer, was fashioned to meet the provisions of the New York Tenement House Law of 1879, which required that every room in new tenements have a window. (The 1867 law required only that every room have *access* to a window.) An indentation on each side of the building gave it the shape of a dumbbell. The indentation, when combined with that of the adjoining building, created an air shaft five feet wide. Each tenement was five or six stories high. Each floor contained fourteen rooms, in two three-room and two four-room apartments, and two water closets in the hallway. Ten of the fourteen rooms had windows bordering the air shafts.

That the dumbbell tenement was an example of housing *reform*—it was the winning entry in a contest to determine the best mass housing design that could fit a 25-by-100 foot lot—dramatizes the tragic state of low-income housing in New York. The largest room in any dumbbell apartment measured only ten-by-eleven feet; and the narrow air shaft, originally designed to provide light and air, acted as a receptacle for garbage, as a breeding place for vermin and insects, and as a duct for fire. The major consequence of the dumbbell was not comfort, but more crowding. Between 1880 and 1893 the density of New York's tenth ward, the heart of the immigrant-filled Lower East Side, increased from 432 to 702 persons per acre. By 1893 most of the ward's 75,000 inhabitants were packed into twelve hundred tenements.

The dumbbell's rapid spread across Manhattan to Brooklyn, and to

Airshaft of a Dumbbell Tenement

This view, taken from the roof of a New York apartment house around 1900, shows how narrow the air shaft between two dumbbell tenements actually was. Such openings could hardly provide the light and ventilation that housing reformers sought. *Public Housing Administration, The National Archives.*

other cities, produced two additional effects. One was the permanent association of the term *tenement* with slum housing. Originally the word had applied simply to any multi-story rental building housing more than three families. Now it became a term of discredit. Second, continuing deterioration of housing conditions in the slums ignited new reform crusades, not the least of which was a move to end the abuses created by dumbbell tenements. Led by Lawrence Veiller, the nation's first full-time professional housing reformer, new investigations and outcries resulted in the passage of the New York Tenement House Law of 1901, which established a revised code of regulations. Among other things the new code replaced the dumbbell's air shaft with a longer, more open court. It also required a separate water closet for each apartment, and it provided stronger fire protection measures. Significantly, however, these regulations applied only to new buildings. The law included a few weak provisions directed at improving light, ventilation, plumbing, and fireproofing in existing tenements (such as requiring landlords to install windows in windowless rooms), but it could not effectively remedy the eighty thousand tenements that covered the five boroughts of New York City.

What happened in New York occurred in other cities on a diminished and not so acute scale. Multi-story tenements, dumbbell or otherwise, did not appear to any great extent until the end of the century, but dilapidated shanties and cellar dwellings multiplied everywhere as swelling populations flooded the housing markets. The situation was particularly severe in Chicago where rear tenements blighted the inner city. These were flimsy shacks constructed in the space between an alley and the rear of the building that fronted the street. Rear tenements probably comprised the worst of all slum housing in Chicago and New York, but they were often overlooked by reformers more conerned with larger structures. In the South much of the only housing available to blacks consisted of old, converted slave quarters that remained in yards and alleyways behind white homes. New Orleans and Charleston had their own kind of rear slums, ignored by white humanitarians.

The successes of Veiller and New York journalists Jacob Riis and Richard W. Gilder in investigating the slums, in arousing public concern, and in prompting legislation generated similar movements in other cities. Civic organizations sponsored investigations and exhibits, and they lobbied successfully for the establishment of housing commissions and regulatory codes in Baltimore, St. Louis, Chicago, Kansas City, San Francisco, Philadelphia, New Orleans, Los Angeles, and Washington, D.C., among others. In some places reformers added a third scheme to their goals for building regulations and model housing. This was decentralization, the removal of poor families from high-density central cities to less congested, more inexpensive land on the urban fringe. Under this plan it was hoped that new, planned communities could grow up around industries that were locating outside city limits. Thus many reformers applauded George Pullman's factory town outside Chicago when it opened in 1880. Unfortunately worker dissatisfaction with Pullman's control over their rents and politics as well as their jobs, the town's financial failure, and disruption from the strike of 1894 buried the experiment under discontent. Thereafter large corporations generally shied away from building decentralized new towns. Planning and housing were returned to private real estate speculators. Schemes to build towns on the model of Ebenezer Howard's English "garden cities" fizzled from lack of capital. The few small projects that were begun, such as the Russell Sage Foundation's Forest Hills Garden built in Queens, New York in 1911, could not reduce costs enough to attract working-class inhabitants. Decentralization, like housing codes and model tenements, never met the expectations of it proponents.

Efforts by reformers to improve housing conditions for low-income residents often reflected middle-class values and in doing so, raised opposition among slum dwellers who held different values. Many could not afford rents for rooms in improved buildings, and tighter housing codes only made their situations more difficult. Because slum buildings were cheap to buy and provided high rates of return, some tenement dwellers saw themselves as potential tenement owners. Costly improvements required by reform codes discouraged investors from purchasing tenements and blocked an avenue of economic mobility for some lower-class members. Moreover, as Roy Lubove has noted, reform efforts to lessen crowding within buildings by imposing co-residence limitations threatened the institution of boarding, one of the most pervasive and important forms of inner city habitation.

The strongest restraint on housing reform was the privatism that governed prevailing attitudes toward property. Americans have always considered the management and disposal of land and buildings as a sacred civil right. Any interference with this right came to constitute a threat to a cultural inheritance. Thus not only did landlords resist and evade housing codes (which tended to be poorly enforced anyway), but also humanitarian reformers avoided any interference with the housing market. Public agencies could neither demolish dilapidated and dangerous buildings, nor construct adequate housing for low-income citizens. Eventually, by expanding their police powers and privileges of eminent domain, governments did begin to assume greater responsibilities for furnishing public housing. As we shall see in later chapters, many of these efforts were clumsy, costly, and even detrimental. Nevertheless the imposition of public initiative was a late, but generally necessary, improvement. During the nineteenth century private builders and speculators had assumed by default the responsibility for housing the flood of urban immigrants. Their profit motives dictated maximizing revenues and minimizing expenditures. The results were crowding, filth, disease, and degradation for the half of the population least capable of improving its lot. Genuine humanitarianism, coupled with fear of disorder, spawned reform crusades. Although these efforts met with, at best, partial success, they at least established greater public responsibility for the health and safety of all of a city's inhabitants.

Although housing reforms improved life in inner city slums only slightly, science and technology, with the aid of public authority, made all cities safer and healthier than ever before. Concern over housing and public health had much in common. Countless surveys revealed that death rates in slum areas doubled and tripled those in other urban districts. Congestion and poorly constructed housing amplified all the problems of urban life: ventilation, fire prevention, sewage disposal, water purification, personal hygiene, and control of disease. Advances in engineering and medicine reduced dangers in almost all these areas, and legislative bodies were willing to use public police power to control and to prevent threats to public safety.

Discoveries by European scientists Koch, Lister, and Pasteur convinced most of the western world that tiny organisms, called bacteria, caused specific diseases, such as cholera, typhoid, diptheria, and tuberculosis. This evidence strengthened the link between sanitation and public health. Since colonial times sanitarians and boards of health had emphasized the need for personal and public cleanliness. Support for sanitation intensified as slum areas spread in the 1860s and '70s. Efforts of men like Dr. Edwin Snow of Providence and George E. Waring, Jr., of New York, who crusaded for public hygiene and for improved sewer systems, succeeded in reducing mortality rates in American cities even before bacteriology won wide acceptance. As knowledge of the germ theory became more common in the 1880s and '90s, state and municipal boards of health (many of which had been established in the aftermath of the cholera, typhoid, and yellow fever epidemics that had ravaged scores of cities during the nineteenth century) could apply scientific certainty to the enforcement of cleanliness regulations.

Increasing knowledge about the origins of diseases also fostered public activities in the field of preventive medicine. Beginning in the 1890s a number of cities established diagnostic laboratories to analyze the incidence of certain diseases and to try to avert their spread. Meat and milk inspections were tightened. Local and state health departments sponsored education programs to alert the public to the causes and prevention of disease. Newspapers, pamphlets, lectures, and school programs explained contagion, personal hygiene, and proper diets. Around the turn of the century various clinics and dispensaries were opened. They provided information on baby care and dental hygiene, and they offered assistance to those suffering from tuberculosis, venereal disease, and minor injuries. Although they brought needed services to many neighborhoods, especially in New York, the clinics and dispensaries functioned mainly as charity institutions. The medical profession and the middle-class public had no taste for any type of general health care that hinted at socialized medicine.

In addition to medical advances improvements in fire protection and in other utilities increased public safety. The Great Chicago Fire of 1871, which consumed nearly 1,700 acres and destroyed over $200 million in property, and the huge conflagration that swept Boston in 1872 attest to the fact that fire remained the principal threat to urban safety. Yet new building codes, architectural developments, and more professional fire fighting forces began to lessen the danger. The New York Tenement House Law of 1867 and subsequent legislation included a number of provisions for fire escape and prevention. New buildings increasingly included fire walls, fire barriers, and steel-frame, fire-resistant construction (although most of these buildings were too expensive for the poor). Much of the drive for better fire prevention was spearheaded by the National Board of Fire Underwriters, organized in 1866. The N.B.F.U. adopted a nationwide policy of drawing local maps, examining ordinances, and inspecting fire fighting equipment as determinants of local insurance rates. This practice stirred cities to upgrade their building codes and fire departments. The old volunteer fire brigades were already giving way to full-time, professional forces. Cities began to purchase steam engines and pumping machinery and to install electric fire alarm boxes, as well as to expand their fire fighting personnel. In addition to fire protection, electricity (especially its use for lighting) and sewer construction promised new benefits in urban health and safety.

By the early twentieth century the United States had achieved the highest standards of mass urban living in the world. But, as Sam Bass Warner, Jr., has noted, neither the benefits nor the facilities reached all urban dwellers evenly. By the 1870s most municipalities had assumed responsibilities for constructing water and sewerage systems and for insuring public health. But public responsibility virtually ended at the borders of private property. Landlords and builders who wanted water and sewers had to pay for connections between their buildings and the water main and trunk line sewer. Owners of newly developed property were assessed for public improvements according to the amount of their land that abutted a street. Those who could afford such facilities, or whose tenants could absorb the costs in their rents, readily installed modern plumbing, heating, and lighting. But for those forced into high-density, low-quality dwellings, modern amenities were much scarcer. Inner city landlords, eager to maximize profits, tried to avoid expensive improvements. And governments remained reluctant to enter the private sanctum of housing construction and property management. Thus inner-city residents, mostly newcomers (native as well as foreign), mostly poor, were at the mercy of the housing market. Over time some of the improvements in sanitation and housing construction trickled down to the slum neighborhoods. For most people, however, the best solution was to escape, to somehow acquire a home beyond the inner core, or to pack up and take a chance that things would be better somewhere else.

THE IMPACT OF INNER-CITY LIFE ON INNER-CITY RESIDENTS

People, crowded into too little space, created the problems in housing, health, and safety outlined above. But urban cores themselves transformed the everyday lives of their inhabitants. The congestion, the streets and neighborhoods, the housing and job markets—all necessitated personal, family, and community adjustments. Some were easy and salutary. They were part of the socialization process that enabled American cities to absorb a variety of peoples and cultures without too much trauma. Other adjustments left scars.

Unlike the residents of the periphery or suburbs, whose environments consisted of single-family, detached houses, slum dwellers seldom knew privacy. Blocks with tenements jammed together, buildings housing a score of families, and apartments inhabited by a dozen people determined personal behavior and development. People had to endure the ways of others who lived so close by. Toleration was not always easy; domestic squabbles and neighborhood fights were common to slum life. Liberals and conservatives of the middle class, accustomed to spacious surroundings, rarely understood how the physical pressures of slum life bred violence as a component of lower-class culture.

Crowding also complicated modes of living outside the tenements. In many areas each apartment building covered the entire lot on which it was built, leaving no room for recreational activity. Housing reformers urged that at least 35 percent of each residential lot be left open, but they could not undo the past and their guidelines were usually ignored. Yards, vacant lots, and playgrounds remained scarce. Children were forced either into the streets, where traffic interrupted their play and threatened their safety, or onto the roofs, where they found privacy but faced more danger. Adults who wished to escape the tenements went to the neighborhood saloon, a custom that unnerved middle-class reformers. Yet by providing the most available premises for relaxation and sociability, the saloon served inner city needs more than any other institution. It proved to be one of the most durable features of the urban environment.

In order to obtain minimal food and shelter, more than one member of a slum family had to work. Frequently this work was performed in tenement sweatshops where whole families would be engaged in the production of clothing, cigars, artificial flowers, or foodstuffs. Here women and children worked long hours at incredibly low wages. Paid according to piecework, they rarely earned more than ten cents an hour, and the average wage was two to four cents an hour. Young children entered the sweatshop system as soon as they could perform simple tasks. For example, an investigator found that three- and four-year-olds could aid a cigar-making operation by straightening tobacco leaves and by putting lids on boxes. Women often had to attend to their domestic duties before, during, and after their sweatshop labor, and many had only five or six hours of rest a day. Conditions were worst in New York where the sweatshop system was most prevalent, but in other cities as well the requisites of subsistence governed the daily routines of slum dwellers and deprived them of leisure time.

Certainly the housing and work patterns of the inner city influenced household composition and family relationships. Residence in a single-family house rather than in quarters shared with others has been a traditional American norm. Historians have only begun to uncover the household patterns of past eras, but it seems quite clear that the norm seldom occurred in the urban cores. The great majority of *families* (kin grouping) were nuclear in structure, consisting only of the head of household, spouse, and children all living in one place. But also, a large number of inner city *households* (including *all* the people inhabiting one residential unit) contained lodgers and boarders. Preliminary evidence has revealed that at any point in time, about one-fourth of all urban households contained outsiders, non-family residents. Countless urban dwellers—perhaps the majority—boarded or lodged with others for at least a few years during their lives. The most common pattern was for young people, usually unmarried migrants who had left their parents' households, to board with an older family whose children were grown. Sometimes, however, whole families boarded. Lodgers frequently stayed until they could obtain quarters of their own; but a number of individuals spent most of their adulthood living with others, either lodging in one place for a long time or shifting from board to board, city to city. Lodging and boarding houses were also common in most cities. The presence of strangers in the urban household, non-kin who shared space, meals, and conversation with the nuclear family, brought not only outside income to the family but also outside contacts and ideas. And the institution of boarding helped ease the migrant's struggle with anonymity in a strange city.

Only a small minority of urban families were extended in composition. Seldom more than 15 or 20 percent contained parents, siblings, aunts, uncles, or cousins in addition to the nucleus of head, spouse, and children. But if examination of family ties is stretched beyond the physical confines of the home, it is clear that many more families were extended in that they maintained close relationships, at least temporarily, with kin who lived nearby. Such relationships appear to have been common among particular ethnic groups who occupied the inner city. Close kin ties between parents and children and between siblings have been discovered among Italians in Boston, Chicago, and Providence. Similar ties existed among East European Jews. Frequently a newly married couple would live temporarily with or near one set of parents or would support a widowed parent or younger sibling. The extended relationships between residential units, called *propinquity,* may have aided adjustment of migrant families to urban life by promoting such activities as visiting, common meals, babysitting, and emotional consolation.

Thus family life provided an important cushion for newcomers to urban society. The two-parent, nuclear household, often augmented by boarders and extended by kin ties to other households in the neighborhood, assumed alone the functions of comfort and support that it had shared with the village community and the church in the American and European countrysides. Urbanization, industrialization, and migration did not crack the resilience of family life. A study of late-nineteenth century Boston has shown that even among Black Americans, a group later identified as "socially disorganized" because of its large proportion of female-headed families, five out of every six households contained a husband *and* wife rather than only one parent.

Although the city did reinforce or augment family life in several ways, the pressures of poverty and slum housing still threatened family solidarity. When they entered the urban job market, most migrant men and women took manual employment that was both dangerous and physically wearing. Long hours of work in poor lighting and poor ventilation induced mental lapses that had harmful results. The incidence of industrial accidents was high in many cities, and there was no compensation to support families whose breadwinners or other members were killed or incapacitated. Moreover, men or women who worked 80 or 90 hours a week without proper rest and nourishment fell easy prey to tuberculosis, pneumonia, and other diseases. The death of the father of a lower-class family at the age of thirty or thirty-five was a common occurrence. Widowhood among the Irish and other immigrant groups was more than a stereotype; it was an imminent reality.

Migration, city life, and poverty also touched young children. The need for supplementary family income pressed many children into the labor market at early ages. Others, who did not have jobs but whose parents worked twelve to fourteen hours a day, roamed the streets away from adult supervision. Some of them became *street arabs*, homeless youths who slept in stairwells and begged in the streets. Older youths joined gangs, formal groupings of both boys and girls that cultivated peer group solidarity but that also harassed merchants, antagonized police, and frightened neighborhoods with their violent activities. But the child laborers, the vagrant boys, and the gangs were minorities. By the end of the nineteenth century, most inner city children went to public schools. Yet here too problems arose, especially among immigrant generations. Children of foreign-born (or even of native-born rural) parents were caught between two worlds. Although the public schools taught values of independence and self-made opportunity, parents often demanded that their children remain obedient and useful family members who would set aside self-fulfillment in favor of working for the benefit of the entire family. Those who chose the schools more easily assimilated into the native middle-class cultural mainstream. Those who held on to their parents' values remained within their ethnic social structure and were generally less upwardly mobile, although important exceptions occurred in areas of politics and crime.

Although the situation of women varied from one ethnic group to another, working-class wives and mothers were the most bound by cultural traditions. Almost all groups assigned women fixed domestic roles and attached them to the household. Of necessity many working class women did take jobs. Here considerable variation occurred between cultures. Irish and Polish women frequently worked away from their families in factories and as domestics. Italians and German Jews, on the other hand, enforced women's family functions. Females in these groups usually took jobs that involved working at home, such as making artificial flowers, sewing, or, as in the case of Italian women in Buffalo, working in family crews in the vineyards and canneries. In most instances unmarried daughters had opportunities for a wider range of jobs (as sales clerks, for example) than did their mothers, who were more confined by male authority and maternal responsibilities.

Finally, movement to and residence inside the inner city influenced

Women's Work and the City

Along with textile mills, piecework production such as this assembly table in the Shrenhat Toy Company of Philadelphia, gave large numbers of urban women work opportunities outside the home by the early 1900s. *U.S. Forest Service, The National Archives.*

social and cultural groups consisting of many individuals, many families. How much cultural baggage did migrants bring with them? How much did life in the city change long-held cultural patterns? Certainly immigrants, particularly those from abroad, sought anchors of familiarity upon arriving in American cities. They often tried to live near friends and relatives. Whole villages were transferred from the Italian or East European countryside to New York, Philadephia, and Chicago. The perpetuation of institutions, feasts, and pageants helped sustain memories of the homeland. Reformers, concerned with the poverty of immigrants, often overlooked the richness of group life that many immigrants sustained.

Yet no group could live in isolation. Socially complex cities fostered contact, exchange, and conflict between people. They altered old customs and spawned new institutions. The necessity of learning the English language, the American ideals taught in the schools, the new patterns of employment, and the bustle of the streets all undermined attempts to recreate Old World life. Almost all groups formed mutual benefit and fraternal societies that provided aid for the sick and paid burial expenses. These organizations, as Humbert Nelli has noted, resembled native American counterparts more closely than they did the middle-class societies that existed in Europe. Foreign language newspapers developed in many cities and helped cultivate ethnic pride and solidarity. But the

A Market on the Lower East Side
Warren Dickerson's view of Hester Street in New York, around 1900, scans a street lined with Jewish shops and peddlers. This photograph reveals a vitality of immigrant life in the city, an informality that often is viewed with nostalgia today. *History Division, Natural History Museum of Los Angeles County.*

papers addressed readers on the basis of nationality, not village or region. And they acquired an American flavor by imitating the style and format of sensationalist English language dailies. Religious institutions also changed, although many old customs proved to be quite durable. The most distinguishing religious factor between Europe and America was the removal of a state church. The voluntary nature of churches in America tended to foster democratization and sectarianism among all religious groups, diluting dogma and elevating personal religious experience. In addition American cities altered the immigrants' material culture. Because they brought little with them, the immigrants were forced to use native goods that made their homes resemble those of all other Americans. This tendency did not necessarily mean that the foreigners were accepting the predominant culture, for they often fashioned American fabrics into European styles and cooked ethnic meals from American foods. Yet convenience and availability forced them to adapt material goods, such as ready-made clothing and mass-produced, Grand Rapids style furniture, that were common to the larger society.

For over a century many Americans have viewed the ethnic neighborhood as one of the strongest institutions of inner city life. The urge for familiarity and cultural identity drove immigrants to seek out their own kind. Very quickly colonies of distinct nationalities formed, most noticeably in cities at or near ports of entry, but also in interior cities from Cleveland to Chicago to Denver. There were Little Italys, Bohemiantowns, Jewish sections, Greek districts, and others. These colonies, or "ghettos" as they came to be called, softened the shock of migration and prepared immigrants for merger into American culture. Yet most colonies were neither as stable nor as monolithic as most people thought because the high incidence of residential mobility kept them in constant flux. Only rarely did one immigrant group comprise a majority of residents in an area one-half to one square mile in size. Little Italy and Polish Town might have contained a plurality of Italians and Poles, respectively, but seldom a majority. Moreover rapid residential mobility scattered residents of these districts to other parts of the city or to other cities, so that even the most homogeneous neighborhoods experienced rapid turnover. They appeared stable only because people moving in were of the same nationality as those moving out. A 1915 survey of Italian and Polish districts in Chicago revealed that nearly half the residents moved each year. And a recent study of Omaha at the turn of the century has shown that members of all ethnic groups who remained in the city fanned out from the central city into many outlying districts well within the span of one generation.

Thus for most immigrant families, residence in a particular ghetto was not a lasting experience. In some cities, principally New York and the congested industrial cities of the Northeast, pockets of single groups did form; and when the immigrants moved, they transferred their whole colony to another district. But generally, residential experiences of immigrants involved dispersion into a number of ethnically mixed neighborhoods. The ghetto's major importance was cultural. It centralized institutions rather than group residence. That is, the churches, clubs, and retail establishments of a single ethnic group frequently located in an area near a bulk of their members and clients but also accessible to the large numbers who lived elsewhere in the city. Thus the secondary commercial centers that sprouted around mass transit routes and intersections often became sites of ethnic business and social activities. The visibility of these institutions gave districts their ethnic identifications even though residential patterns were mixed and unstable.

One urban group, however, did experience the ghetto as a place of confined, ethnically uniform residence, as well as a center for cultural institutions. Black Americans were physically isolated from the rest of urban society. Unlike all other immigrant groups in industrial America, the black residential experience was one of contracting, rather than expanding, dispersion. Supporters of discriminatory housing markets and other types of segregation denied blacks the opportunities afforded white groups. Although ethnic neighborhoods in most cities were dissolving in the early twentieth century, black ghettos were growing in size and homogeneity. By 1920 ten Chicago census tracts were over 75 percent black. In Detroit, Cleveland, Boston, Los Angeles, and Washington, D.C., two-thirds or more of the black residents were jammed into only two or three wards. Like the immigrants, blacks developed a number of clubs and associations that reinforced racial unity. Some of these individuals and organizations sounded a new note of militance after 1890. Activities ranged from boycotts against segregated streetcars in the South to support for black entrepreneurship and retaliation against white violence in the North. But more commonly the ghetto bred frustration, submission, and escapism. Color, more than anything else, distinguished Afro-American communities from those of all other groups who entered the inner cities. Color was not cultural baggage; it was an indelible legacy.

PATTERNS OF SOCIAL MOBILITY

If immigrants came off the farms and from abroad seeking security and an improvement in their life styles, what were the chances that these hopes would be fulfilled? At the end of the nineteenth century, beliefs remained strong that there was an open road from the bottom of society to the top, or at least the middle. The century's expanding industrial economy spun off new jobs, new markets, new areas for investment. Although hard times punctured the booms with unprecedented frequency—there were serious, though temporary, declines in each of the four decades preceding World War I—the euphoria of expansion dulled sour memories.

Yet dark clouds persisted. By the late nineteenth century the spread of slum decay, the power and impersonality of giant factories, and the ever-widening gulf between rich and poor withered the dreams of many. In addition the social complexity, churning neighborhoods, and competition for space and jobs, so common to city life, fanned hostilities between newcomers and those who considered themselves guardians of the "American Way." Popular opinion came to fear that immigrants were displacing native workers, driving down wage rates, deteriorating residential districts, subverting traditional morality, and threatening political order. Newspapers and even some "scientific" theory reinforced vicious stereotypes that depicted Italians as swarthy and stupid, Irish as lazy and drunkardly, Jews as greedy and cunning. In the 1880s influential reformers like Charles Loring Brace and Josiah Strong voiced strong fears that heightened waves of foreign newcomers would bring down American civilization. After the turn of the century Madison Grant, director of the New York Museum of Natural History, warned that among the new immigrants were

> a large and increasing number of the weak, the broken and the mentally crippled of all races drawn from the lowest stratum of the Mediterranean basin of the Balkans, together with the hordes of the wretched, submerged populations of the Polish ghettos. Our jails, insane asylums and almshouses are filled with this human flotsam and the whole tone of American life, social, moral and political has been lowered and vulgarized by them.

These beliefs, plus the activities of nativist organizations, such as the American Protective Association and the American Patriotic League, worked to impede immigrants' (particularly Catholics') chances for betterment. In addition as blacks sought their fortunes in southern and northern cities, the effects of racism stifled their opportunity and pinned them to the very bottom of urban society.

Historians have now proven that the rags-to-riches path was not very well worn—either before or after the Civil War. Andrew Carnegie and Henry Ford were aberrations. Most men at the pinnacle of society possessed advantages from the start; they did not rise from backgrounds of poverty. Yet beneath the peaks there was considerable movement. Some people climbed up the socio-economic ladder, if only a rung or two. Others skidded downward. Still others rose only to slip back. Success was the goal of all groups who poured into American cities. The

extent to which they attained that goal opens a window to some meaningful experiences of urban life.

There are three major types of socio-economic mobility: geographical,
occupational, and property. Although an individual's experiences could
have involved a combination of these categories, it is possible to view
them separately. The magnitude of geographical mobility in the half-
century after the Civil War has been detailed in earlier pages. A kind of
wanderlust, an extraordinary transience, of the entire population has
distinguished this country's history as much as its frontiers, its political
institutions, and its cultural pluralism. The major purpose of migration
has been to seek the road to a better future. "In our lexicon," George
Pierson has written, "movement means improvement." Of course there
was always a gap between hope and reality. Students of migration have
not been able to trace very many people from city to city, but some
evidence suggests that many who left one town for another, particularly
the unskilled, never made a move upward. Still the belief in opportunity
beckoned people to move. So much so that as early as 1847 one foreign
traveler wrote, "If God were suddenly to call the world to judgment He
would surprise two-thirds of the American population on the road like
ants." Moreover movement from place to place within a single city often
brought tangible improvement as families set out in search of their dream
house.

Most studies of social mobility have focused on occupational change
because a person's job furnishes the most available gauge of his or her
status. Within this category are two subtypes: individual, the changes
over one person's lifetime; and generational, the difference in occupational attainments between fathers and sons. At the outset it must be
emphasized that constant economic change and growth vitalized urban
job markets, especially for skilled and white-collar labor. To be sure
mechanization and new products pushed some callings into obsolescence,
but the expansion of other areas more than compensated for the con-
traction. Thus in most cities upward mobility outweighed downward.
Although many rose from blue-collar positions into lower-middle class
jobs—foremen, clerks, salesmen, petty merchants—very few middle class
members or their sons slipped into manual categories. This trend was
reinforced by the influx of unskilled newcomers, immigrants in northern
cities, blacks in southern cities, who filled the lower ranks of the labor
force and formed a base upon which those more advantaged could climb.

Determining whether or not an individual advanced from a manual
to a nonmanual occupation has been the handiest method of gauging
significant upward mobility. Conversely, a skid from nonmanual to
manual ranks has signaled downward mobility. Although historians have
just recently begun to apply these measures to data from the past, it

appears that at the end of the nineteenth century an individual's chances for upward movement of this kind were moderate but steady. The possibilities of downward mobility, however, were quite low. In newer cities of the interior, such as Atlanta or Omaha, about one in five white males rose from manual to nonmanual callings over a ten-year period—that is, assuming he stayed in the city for that long. For residents of older cities of the Northeast, the chances were about one in seven. Incidences of downward mobility varied more widely but generally occurred about half as frequently as upward mobility.

These rates—derived for only a handful of cities—apply to all ethnic groups, including Anglo-Saxon Protestants, taken together. The trends for separate groups varied. Generally, native-born men were more likely to rise occupationally than foreign-born. Such a difference appears obvious given the immigrants' lack of skills and capital and the hostilities they encountered in some areas of employment. But patterns were not entirely uniform or consistent. For example, in Omaha in the early 1900s, a number of Jewish and Italian immigrants became petty merchants and thereby moved into proprietor or nonmanual ranks from blue-collar jobs. A similar trend had occurred earlier among Germans in Poughkeepsie. These cases occasionally gave immigrants higher upward mobility rates than natives. But the foreign-born tended to fall from white-collar to blue-collar status more often than natives. Although different groups advanced and fell at different rates, and although circumstances varied according to the social and economic conditions of a particular place, the evidence gathered thus far suggests that manual-to-nonmanual mobility was moderate but fairly constant from 1850 to 1920.

Two other paths of upward mobility occurred more frequently than the one described above. Sons of blue-collar workers attained white-collar status more frequently than did their fathers. In Boston, Indianapolis, and Poughkeepsie between 1880 and 1910 at least one-fourth of manual laborers' sons were able to improve their positions significantly over those of their fathers. Like career mobility, rates of intergenerational mobility varied considerably from city to city. Yet that they were consistently higher than those measuring individual career mobility suggests that a number of men were able to escape a permanently low status passed down from one generation to another. Also, many men who did not achieve significant mobility managed to climb just a notch or two: from unskilled jobs to semiskilled; from semiskilled to skilled; from clerks to managers; or from salesmen to proprietors. It has been difficult to determine which occupational changes would have represented improvement at this level, mainly because wage rates and income data are unavailable. Yet most research has suggested that the bulk of mobility occurred in small increments.

Even those who were unable to rise occupationally might still have been able to experience economic and social mobility through property acquisition. Although inestimable numbers of urban dwellers lived on the margins of subsistence, many owned property. Wage rates generally rose from the 1860s onward, and countless families either purchased real estate or bought personal property or accumulated savings. One study has revealed that of a sample of Irish laborers who remained in the same ward of Providence between 1860 and 1870, 85 percent owned property, most of it personal and most of it acquired over the ten-year period. Stephan Thernstrom has estimated that a majority of laboring families who lived for ten years, during the 1860s and '70s, in Newburyport, Massachusetts, had savings accounts, and more than a third owned real property. It is important to note in these examples the relationship between property holding and residential stability. Property ownership among migrants has been much more difficult to uncover. It seems logical that migrants must have held less, although the hypothesis that people do not move because they have a "stake in society" has not been proven. Nevertheless property ownership undoubtedly presented many families with a source for upward mobility when occupational avenues were closed.

White males of all origins had opportunities to inch upward. Blacks encountered many more barriers. Confined mostly to menial and domestic jobs—much more so than before the Civil War—, they found their way into basic trades only as strikebreakers. Trapped in the lowest-paying jobs, blacks could accumulate capital far less easily than whites. Consequently a smaller fraction of them held property. Proportions of black owners in Atlanta, Poughkeepsie, and Birmingham at the end of the nineteenth century were only one-half to one-fourth those of working-class whites. Few blacks owned property that was valued as high as that of any white. Women were also excluded from the main routes of social mobility. When husbands and fathers moved up, the women in their families were pulled along into higher statuses. Yet her *occupation* seldom defined family rank; it was more of a supplementary appendage. Because the types of jobs open to women were limited—mostly factory, sweatshop, domestic, or petty clerical work—, female heads of households were pinned to working-class ranks—unless they were widows of men who had been in higher stations.

What were some of the consequences of the movement that did occur? For one thing, social mobility did *not* eliminate poverty. Economic freedom and mobility produced greater distinctions between rich and poor, rather than more equality in urban society. Although few members of the middle class fell into the lower class, downward mobility did occur within the lower ranks, with somber results. Unemployment frequently ran high in the industrial cities, and loss of job or physical incapacitation of a family's breadwinner could plunge it into destitution. Additionally, huge numbers of people entered urban society at the lowest levels and never rose. Thus the absolute numbers of urban poor constantly expanded in spite of the opportunities that the American economy promised.

As cases of dependency multiplied, public attitudes toward the poor hardened. Economy-minded officials and their middle-class supporters began to attack forms of outdoor relief. Believing direct grants of money and provisions encouraged pauperism, several cities abolished outdoor relief by 1900; and several others made such grants only in return for work. Cities turned to institutions—poorhouses, almshouses, juvenile homes, and special homes for the blind, deaf, mentally ill, and physically handicapped. The trend was for states to assume management of these institutions, but efforts by state boards to administer "scientifically" (that is, to change the poor into productive citizens) usually fizzled. Increasing destitution and dependence exacerbated the trends that had developed before the Civil War. Rehabilitation, costly and demanding, lapsed into confining, isolating, and retaining social undesirables from the outside world.

Reflecting the larger trend toward efficient, scientific administration of all forms of organized activity at the end of the nineteenth century, private social welfare organizations emphasized coordinated, systematic efforts to relieve poverty. By the 1890s many major cities contained a Charity Organization Society (COS) that organized communications among local charities, established agencies to find jobs for the unemployed, and sent employees to ascertain that every dependent was truly needy. These activities reflected the longstanding moralistic attitudes toward poverty: the belief that individual weaknesses, such as drunkenness and laziness caused poverty. Yet the emphasis on investigation and close supervision of the poor stressed by the COS induced conclusions that low income, low-quality housing, and inadequate sanitation, rather than individual failure were responsible for dependence. The investigations led welfare agencies to support reforms that sought to relieve the environmental problems afflicting the poor. These efforts slightly improved slum and factory conditions, but public attitudes resisted large-scale change. According to Raymond Mohl, "reformers suffered in the long run from the constraints imposed by a society that was unprepared and indisposed to accept responsibility for those who were unable to survive in a competitive system." Both the downwardly mobile and those immobilized at the bottom still had to fend for themselves.

The kinds of hardship that were so common in the inner cities of industrial America produced two sets of reactions: pessimism and resignation born of despair, and unrest and violence born of frustration. Urban areas in the half-century following the Civil War suffered from crime and civil discontent. Several cities experienced labor violence in the 1870s and 1890s. New Orleans experienced a race riot in 1866 and an anti-Italian riot in 1891. There were race riots in Wilmington in 1898 and in Atlanta in 1906. Over fifty people were killed in Cincinnati in 1884 as a result of a three-day riot that burst out after an attempted lynching.

But the extent of these incidents was much smaller than conditions should have warranted because two factors—"safety valves"—relieved the pressures of social unrest. First, the possibility of geographical mobility left open a means of escape. America is not only a nation of immigrants but a nation of migrants. If life was unsatisfactory in one place, the grass was always greener somewhere else. More importantly, nearly everyone could—and countless people did—seek greener grass in the cities. Migration patterns reversed Frederick Jackson Turner's theory that open land in the West calmed urban tensions by drawing away the discontented. Instead, cities attracted those disappointed with farm life and those fed up with life in another city. To be sure, many dreams were wistful, and many migrants found only more of the same at their destinations. But how was improvement to be measured? The man who moved from the textile mills of Manchester, New Hampshire, to the grain mills of Minneapolis may not have increased his income; but he may have moved his family from a three-room dormitory apartment to a four-room rented house and have paid a penny for a loaf of bread instead of two cents. Each city had its attractions, mythical and real. It took over a thousand dollars to start a farm but only a few dollars for a railroad ticket to Chicago or Kansas City. Why not go? Life there couldn't be worse.

Second, the existence and hope of upward mobility soothed the sores of urban dissatisfaction. As Stephan Thernstrom has written, "It is not equality of *condition* but equality of *opportunity* that Americans have celebrated." In spite of the widening gap between the very rich and the very poor, the American economy left room for upward movement: if not at the top, then in the middle: if not for new entrepreneurs and industrialists, then for workers in new trades and services and for white-collar laborers in the new commercial, industrial, and public bureaucracies. Even if there seemed to be no hope of individual improvement, things might be better for the next generation. Often they were. The big success story, the rise from bottom to top, was usually a myth. But improving one's status by taking a new job, acquiring some real estate, or buying a horse and wagon was altogether possible.

Thus as Professor Thernstrom has so forcefully argued, mobility—both geographical and socio-economic—dampened class conflict in American cities. The ability of people to edge upward within or, occasionally, out of lower-or working-class ranks prevented the formation of a permanently oppressed proletariat (with the exception of nonwhites). Moreover these conditions did not foster a "revolution of rising expectations" because most dissatisfied people did not stay in one place long enough to develop common identity with those similarly discontented. Although working-class protest existed in American cities, it proved difficult to organize, as many Socialists painfully discovered. Yet one kind of organization within urban cores was successful, because it often addressed the experiences of inner-city life. This institution was the political machine.

BIBLIOGRAPHY

The literature on immigration and its impact on urban society is too voluminous to list briefly. Among the most important works from an urban perspective are Marcus Lee Hansen, *The Atlantic Migration, 1607–1860* (Cambridge: Harvard University Press, 1940); Hansen, *The Immigrant in American History* (Cambridge: Harvard University Press, 1940); Oscar Handlin, *Boston's Immigrants: A Study in Acculturation* (Cambridge: Harvard University Press, revised ed., 1959); Handlin, *The Uprooted* (Cambridge: The Belknap Press of Harvard University Press, 1954); Moses Rischin, *The Promised City: New York City's Jews, 1870–1914* (Cambridge: Harvard University Press, 1962); Humbert S. Nelli, *The Italians in Chicago, 1860–1920: A Study in Ethnic Mobility* (New York: Oxford University Press, 1970); Donald B. Cole, *Immigrant City: Lawrence, Massachusetts, 1845–1921* (Chapel Hill: University of North Carolina Press, 1963); Rudolph J. Vecoli, "*Contadini* in Chicago: A Critique of *The Uprooted*" *Journal of American History*, 51 (September 1964), 404–17; Gerd Korman, *Industrialization, Immigration, and Americanization: The View from Milwaukee, 1866–1921* (Madison: State Historical Society of Wisconsin, 1967); and David Ward, *Cities and Immigrants: A Geography of Change in Nineteenth-Century America* (New York: Oxford University Press, 1971). The nativist reaction to immigrants is best examined by John Higham, *Strangers in the Land: Patterns of American Nativism, 1860–1925* (New Brunswick, N.J.: Rutgers University Press, 1955); and Ray Allen Billington, *The Protestant Crusade, 1800–1860: A Study of the Origins of American Nativism* (New York: The Macmillan Company, 1938). For works on internal migration, see those listed under geographical mobility in Chapter 3. Important studies of black migration include Gilbert Osofsky, *Harlem: The Making of a Ghetto* (New York: Harper & Row, 1966); Allan H. Spear, *Black Chicago: The Making of a Negro Ghetto, 1890–1920* (Chicago: University of Chicago Press, 1967); John M. Bracey, Jr., August Meier, and Elliot M. Rudwick, eds., *The Rise of the Ghetto* (Belmont, Calif.: Wadsworth Publishing Co., 1971); and Hollis Lynch, ed., *The Black Urban Condition: A Documentary History, 1866–1971* (New York: Crowell, 1973). The rise of ethno-religious identifications is analyzed by Sam Bass Warner, Jr., *The Urban Wilderness: A History of the American City* (New York: Harper & Row, 1973); Nathan Glazer and Daniel Patrick Moynihan, *Beyond the Melting Pot: The Negroes, Puerto Ricans, Jews, Italians, and Irish of New York City* (Cambridge: M.I.T. Press, 2nd ed., 1970); Robert D. Cross, *The Emergence of Liberal Catholicism in America* (Cambridge: Harvard University Press, 1959); Henry F. May, *Protestant Churches and Industrial America* (New York: Harper, 1949); Oscar Handlin, *Adventure in Freedom: Three Hundred Years of Jewish Life in America* (New York: McGraw-Hill, 1954); and Nathan Glazer, *American Judaism* (Chicago: University of Chicago Press, 1957).

For analyses of housing, slums, and public health, see Roy Lubove, *The Progressive and the Slums: Tenement House Reform in New York City, 1890–1917* (Pittsburgh: University of Pittsburgh Press, 1962); Robert Bremner, *From the Depths: The Discovery of Poverty in the United States* (New York: New York University Press, 1956); Jacob Riis, *How the Other Half Lives* (New York: C. Scribner's Sons, 1890); James Cassedy, *Charles V. Chapin and the Public Health Movement* (Cambridge: Harvard University Press, 1962); and Barbara Rosenkrantz, *Public Health and the State: Changing Views in Massachusetts, 1842–1936* (Cambridge: Harvard University Press, 1972). Some valuable work on urban family life has been done by John Modell and Tamara K. Hareven, "Urbanization and the Malleable Household: An Examination of Boarding and Lodging in American Families," *Journal of Marriage and the Family*, 35 (August 1973), 467–79; Virginia Yans McLaughlin, "Patterns of Work and Family Organization: Buffalo's Italians," *Journal of Interdisciplinary History*, 2 (Autumn 1971), 299–314; and Elizabeth H. Pleck, "The Two-Parent Household: Black Family Structure in Late Nineteenth-Century Boston," *Journal of Social History*, 6 (Fall 1972), 1–31. Immigrant residential experiences and social mobility are examined in Sam Bass Warner, Jr., and Colin B. Burke, "Cultural Change and the Ghetto," *Journal of Contemporary History*, 5 (October 1969), 173–87; Howard P. Chudacoff, "A New Look at Ethnic Neighborhoods: Residential Dispersion and the Concept of Visibility in a Medium-Sized City," *Journal of American History*, 60 (June 1973), 76–93; Stephan Thernstrom, *The Other Bostonians: Poverty and Progress in the American Metropolis, 1880–1970* (Cambridge: Harvard University Press, 1973); Richard J. Hopkins, "Occupational and Geographic Mobility in Atlanta, 1870–1896," *Journal of Southern History*, 34 (May 1968), 200–213; and Sidney Goldstein, *Patterns of Mobility, 1910–1950: The Norristown Study* (Philadelphia: University of Pennsylvania Press, 1958).

5
THE RISE OF
BOSS POLITICS

Insiders called it "the organization"; outsiders called it "the machine." Whatever the nomenclature, "it" was a political association that operated outside of, but often controlled, the legally established government. Its specific tasks were to serve the needs and wants of its constituents and to perpetuate its own existence by obtaining, maintaining, and centralizing political power. The effectiveness of the political machine depended upon the genius of its leaders. They built the organization, managed it, and determined its policies: they were the bosses.

From the beginning bosses were maligned. Reformer-journalist William Allen White described Richard Croker of New York as "a dull, emotionless prosimian bulk of bone and sinew—a sort of human megatherium who has come crashing up from the swamps splashed with the slime of pre-Adamite wickedness!" Other bosses were portrayed as crude, ruthless, power-bent and money-hungry barons who surrounded themselves with cronies and sycophants. Often such reputations were deserved. The graft, fraud, and thievery that swirled around bosses, and that they often encouraged, outraged middle-class moralists. Yet the boss system had merits. If it had been as hateful as its detractors believed, it would not have lasted as long as it did. Bosses and machines acquired power because they could manipulate people and situations. They stayed in power because they accomplished things which the people—or at least a large segment of the people—wanted.

125

Elements of bossism existed as early as colonial times, yet it was not until after 1850 that conditions were ripe for the use of boss politics in cities. Largely responsible were the new trends already detailed here: the huge increase in urban populations, accelerating industrialization, commercial expansion, technological change, immigration, and the rise of tenement neighborhoods. The myriad of new households and businesses strained existing services and created an urgent need for more water, gas, and sewer systems, more policemen, firemen, and teachers, more streets, schools, and government buildings. How would these improvements be financed? Modernization had split urban communities into a number of competing interest groups. Who would determine public priorities?

Secondly, many cities suffered from obsolete governmental forms and from political chaos. After 1820 most new city charters copied the federal form of government: two legislative councils elected from districts (wards) and an executive (mayor) elected at-large. Although the scope of the mayor's authority varied from city to city, he generally held powers of veto and of appointment. Usually, however, bicameral urban governments proved inefficient. Mayors were unable to overcome particularistic interests of councilmen, and both branches fought constant battles with state governments over the exercise of power. As the creators of cities, states jealously guarded their powers to determine their cities' needs and to control finances by limiting local taxing and bonding powers. Consequently most cities had to expand their functions in piecemeal fashion by petitioning the statehouse for charter amendments. Also, as new needs called for new officers, a confusing array of boards and commissions piled on top of each other. Some were appointed by the state, some by the mayor, some by the city council, and some were elected by the people. Jersey City's charter was amended ninety-one times in forty years, and at one time thirty separate boards administered public functions in Philadelphia.

Governmental confusion and economic change tended to fragment political leadership. By the middle of the nineteenth century local entrepreneurs—merchants, manufacturers, contractors, and real estate operators—vied for political control in order to steer public policy in directions suited to their own interests. At the same time, other businessmen extended their outlooks beyond local matters. Because their concerns focused on interurban and interregional networks of transportation, finance, and communications, these business elites often withdrew from local affairs. Expansion of the franchise from 1820 onward created a mass of new voters with their own political goals and leadership. These groups, their numbers swelled by immigration, often found themselves at the center of prime social and economic issues: temperance, working conditions, nativism, religious and moral debates, and public education. Independent political parties sprouted around these issues—the Free Soil, Know-Nothing, and numerous workingmen's parties—and confounded leaders of the two major parties. A different kind of leader emerged from the newly enfranchised electorate. He was frequently a self-made man who zealously pursued the cause of his constituents. But also, because of the hostility he encountered, he was often unscrupulous in his quest for power. The old leadership, the mercantile and professional elites of the early nineteenth century, also changed. Some withdrew from politics altogether, while others turned to humanitarian causes such as hospitals, schools, and prison reform.

A third ingredient that contributed to the new political situation was the way in which the American dream and its urban reality affected immigrants, particularly the Irish. Oscar Handlin has asserted that in the Old World, government was very distant from peasants' everyday lives. The State seemed to exist only for the benefit of the rich and powerful. In the minds of most the government was an exploiter; its main functions were to collect their taxes, to force them to labor on public projects, and to conscript them into the army. In Ireland, where peasants had long chafed under the brunt of what they considered to be unjust British rule, people developed a network of illegal activities to vent their discontent. They formed secret societies and used bribery and sabotage to defend themselves against oppressive landlords and politicians.

But in America the immigrants found a different conception of government. In the Land of Liberty, they were told, anyone (any male, that is) could share in the selection of his rulers by becoming a citizen and voting. But naturalization and the franchise did not automatically turn immigrants into the republicans envisioned by the Founding Fathers. Rather, the newcomers added their own flavor to politics. The Irish—the most politically active group—transferred their old institutions to American cities where, as Daniel Boorstin notes, they "organized not against but within the government." They brought well-known attitudes and customs with them: a belief that the existing government was not wholly legitimate, a penchant for tight, hierarchical organization, a readiness to resort to illegal acts or even violence to achieve desired ends, and an intense loyalty to the organization to which they belonged. The Irish discovered that numbers, particularly numbers of votes, created power in a democratic system. Long accustomed to viewing government as external and exploitive, the Irish created their own political organizations that could use numbers to achieve ends beneficial to them.

These elements contributed to the rise of boss politics by creating three needs: The multiplying social and economic sectors of the city required someone to act as a broker between a large number of rival interests and to establish order and communications between people, districts, and institutions. The increasingly complex urban environment needed an agency that would devise policies and make decisions for the entire community. These were the tasks of an established government, but city administrations had become sluggish and disorganized. Immigrants who had filled urban cores needed some agency to attend to their problems of poverty and bewilderment. Political machines and their bosses met these needs because they centralized decision making and directed their activities to those areas that traditional governments had been unable or unwilling to approach.

Until the middle of the nineteenth century politics in this country had never been regarded as a profession. Men who participated in public life usually had successful private careers behind them. They had entered politics motivated by an obligation to serve the community. Prevailing attitudes considered politics a temporary activity. If a man lost an election, he could always fall back on his private vocation. Urban conditions and the growth of machines in the industrial era changed this notion. Cities had become factionalized, producing what Sam Bass Warner, Jr., has called a "specialization of leadership." As Zane Miller has written, "Unable to create broad-based and effective coalitions, politicians accomplished what they could by using patronage, special favors, and bribery to persuade individuals and groups to cooperate on specific projects." Politics became a full-time profession based on service—service to one's relatives and neighbors, to one's business associates, and to oneself. This was what sustained the machine and what distinguished it from a political party.

STRUCTURE AND FUNCTIONS

Critics depicted political machines as monolithic mobs and bosses as despots who dictated every act, every crime. The images were seldom true. Like most other political organizations, machines were coalitions. They only appeared homogeneous because their leaders kept the component parts well-oiled, preventing friction and dissolution. Most big city machines were federations, consisting of smaller machines organized at the levels of wards, precincts, and even blocks. The bosses who became the subjects of muckrakers' exposés were not autocrats who ruled their domains with iron hands. Rather, they were executives, chairmen of boards, and brokers who coordinated whole hierarchies of smaller bosses.

The ward and precinct bosses derived their power directly from the neighborhoods. They were the ones who mustered numbers and utilized votes as a marketable commodity. In order to offer their constituents more, smaller bosses allied into a larger organization under the aegis of a city-wide boss. It was the city boss' job to keep order within this organization, but often unity proved impossible. For example, throughout much of its early history, Chicago changed so rapidly and spawned so many diverse power bases that a single city-wide machine could not be formed until well into the twentieth century. On the other hand, the establishment and growth of Tammany Hall in New York in the early 1800s provided a framework within which lower-class political interests could combine. In most instances an agent who could weld the various local organizations into a more powerful machine could promise unprecedented benefits to all. Such promises gave city bosses their power.

Yet bosses held their positions as leaders of coalitions only by the support and good will of others. Their power was not absolute; it was checked by the lower bosses who operated the gears of the machine. Moreover, the entire system was based on neighborhood support. Corruption and chicanery gave bosses influence and leverage, but they sustained their power only because they provided services that many people wanted and needed. Although machines thrived on the vulnerability and manipulation of the needy and ignorant, bosses could not lead their constituents where they did not want to go. Bosses who forgot these limitations fell.

The specific functions of boss politics flowed in two directions. In return for votes, machines personalized government for immigrants and other constituents. In return for material gratuities, machines granted privileges to segments of the business community. Both sets of functions reinforced traditional American notions of privatism.

Immigrants looked to politics not for the fulfillment of some abstract ideal but for individual and group benefits. Bosses understood this attitude, and they became specialists in personal relations. Bosses often were immigrants or sons of immigrants; they knew the inner city and its needs first hand. They built their constituencies with jobs, largess, and personal services. Bosses controlled jobs through their control of government offices. The urban economy pushed immigrants into unskilled employment, and a large proportion of this employment fell under the auspices of public officials. The decades between 1870 and 1920 witnessed a flurry of public and private construction in the cities. Local officials on public works boards and in inspectors' offices could easily convince contractors and other employers to hire men faithful to the machine. Bosses and their associates could also provide constituents with jobs on the expanding public payroll. Men who received jobs as a result of machine influence were always reminded where their jobs came from. Some were required to express their appreciation by making a contribution to machine coffers. This was especially true for public employees—

policemen, firemen, teachers, clerks, and janitors. All were expected to remember the machine on election day.

However, there were always many more people who wanted favors than there were jobs to be distributed. Consequently bosses maintained their popularity by offering forms of public benevolence. Through their control of city councils, they appropriated funds to make neighborhood improvements such as parks, playgrounds, and bathhouses. They often took neighborhood children on summer picnics and sponsored free days at the amusement park, and they distributed turkeys and other food on Easter, Thanksgiving, and Christmas. Each boss had his own style. James Michael Curley, mayor and boss of Boston in the early twentieth century, wrote of how he would approach an old, bent woman who was plodding down the street by saying, "A woman should have three attributes. She should have beauty, intelligence, and money." As he handed her a silver dollar, he would add, "Now you have all three." Reformers objected to these forms of what they called "mass bribery." Yet no one else was interested in providing welfare to the poor in such a personal way.

Machines also rendered intangible services that aided immigrants in a bewildering world. Bosses installed themselves as buffers between slum dwellers and the law and were increasingly expected to smooth over difficulties and to obtain exemptions from the law. The boss could convince authorities to look the other way when a neighborhood saloon wanted to stay open after hours or on Sundays, or he could prevent police harassment of a gambling house or other vice establishment. Most importantly, the boss intervened when one of his constituents ran afoul of the law. When an immigrant was arrested for intoxication, vagrancy, robbery, or assault, the boss would be the only person who could provide assurance, counsel, and, in many cases, bail. When a youth was brought in for disturbing the peace, the boss could go to the station house, talk to the officers, convince them that the young man came from an upstanding family, and secure his release. This kind of intervention gave slum dwellers a sense of importance, confidence that someone was on their side, a feeling that they were getting a break in an otherwise oppressive system.

Bosses cultivated mass attachment by making their power visible and accessible. They were joiners and boosters, card-carrying members in a host of ethnic and neighborhood associations. They set up their own clubs, often in a corner saloon, where a person could go to get help. Bosses held open house in these informal offices, distributing jobs and food, and calling constituents by their first names. They appeared at wakes and weddings, and they readily offered cash to defray funeral expenses or to start a pair of newlyweds on the right foot. No wonder a boss' achievement, including the appearance of his name in the news-papers, reflected the glory of the neighborhoods. The immigrants accepted the boss as one of their own. He spoke for them. National political issues were unimportant. A boss who became too interested in the tariff, public land policy, or the amount of silver in national currency soon lost his neighborhood following. In the streets and tenements only local and personal issues counted—bathhouses, extra jobs, Mrs. Kelly's boy Tim. Here the success of a politician was measured by two canons: "He gets things done" and "He keeps his word."

Immigrants and the poor formed one special interest group served by political machines; the business community was the other. The urban boom that spread across the country after the Civil War unleashed torrents of construction and commercial activity. Population growth and geographical sprawl forced cities into a frenzy of physical expansion. Huge profits lay waiting in new services and utilities. Politicians could now determine who received those profits. By making these decisions bosses enriched themselves and financed their personal politics while also directing urban growth.

The increased need for municipal services had resulted in an expansion of public agencies to administer them. By securing public offices and the patronage attached to them, machines could distribute political favors to their advantage. They could control the letting of contracts for public works, such as streets, sewers, and buildings. They could influence the granting of streetcar, gas, telephone, and electricity franchises. They could juggle tax assessments for favored property owners. They could select printers, banks, and other firms who would receive city business. These privileges had their price: favored businessmen were expected to pay the machines for their contracts and franchises. Outsiders called the practice bribery. Bosses called it gratitude. Often the politicians padded public contracts, so that it was easy for chosen firms to kick back huge sums to the bosses and their treasuries. Outsiders called this graft. Bosses doctored the ledger books to hide it.

There were two kinds of graft. *Honest graft* or *boodle* was simply investment capitalism—only the kind that maximized profits while eliminating risk. From their positions within government machine politicians had an advantageous view of where lucrative investments in real estate and utility companies could be made. Moreover, they could set policies that would assure the success of such investments. As George Washington Plunkitt, one of Croker's underlings, explained,

Just let me explain by examples. My party's in power in the city, and it's goin' to undertake a lot of public improvements. Well, I'm tipped off, say, that they're going to lay out a new park at a certain place.

I see my opportunity and I take it. I go to that place and I buy up all the land I can in the neighborhood. Then the board of this or that makes its plan public, and there is a rush to get my land, which nobody cared particular for before.

Ain't it perfectly honest to charge a good price and make a profit on my investment and foresight? Of course it is. Well, that's honest graft.

Dishonest or *dirty graft* derived from participation in explicitly criminal operations. It usually consisted of shakedowns and payoff from gambling and vice operations in return for protection from police harassment. This was the most sordid activity of boss politics, but it was difficult to avoid. Bosses were specialists in gaining exemptions from the law, and the line between who was to receive such favors and who would not seldom was drawn. Payoffs from gambling, prostitution, and illegal liquor trade provided the most available revenues for machines. Many bosses operated vice establishments themselves, and many entered politics from backgrounds in illicit activities.

In addition to functioning as service agencies and as dispensaries of political favors, machines provided important avenues of social mobility to immigrants. Politics posed few barriers of discrimination. Any man who commanded enough votes could attain office. Moreover, because machines transformed politics into a profession that reflected the glory of the neighborhoods, membership in the machine elevated an individual and opened opportunities to him—whether he ran for office or not. Every boss needed henchmen to carry out various operations. It was usually easy for an underling to grab a little of the honest or dishonest graft as it floated by. And there was usually room at the top for the energetic, bright young man.

Participation in politics seemed particularly attractive to the second generation of immigrants. As Oscar Handlin has related, the sons of immigrants were a restless generation. A number of them recognized that their lack of skills, of education, and of capital frustrated their desires to move ahead in a supposed land of opportunity. They often felt the lash of discrimination and the chains of poverty. Yet their schoolbooks told them that government existed for the people, and machines offered them the opportunity to serve—and be rewarded for their service. So they entered politics because the machine promised that success of the organization would also mean personal achievement. The magnetic force was the prestige that the machine could bestow, not only to the individual but to his family and to his neighborhood. Prestige, service, loyalty, accomplishment—these were what the machine offered to inner-city residents, and these were what enabled the boss system to withstand heated attacks for so many years.

The essence of boss politics is best described by example. Each boss and each organization had unique features and personalities. Functions remained relatively constant, however. Sometimes the boss exerted power from an elected office. More frequently, he pulled strings from backstage, attaching public officials to him by bonds of loyalty and patronage. Bosses could operate within the Republican party as well as in the Democratic, although most machines developed as Democratic because of that party's attraction for workingmen and immigrants. Yet Democratic bosses felt no discomfort working out contracts and deals with Republican businessmen. All bosses pursued power and advantage, but some showed genuine concern for their constituents, while others devoted more attention to dishonest graft and self-serving. Still all bosses used politics as a vehicle for personalized service, and they dispensed political favors on a cash and carry basis.

Modern urban bossism was reared in New York's Tammany Hall. The Society of St. Tammany evolved from an Anti-Federalist social club in the 1790s into a political organization that courted the expanded working-class vote by supporting popular issues of the 1830s. During the depression that followed the Panic of 1837 the Tammany Club distributed food, fuel, and clothing to the city's poor. It continued its relief services into the 1840s, paying particular heed to the increasing numbers of Irish immigrants. By this time Tammany had become a powerful wing of the Democratic Party in New York, and it used its charitable activities to win votes for its candidates. As the club acquired power, it exercised increasing control over local patronage. Party leaders consulted Tammany in the choice of candidates, and elected officials followed Tammany dictates in the distribution of government jobs, rewarding loyal Tammany members who worked for the cause of the club and of the party.

William Marcy Tweed was the first man to centralize control of the Democratic Party under Tammany Hall. His achievement enabled him and his organization to run the entire city of New York and to milk its treasury of some $200 million—in about six or seven years. Unlike later bosses Tweed did not emerge from a background of poverty. His father was a middle-class craftsman and former treasurer of the Tammany Society. Tweed became leader of a neighborhood gang, later of a volunteer fire company. His strength and popularity caught the attention of Tammany leaders, and Tweed was elected to the City Council at twenty-eight and to the U.S. House of Representatives at thirty. The debates of Congress bored Tweed, and he did not seek reelection. Instead, he returned to New York and resumed his rise within the Tammany machine.

By the late 1860s Tweed had combined cunning and luck to win control of the entire city administration and part of the state legislature. He maneuvered his way into the chairmanship of Tammany and consolidated his power by boosting associates into public office through election or appointment. Once in command this crew became known as the Tweed Ring. The top echelon consisted of Tweed and four men. George Barnard, a graduate of gambling houses and minstrel troops, became City Recorder and was elevated to the State Supreme Court. Richard B. "Slippery Dick" Connolly, an Irish immigrant, was City Comptroller. Peter "Brains" Sweeney was City Chamberlain and had the task of depositing city funds in selected banks. Abraham Oakey Hall, actor, poet, and dandy was District Attorney and later Mayor of New York.

Tweed and his men worked daily to maintain their positions, but the machine was in full flower at election time. To insure victory it perfected three kinds of voting fraud. First, repeaters, supplied with names that had already been falsely registered, were hustled around to several polling places to cast their ballots. Second, Tammany-appointed election officials bought off Republican counterparts and manipulated vote tallies (following the proverb coined later in the century that "a vote on the tally sheet is worth two in the box"). Third, the machine made special efforts to naturalize immigrants so they could vote. It established neighborhood naturalization committees, paid fees, expedited paper work, and provided witnesses—for prospective citizens who pledged to vote for the Democratic Party and Tammany candidates. Judge Barnard was usually listless on the bench, but he became a frenzied worker the month before an election. In October, 1868, he naturalized an average of 718 future Democrats a day. It was estimated that one-sixth of the votes cast in New York City that year were fraudulent.

With his henchmen entrenched in office Tweed was ready to start his notorious assault on the public treasury. In 1870 he used his influence over the General Assembly to obtain a new charter for New York City. Among other things, the charter gave the mayor greater powers of appointment and created a Board of Audit that would handle all bills paid by the city and county. The charter cost Tweed $600,000 in bribes, but it was worth it. With the mayor's office and Board of Audit in the hands of Tweed men, contracts could be padded and kickbacks demanded. One of the richest bonanzas was the construction of a new county courthouse. By the time the Tweed Ring had finished inflating appropriations, the building had cost a total of $12,500,000, including $7,500 for thermometers, $190 apiece for cuspidors, $404,347 for safes, $41,190 for brooms and other "articles," and $2 million for plastering. In contrast, a similar courthouse was built in Brooklyn at the same time for $800,000. In 1871 at age forty-seven, Bill Tweed, bald and weighing over 300 pounds, reputedly was worth $12 million. He had a Fifth Avenue Mansion, a Connecticut estate, a steam yacht, a well-stocked stable, and a blond mistress. But he always had enough money for others. In 1870 he spent $50,000 on the poor of the Seventh Ward. He reportedly raised a million and a half dollars for the Catholic Church. And his wallet was always open to Tammany candidates in need of campaign funds. Tweed clearly recognized that in industrial America power and money were inseparable. He did not set the standards of his day. He merely embellished those established by the rising business powers. As one writer has remarked, "Property and cash were the gods of America, to be stolen and spent, multiplied and glorified." Both politicians and businessmen participated in the ritual.

Tweed's career climaxed early in 1871 when an investigating committee found him innocent of misusing city funds in the 1870 elections. Then on July 18, the *New York Times,* acting on information divulged by a disaffected sheriff, Jimmy "The Famous" O'Brien, printed "reliable and incontrovertible evidence of numerous, gigantic frauds on the part of the rulers of the city." The exposés of boodling, bribery, and embezzlement continued for over a month. A committee of seventy community leaders, headed by Samuel J. Tilden, investigated and publicized the extent of wrongdoing. As a result Judge Barnard was impeached, Mayor Hall was indicted, and several other Tammany lieutenants fled to Paris. After a frenzied attempt to cover his tracks, Tweed was arrested. He eventually was convicted on 104 counts of fraud and bribery and sentenced to twelve years in prison.

Tweed's jailers allowed him to make periodic visits to his family while he served his term. While eating dinner at his son's home one evening, Tweed excused himself and went upstairs. No one saw him again until several days later when he was picked up in Spain and shipped back to New York. Back in jail, Tweed offered to make a full confession in return for freedom to return to his family. Samuel Tilden, now governor, refused the request, but Tilden's successor, Lucius Robinson, agreed. Tweed confessed, but Robinson reneged, saying Tweed would be released only when he had paid back the state $6 million. Tweed refused, and instead donated huge sums to charity. He died of pneumonia in prison in 1878.

The Tweed Ring left confusion and debt in its wake. Between 1867 and 1871 New York City's debt soared from $300 to $900 million, and its account books were left in chaos. Yet all the sordid stories tell only a part of Tweed's impact on the city. Whatever his motives, Tweed saw that important things were accomplished. New York City was growing too fast for existing institutions to meet its needs. Tweed's regime bypassed traditional forms of administration. In doing so it extended streets, granted franchises to transit and utilities companies, developed Central Park, and generally oversaw the physical expansion of the city. It also secured revision of the city's antiquated government with charter reforms that, at least in theory, increased local efficiency. Amidst all this improvement the boss and his henchmen lined their pockets at public expense. Yet Tweed's accomplishments outdistanced those of all leaders who had preceded him in New York. He succeeded by coordinating physical growth with an organized, though expensive, political plan. He used numbers and votes, however fraudulently, to build his power, and he played the role of broker between business and government with optimal skill. Most importantly, to the poverty-stricken worker who received a free meal and a couple of dollars on election day or whose family received a basket of food at Christmas, Tweed was a hero, someone who cared.

The demise of William Marcy Tweed did not signal the end of Tammany Hall. "Honest" John Kelly succeeded him as head of the machine, and after a brief hiatus Tammany candidates moved back into positions of power. In some ways Tammany Hall and similar machines elsewhere changed after 1880. Their graft and corruption became less flagrant, and they used the expanding municipal bureaucracy and the ever-pressing need for services to cement their influence—or clout, as it came to be called. But machines still based their existence on numbers, jobs, and favors.

Richard Croker was typical of the late-nineteenth century boss. Born in Ireland in 1843 he sailed to the United States with his parents at the age of three. He grew up in the slums of Lower Manhattan, dropped out of school when he was thirteen, and joined the Fourth Avenue Tunnel Gang. Here he learned the lessons that prepared him for his political career: discipline through loyalty, reputation through results, and leadership through strength. Using his forceful personality and uncanny pugilistic skill, Croker became the gang's leader and was recruited into Tammany Hall in the 1860s. Starting as an attendant to Judge Barnard, Croker worked his way up through the machine until he became Tammany's—and the city's—boss in the late 1880s.

Croker was a very able politician. He could win a point with affable charm or with vicious attack; he also knew when to compromise. His candor often won the respect of his enemies. Reformer Lincoln Steffens wrote, "Richard Croker never said anything to me that was not true, unless it was a statement for publication." The reverence that the city's populace paid him was enormous. When he took his annual European vacation, thousands saw him off. When he attended the opera annually on Jefferson's birthday, the orchestra played "Hail to the Chief" while he took his seat.

Unlike Tweed, Croker did not steal outright from the public treasury. Rather, he perfected the use of honest graft. By using his control over city purchases and contracts, Croker could convince favored business-men to grant stock in their companies to the boss and his associates or to offer tips on promising investments. Croker distributed his profits around the organization but also kept some for himself. By the early 1890s he owned a farm stocked with thoroughbred horses, a private pullman car, and seven homes—even though he had no visible means of support after retiring from the public payroll in 1890. At first most of Croker's sup-porters took pride in this affluence: Dick Croker was one of them, a man who rose from the slums, a man who kept his word and got things done. Why shouldn't he reap the rewards of advantage? As Alfred Connable and Edward Silberfarb have written, "Rewarded by city jobs, peddling licenses, free lawyers, and sumptuous Tammany picnics, most immi-grants were bored by abstract reform talk about privileged corpora-tions paying off the city, charging high rates for inadequate service, and providing cheap workmanship that endangered public safety."

Honest graft could not sustain the whole machine, however. Croker welded his underlings to him by permitting them to participate in dirty graft. He generally overlooked the activities of his 90,000 precinct work-ers—many of them policemen, firemen, and other civil servants—as long as they carried their districts for Tammany candidates on election day.

Croker had many friends but also some enemies. In 1894 these op-ponents managed to dent Tammany's power for the first time since Tweed's demise. At the instigation of Thomas Platt, U.S. Senator and chairman of the Republican State Committee, a committee under the chairmanship of State Senator Clarence Lexow began an investigation of police corruption in New York City. The Lexow Committee's hearings—6,000 pages of testimony—detailed an extraordinary degree of police graft and accomplished just what Platt desired—disenchantment with the machine. But Croker stayed one step ahead. He sensed the public mood and resigned as Tammany's chairman so as not to be linked to an elec-toral defeat. In the mayoral election of 1894, the reformers' candidate, Republican merchant William Strong, won by 45,000 votes. After the election Croker sailed to England for a three-year vacation.

Mayor Strong and his new police commissioner Theodore Roosevelt managed a few reforms, but their strict enforcement of the law made many people long for the looser Tammany days. In September, 1897, with the Lexow revelations buried, Richard Croker returned to New York and reestablished his control over Tammany. He was just in time. The State Legislature had given the city a new charter that on January 1,

1898 would consolidate Brooklyn, Queens, Staten Island, and the Bronx with Manhattan. The winner of the 1897 mayoral election would administer a Greater New York City of over three million people. The reformers entered Seth Low, president of Columbia University and former mayor of Brooklyn as their candidate. Croker and the Democrats selected a political unknown, Judge Robert Van Wyck, and frankly aimed their campaign at the tenement districts where reform crackdowns had been heaviest.—Their slogan was "To Hell with Reform!"—The strategy worked. The close election was decided by a Democratic landslide in the inner wards. Croker and Tammany again ruled the city.

Croker's triumphant return damaged his political savvy, for he began to make mistakes, something successful bosses could not afford. First, he divorced his wife and moved into the Democratic Club on Fifth Avenue, where he kept a court, forcing lieutenants to visit him in their best dress and to remain standing at dinner until the boss was seated. Then Croker tried unsuccessfully to lead his machine into state and national politics. He pressured his organization to work for a Tammany candidate running against Teddy Roosevelt for governor in 1898, and he backed William Jennings Bryan for president in 1900. In both instances Croker's ignorance of larger issues and his antagonistic speeches hurt him and his candidates. Third, reformers revived public disaffection with the machine in New York City. An investigation led by Assemblyman Robert Mazet exposed Croker's connections with a firm that furnished most of the city's ice and was planning to double its prices to consumers. Croker's participation in the scheme was still honest graft, but it was the kind that directly drained the pockets of ordinary working-class families. Moreover exposés revealed that dirty graft had again spread throughout the city. These occurrences loosened Croker's grip on his machine. When Seth Low defeated the Tammany candidate for mayor in 1901, Croker again sailed for England.

Croker had presided over some thirty-five district leaders. The career of one of these smaller bosses, Timothy D. Sullivan, illustrates how the city boss was a broker and how his power could be checked. "Big Tim" Sullivan was a second generation immigrant, born in the Bowery and raised by his widowed Irish mother. Like Tweed and Croker he left school at an early age and became the leader of a gang. His leadership and brawn gave him ready entry into Tammany Hall. He became a political prodigy and was elected to the State Legislature in 1886 when he was twenty-three years old. He later served a term in the U.S. House of Representatives, but like Tweed he could not stomach life in Washington and returned to New York after two years.

Back in New York, Sullivan secured control over the Lower East Side and Bowery districts by soliciting support from the Jewish immigrants who were replacing some of the Irish residents. He used his political leverage with Tammany to place his supporters on public payrolls and to open a string of profitable gambling halls. He also cultivated his personal appeal with consummate skill. He arranged bails, sent food and medicine to the sick and feeble, gave shoes to needy school children, and sponsored annual summer picnics. His Timothy D. Sullivan Association was a poor man's social club that operated out of neighborhood saloons. The Sullivan clubhouses became distributing centers for those who needed jobs, food, and other services, as well as for political machination. Sullivan built his machine on trust and loyalty—he was a man who kept his word. It was said that he was so well-liked that his portrait hung in nearly every building in his district.

Like other district bosses Sullivan generally stood behind Boss Croker. But Big Tim had such a loyal following that he could assert his independence if he so desired. On one occasion Sullivan threatened to withhold the huge payments that his gambling and prostitution ring made to Tammany Hall unless Croker would restore an ousted police chief to power. Later Sullivan touted his own aldermanic candidate over an incumbent who was a loyal Croker ally. When Sullivan's candidate won, the district boss reputedly boasted, "Croker ain't the whole thing." Yet after Croker's fall Sullivan shirked the opportunity to become city boss, preferring to influence the policies of City Hall from his own district and to look after his multimillion dollar vice operations. He kept his independence until 1912 when he became ill and was committed to an insane asylum. He shortly escaped but was apparently struck by a freight train and was found dead in a railroad yard. His funeral attracted over twenty-five thousand mourners.

New York City provides the most colorful showcase for the examination of machine politics, but bossism flourished in many other cities as well. Moreover, machines were not peculiar to the Democratic Party. Philadelphia had "King" James McManes, a Republican who controlled the city's fiscal policies and electoral politics from the late 1860s until 1881. McManes achieved and exercised his power by becoming the leading figure on a municipal board that superintended the city's gas utility. Using his authority over the distribution of jobs and letting of contracts, McManes spread his influence to other city departments. He required city employees to kick back a portion of their salaries to his organization, and he manipulated elections for his own benefit. Like other bosses, McManes took care of himself. During his reign he reputedly earned two and a half million dollars, mostly from payoffs from favored contractors. Also like other bosses McManes alarmed opponents by his lavish expenditure of public funds. Between 1860 and 1880 Philadelphia's municipal debt swelled by 350 percent. Although much of the money facilitated the

physical expansion of the city, a number of Republican businessmen became outraged. They formed a Committee of One Hundred and fused
with local Democrats to defeat machine candidates in the 1881 elections.
McManes retired to enjoy his private fortune, but bossism returned to
Philadelphia later in the decade.

Chicago had its own brand of machine politics. Practically every ward
boss was an independent entrepreneur, each courting his constituency in
his own style. Johnny Powers of the Nineteenth Ward was known as
"The Chief Mourner" because of his attendance record at funerals.
Michael "Hinky Dink" Kenna of the First Ward served free lunches in
his saloon. His partner, "Bathhouse John" Coughlin, received his nick-
name for the kind of services he sponsored. "King" Michael McDonald
offered open gambling houses. "Blond Boss" William Lorimer worked
to remove prejudices against Jews and other immigrants on Chicago's
West Side. Although all but Lorimer were Democrats, no individual was
able to fuse these men into one city-wide machine. Carter Harrison and
his son Carter II held the mayoralty off and on through three and a half
decades and cultivated faithful support among immigrants by champion-
ing "personal liberty"—meaning toleration of drinking and gambling. But
neither Harrison could overcome the independence of the ward bosses.

Still, machine politics in Chicago contained familiar features. Political

Two Chicago Ward Bosses
Michael "Hinky Dink" Kenna and "Bathhouse John" Coughlin were bosses of
Chicago's First Ward, the notorious "levee" district. *Courtesy Chicago Historical
Society.*

power was derived from numbers and favors. City employees paid part of their salaries to the boss who got them their jobs. Boodling and graft were common. Powers maintained a mutually profitable relationship with streetcar companies, particularly with traction magnate Charles Tyson Yerkes. Roger Sullivan, one of the most powerful bosses of early twentieth-century Chicago, specialized in granting favors to—and receiving gratuities from—banks and gas companies. The lack of a strong city boss, however, produced two extremes of instability. On one hand, it was somewhat easier for reformers to gain a foothold in Chicago politics because they did not have to battle a single, entrenched machine. Yet on the other hand, because there were so many bosses, so many enemies, reformers found it difficult to mount a unified attack against every boss, and their footholds quickly eroded.

It is important to note that bossism was not confined to the very large cities. Small cities also needed leaders who could coordinate political power, mediate between immigrants and their new environment, and organize physical expansion. In Omaha, Nebraska, Tom Dennison built an inner city Democratic machine that influenced local politics for nearly three decades after the turn of the century. Dennison used politics to protect a special interest, his multimillion dollar vice business. By appealing to immigrant voters of the inner wards (Dennison's saloons would often be the only places where immigrant workers could cash their paychecks) Dennison could place his lieutenants in high offices and through them act as a broker between the city government and the business community. As in other cities the boss accumulated boodle from firms receiving city business and contracts. Dennison remained in power from the early 1900s to the late 1920s (with only a brief hiatus between 1918 and 1921), and retired to California a wealthy man.

Practically every major city experienced a period of boss rule some time after 1880. In Pittsburgh Christopher Magee supervised a Republican machine that lasted for half a century. In San Francisco Abe Ruef, whose Jewish ancestry and college training distinguished him from other city bosses, operated from within the Union Labor Party to acquire complete control of the city in the early twentieth century. Martin Behrman of New Orleans directed most local affairs between 1900 and 1920 from his posts as mayor and as leader of the Democratic Choctaw Club. The Pendergast brothers, Jim and Tom, spread their influence from Kansas City's river wards to the entire city. The reigns of Jim and, later, Tom lasted from the late 1880s to the late 1930s. Edward H. Crump rose to power in Memphis around 1910 and was not ousted until the 1940s. In Jersey City Frank Hague ruled from 1917 to 1947 under the slogan, "I am the law." The list could continue indefinitely. Like all the others these men were coordinators, not dictators. They presided over federations, not over autocracies. They directed their attention to a full range of services—from Thanksgiving turkeys to business franchises to gambling dens.

AN APPRAISAL

Around 1900 George Washington Plunkitt, one of the district bosses under Richard Croker, remarked, ". . . when a man enters politics he should get something out of it." Some twenty-five years later, Jimmy Walker, mayor of New York, reputedly said, "There comes a time in politics when a man must rise above principle." To those outside the machine these statements expressed the ends and the means of boss politics. The goals were power and individual gain. The methods were fraud, deception, extortion—any legal or illegal tactic to secure and perpetuate power. To their opponents bosses seemed to have no higher purposes, no ideologies.

No doubt the vote frauds, the support of vice and crime, the graft, and the unsavory alliances with privileged businesses offended values of thrift, fair play, and fidelity to the law. Yet an assessment of boss politics must extend beyond issues of morality and fair play. Men like Croker and Tim Sullivan would not have lasted as long as they did if they had not served real needs of large segments of the urban population. Machines were less immoral than amoral, less illegal than extralegal. They were not reactionary but pragmatic, not one-dimensional but flexible. Moreover, bosses did express higher goals, if not in their words than in their deeds. Bosses were *both* villains and heroes—and something more.

The larger purposes of machines can be divided into the politics of order and the politics of reconciliation. Bosses and their organizations tried, and often succeeded, to bring order to decentralized urban administration by superimposing a personalized, hierarchical structure on loosely constructed city governments. As Daniel Patrick Moynihan has noted, the way in which machines maintained their power often appeared tyrannical, but the ruling principle was not despotism but order. It is easy to find complexities in any society in any era. But most historians agree that the last half of the nineteenth century was a particularly dynamic and confusing period in American history. Bosses eased the political and economic strains in cities by rebuilding communications. Bosses thrived on alliances, and they fully recognized that businessmen and politicians together could manipulate government for their mutual benefit. Thus machines served the interests of legitimate and illegitimate businesses whose activities needed order in a complicated, competitive world. The services were costly to the public. But they also built streets and streetcar systems, sewers and gas lines, parks and schools.

Perhaps more importantly, machines reconciled urban newcomers to their environment. Boss politics provided a means for immigrants to secure their best interests and opened a path upward when lack of education or vocational skills closed other avenues of social mobility. The jobs, handouts, and personal relationships humanized politics for deprived classes. The system depended on an ethic of loyalty, cultivated in the blocks and neighborhoods. More than the industrial machine, the political machine required constant attention. As George Washington Plunkitt preached, "[The boss] plays politics every day and night in the year, and his headquarters bears the inscription, 'Never Closed.'" Bosses knew what happened in the streets and alleys, in the tenements, and in the taverns as well as what happened in government and business offices. They knew the needs of slum dwellers, and they tried to fill these needs when few others seemed to care. Charities and government agencies also tried to help, but they were obsessed with determining the worthiness of welfare recipients. Bosses asked no questions.

Martin Lomasney, boss of Boston's South End, once told Lincoln Steffens, "There's got to be in every ward somebody that any bloke can come to—no matter what he's done—and get help. Help, you understand, none of your law and justice, but help." Here was the ideology of boss politics: positive government, the belief that government existed to help people. Bosses transformed politics into a full-time, professionalized service. As a result the people served by bosses came to expect all governments to attend to the personal problems of everyday life:—jobs, food, relief, and social services. Before the advent of social security, unemployment insurance, medicare, food stamps, or Aid to Families with Dependent Children, bosses and machines made meaningful attempts to distribute relief and welfare. Many people, even in the worst slums, never used these services, but they knew they could receive help if they needed it.

Bosses almost always operated under a barrage of criticism. Yet their ability to remain in power, often long after their enemies had faded, stemmed not only from their services, but from their flexibility and pragmatism. They adjusted to change as often as they fought it. Because their services were directed at newcomers, machines seldom were depleted by residential mobility. Those who moved out of a boss' realm but remained in the city might remember the machine and vote for its candidates for city offices. But those who moved into the boss's wards needed the machine's help and were also ready recruits for the organization. Moreover as neighborhoods changed, bosses often changed with them. When Jews began to replace the Irish as the predominant group on New York's Lower East Side early in Tim Sullivan's political career, the boss learned Yiddish and modified his appeal in order to win votes in changing neighborhoods.

Bosses adjusted in other ways as well. When a measure to install a city commission government threatened to subvert Tom Dennison's control of Omaha in 1912, the boss did not fight public sentiment. He merely entered his own slate of candidates for the commission who then dominated the body for the machine's benefit. Boss Crump solidified his grip on Memphis in the same way when a new city charter established a commission form of government in 1909. Bosses could also show forgiveness to those who tried to unseat them. After a reform crusade failed to remove Johnny Powers from the Chicago City Council in 1896, Powers offered jobs to almost every prominent member of the losing camp. Acts like this and utterances like Mayor Walker's disdain of principle reflected a cynicism that only hardened the opposition against boss politics. Yet on the other side of such cynicism was a kind of self-satire, a refusal to take everything and everybody too seriously. Such whimsey gave bossism its color and appeal.

Bosses did not uniformly oppose all reforms. Rather they were selectively pragmatic. Certain reforms were clearly inimical to machine operations. Civil service, for example, threatened the patronage foundations of machines by requiring prospective jobholders to take examinations that could reveal their incapacities. Bosses also tended to avoid reform in the area of public education, preferring instead to support the more immigrant-populated parochial schools. Temperance and vice laws were strongly opposed. Yet bosses could coexist with reformers on other issues. Bosses occasionally acquiesced to changes in the structure of city governments because they could appropriate new forms for their own advantage; and they supported the Seventeenth Amendment, which provided for the direct election of U.S. senators, because the amendment would end the monopoly that rural-dominated state legislatures had exercised over the selection of senators. In Cincinnati, George B. Cox, a Republican boss who held power from 1885 to 1911, began his career by forming an alliance between neighborhoods just outside the slums and reform Republican districts of the periphery. Although Cox later lost his suburban backing, he acepted the advice of his reform allies for many years and supported causes such as the secret ballot, housing reform, Sunday closing laws, and voter registration. Charles Francis Murphy, Croker's successor as chief of Tammany, was another boss who gave his blessing to some reform. He supported the Seventeenth Amendment, suffrage for women, public ownership of utilities, and laws to improve working conditions for laborers. Even Big Tim Sullivan once dashed to the State House in Albany to cast a decisive vote in favor of a bill limiting working hours for women to fifty-four a week. (He said he did it because, "I had seen me sister go out to work when she was only fourteen and I know we ought to help these gals by giving 'em a law which will prevent 'em from being broken down while they're still young.") As J. Joseph Huthmacher and John D. Buenker have demonstrated, men like Cox, Murphy, and Sullivan understood their constituents' needs and desires for welfare and labor reform. The bosses' support for such laws helped fashion what became known as "urban liberalism."

Although many of the features of boss politics remain today—especially in cities which still elect city councilmen on partisan and ward bases—, the institution has changed considerably over the past half century. In many places reformers succeeded in destroying ward bosses by instituting city-wide, or at-large, elections of local officials that undermined the influence of precinct and neighborhood organizations. Moreover, city governments, federal agencies, and labor unions have taken over most of the machine's welfare and social services. Yet in many places the boss still retains one of his primary functions—that of broker, of providing a bridge between various sectors of the complex urban society. He remains an important figure in the distribution of the jobs and favors and relief that other agencies now create.

In the years between 1860 and 1920 political machines accomplished many things for American cities at great social and economic costs. Just how these benefits and costs can be weighed against each other will long remain a topic of debate. On one side stands the enormous expansion of urban facilities that bosses initiated and supervised. On the other side stand the cheating, frauds, and twisted laws. Machines gave millions of ordinary urban dwellers confidence that someone in the power structure cared about them. Bosses were not the only leaders who tried to cement group loyalty with personal beneficence: a few industrialists like John Henry Patterson of the National Cash Register Company in Dayton, Ohio and H. J. Heinz, the food producer, sponsored company picnics, concerts, and some kind of welfare. But bosses had to direct themselves to a broader, more heterogeneous constituency. It has been suggested that because bosses acted as buffers between different economic interests and between different social groups they may well have eased the pressures that could have arisen from ethnic and class conflict and thus prevented socialism and other forms of revolutionary change from occurring. On the other hand, however, machines were not all-tolerant. They could be exclusive, often favoring some groups at the expense of others. Irish-dominated machines in New York, Chicago, New Orleans, New Haven, and Detroit ignored Italians and Poles for many years and only grudgingly surrendered a few jobs and offices to such newer immigrant groups. Blacks seldom were wooed by bosses. (The major exception occurred in Chicago where Mayor William Hale Thompson, a Republican, built a solid following in the black ghettos between 1915–1923 and 1927–1931). These "outsiders," plus those insiders who dared to resist the boss's wishes, were the truly disadvantaged, for they were excluded from whatever helpful services machines could render. Yet numbers counted, and any large groups that sought entry to the business of politics usually received it.

Bosses cannot be judged by their sordid activities alone. They arose in an age when "respectable" industrialists and merchants trampled opponents and manipulated the public—all in their quest for dollars and power. Nor should bosses be revered for preserving social and political order. America's political institutions remained viable in spite of, as well as because of, machines and bosses. More fundamentally, bosses can be characterized as catalytic agents. Their attempts to meet real needs—attempts that were sometimes humane and sometimes criminal—dramatized the problems of modern urban society and provoked wide-ranging thought about how cities and their needs should be managed in the future. Such thought bred the urban reformer.

BIBLIOGRAPHY

Although scholars have not yet attempted comprehensive studies of all aspects of boss politics, a number of articles and monographs have provided valuable insight into bosses and their machines. For general interpretations, see Richard C. Wade, "Urbanization," in C. Vann Woodward, ed., *The Comparative Approach to American History* (New York: Basic Books, Inc., 1968); Robert K. Merton, "Latent Functions of the Machine," in Merton, *Social Theory and Social Structure* (New York: The Free Press, rev. ed., 1949), pp. 71–82; Elmer E. Cornwell, Jr., "Bosses, Machines, and Ethnic Groups," in Lee S. Greene, ed., *City Bosses and Political Machines*, Vol. 353, *The Annals of the American Academy of Political and Social Science* (Philadelphia: American Academy of Political and Social Science, 1964), 28–34; and Eric McKitrick, "The Study of Corruption," *Political Science Quarterly*, 72 (December 1957), 502–14. See also the sections on bossism in Zane L. Miller, *The Urbanization of Modern America: A Brief History* (New York: Harcourt Brace Jovanovich, Inc., 1973), and Daniel J. Boorstin, *The Americans: The Democratic Experience* (New York: Random House, Inc., 1973). Anthologies and group studies include Blaine A. Brownell and Warren E. Stickle, eds., *Bosses and Reformers: Urban Politics in America, 1880–1920* (Boston: Houghton Mifflin, 1973); Bruce M. Stave, ed., *Urban Bosses, Machines, and Progressive Reformers* (Lexington, Mass.: Heath, 1972); and Harold Zink, *City Bosses in the United States: A Study of Twenty Municipal Bosses* (Durham, N.C.: Duke University Press, 1930).

Among individual machines Tammany Hall has received the most attention from historians, most notably, Jerome Mushkat, *Tammany: The Evolution of a Political Machine, 1789–1865* (Syracuse: Syracuse University Press, 1971);

Seymour Mandelbaum, *Boss Tweed's New York* (New York: Wiley, 1965); and Alexander B. Callow, Jr., *The Tweed Ring* (New York: Oxford University Press, 1966). Alfred Connable and Edward Silberfarb, *Tigers of Tammany: Nine Men Who Ran New York* (New York: Holt, Rinehart, and Winston, 1967) is a lively, popular account. William L. Riordon, *Plunkitt of Tammany Hall* (New York: Dutton, 1963) is a delightful memoir of a boss and includes a perceptive introduction by Arthur Mann. Also useful is Theodore F. Lowi, *At the Pleasure of the Mayor: Patronage and Power in New York City, 1898–1958* (New York: The Free Press, 1964). For works on Chicago, see Joel A. Tarr, *A Study in Boss Politics: William Lorimer of Chicago* (Urbana: Unviversity of Illinois Press, 1971); Harold F. Gosnell, *Machine Politics: The Chicago Model* (Chicago: University of Chicago Press, 1937); Allen F. Davis, "Jane Addams *vs.* the Ward Boss," *Journal of the Illinois State Historical Society,* 53 (Autumn 1960), 247–65; and Lloyd Wendt and Herman Kogan, *Lords of the Levee: The Story of Bathouse John and Hinky Dink* (Indianapolis: Bobbs-Merrill, 1943). Mike Royko, *Boss: Richard J. Daley of Chicago* (New York: Dutton, 1971) is a popular account of a well-known modern boss.

Other important studies include Zane L. Miller, *Boss Cox's Cincinnati: Urban Politics in the Progressive Era* (New York: Oxford University Press, 1968); Lyle W. Dorset, *The Pendergast Machine* (New York: Oxford University Press, 1968); Joy J. Jackson, *New Orleans in the Gilded Age: Politics and Urban Progress, 1860–1896* (Baton Rouge: Louisiana State University Press, 1969); William D. Miller, *Mr. Crump of Memphis* (Baton Rouge: Louisiana State University Press, 1964); and William D. Miller, *Memphis During the Progressive Era, 1900–1917* (Memphis: Memphis State University Press, 1957). For a provocative analysis of what happened to bosses and machines during and after the 1930s, see Bruce M. Stave, *The New Deal and the Last Hurrah: Pittsburgh Machine Politics* (Pittsburgh: University of Pittsburgh Press, 1970). A valuable and revisionist interpretation of boss' relationships with reform can be found in John D. Buenker, *Urban Liberalism and Progressive Reform* (New York: Charles Scribner's Sons, 1973).

6

THE DISPOSITIONS OF URBAN REFORM

HONESTY AND EFFICIENCY IN GOVERNMENT

American urbanization between 1870 and 1920 brought startling social and material changes. Migration, immigration, industrialization, and technological innovation converged to infuse cities with excitement and opportunity. The new conditions, however, aggravated old problems of poverty, crowding, and social tension. The dysfunctions of industrial urban society alarmed many of the middle-class whites now inhabiting the periphery. Josiah Strong, a Congregationalist minister from Cincinnati, Ohio, expressed a common feeling when he wrote in 1885, "The city is the nerve center of our civilization. It is also the storm center. . . . (It) has become a serious threat to our civilization." Such concern prompted reforming efforts to improve social, political, and economic conditions. These movements were not confined to a singular issue or cause or to the more affluent classes; they included important support from working classes, many of them immigrants, who helped fashion reform into an ideology of urban liberalism.

Boss politics, with its legions of foreign-born supporters and its proclivity toward extralegal activities, posed a threat to the established classes who inhabited the urban outskirts. Largely native-born and Protestant, these people viewed what was happening in inner-city districts with rising apprehension. They feared that immigrant-dominated political machines were subverting social and political order and that illicit collusions between government and big businesses were undermining fiscal stability. Some residents of the periphery were the very businessmen who were benefiting from associations with local politicians; but most abhored the illegality and special privilege that had infected city government, and they equated bad politics with bad business. The remedy that business-oriented groups offered was civic reform, changes in the governmental structure to ensure honest and efficient administration. Civic reform was one of the strongest branches of the crusade for better urban conditions. It was also one of the most paternalistic and naive.

Mr. Dooley, the fictional Irish saloonkeeper created by Chicago newspaper columnist Finley Peter Dunne, observed in 1902, "A man that'd expict to thrain lobsters to fly in a year is called a loonytic; but a man that thinks men can be tur-rned into angels by an iliction is called a rayformer. . . ." There was a painful degree of truth to this satirical definition. Incensed by local corruption in the years after the Civil War, business leaders organized to root out bosses and to replace them with the "best men" to handle the affairs of expanding cities. The Committee of Seventy, which ousted the Tweed Ring from New York in 1871, and the Committee of One Hundred, which exposed the McManes machine of Philadelphia in 1881, consisted of well-known merchants, lawyers, and journalists who believed they were acting in the civic interest and in the name of morality. They blamed bosses and machines for polluting the American system, and they wanted to cleanse politics by restricting the voting franchise with property qualifications and literacy tests. Men like E. L. Godkin, editor of *The Nation*, Samuel Bowles, III, editor of the *Springfield Republican*, and Moorfield Storey, a Boston lawyer and publicist, distasted politics; but they became active reformers in the early 1870s because they believed that only men like themselves, wealthy and refined, should have the responsibility for maintaining democracy.

Yet the roots of reform went much deeper than antagonism to political corruption; they paralleled larger changes within the whole of American society. The expanding scope of economic activities had necessitated policies that would reduce waste and inefficiency. The establishment of such policies is called *rationalization*—the process that applies centralized, bureaucratic control to financial, commercial, and industrial organization. One of the most influential preachers of rationalization in the late nineteenth and early twentieth centuries was Frederick W. Taylor whose book, *The Principles of Scientific Management* (1911), applied the Gospel of Efficiency to factory operations and transformed manufacturing into a science. Taylor's crusade was only one of several such movements. Principles of rationalization had been used by John D. Rockefeller and his associates when they created the Standard Oil Trust in 1882, combining several corporations into a more profitable (and monopolistic) enterprise. About the same time, Gustavus F. Swift revamped the meatpacking industry by breaking down the production of dressed meats into simple, uniform tasks. He also organized his operation more effectively by acquiring control over the transportation and marketing of his products. Bankers and merchants were making financial transactions more efficient by using checks and negotiable bills instead of cumbersome commercial paper.

To business-oriented reformers efficiency in government was as necessary as economic rationalization, and, as in business, efficiency meant economy. These people were convinced that city governments had become inefficient because irresponsible officials were squandering public treasuries and burdening taxpayers with huge debts. In times of prosperity many cities—often, but not always, at the instigation of bosses—spent lavish sums on public buildings, streets, sewers, and other improvements. But when depression struck, as it did severely in 1873–78 and 1893–97, cities were left with huge commitments and with insufficient revenues to pay off their debts. According to Charles N. Glaab and A. Theodore Brown, the debts of the nation's fifteen largest cities rose by 271 percent in the ten years after the Civil War, while their populations grew by just 70 percent. As time passed and as cities financed more of their expenditures by borrowing money, an increasing percentage—often as much as one-third—of annual budgets was used to pay the interest on bonded indebtedness. Occasionally the situation became crippling. In 1878 depression and a third yellow fever epidemic in five years forced the city of Memphis to default on its interest payments. The state then revoked the city's charter and assumed control of its fiscal operations.

It is no wonder, then, that men interested in efficient government constantly demanded fiscal retrenchment and more careful control of debt. When they succeeded in attaining positions of power, their goals of prudent management became near obsessions. For example, Grover Cleveland, who rose to national prominence when his concern with reform gave him the mayoralty of Buffalo in 1881, conceived of his mission almost exclusively as safeguarding the public purse and defending the rights of property. Almost four decades later Edward P. Smith, a lawyer who became mayor of Omaha when reformers managed temporarily to dislodge Boss Tom Dennison's machine, stated, "I have no desire or ambition to have my administration known as a 'reform' administration. I want it known as a clean administration and a business administration . . . My job is to sit on expenditures."

Driving out irresponsible leaders often presented a dilemma, for replacing the boss meant beating him at his own game—party politics, a game which many reformers considered despicable. Their solution was to advocate removal of party politics from municipal administration. With help from sympathetic state governments, civic reformers sometimes were able to secure charter amendments that provided for structural changes such as nominating and electing city officials on nonpartisan bases (no candidate could run for office under a party label), separating municipal elections from state and national elections so they would be held at different times of the year, and establishing civil service that would determine qualifications for appointed officials by their fitness for office rather than by their party affiliations. The argument behind these changes was that a city did not need a Republican or Democrat to build a school or lay a sewer; responsible local government was no place for party politics. Nonpartisanship became a major objective of the many city clubs and civic leagues established in cities across the country at the end of the nineteenth century.

To these organizations, consisting mostly of Republican businessmen, the city was like a corporation, to be managed according to strict business principles. This attitude helped to produce two major structural reforms: the commission and city manager forms of administration. In 1900 a hurricane and flood ravaged Galveston, Texas. To speed the city's recovery the state legislature replaced the ward-based city council with a commission of local businessmen, each of whom administered a different branch of municipal affairs. The system worked so effectively that the city adopted it permanently, electing the seven commissioners on an at-large (citywide rather than ward representation), nonpartisan basis. Although by combining legislative and administrative functions the city commission plan destroyed traditional separation of powers, it won wide support from civic reformers because it operated like the board of directors of a corporation. Within ten years over 100 communities, mostly small cities where ward organizations were weak, adopted commission plans. The cases of Kansas City, Omaha, and Memphis proved, however, that city commissions could not always escape machine politics. In these cities bosses simply filled commission seats with their henchmen, thereby preserving control.

The other structural innovation grew out of business reverence for expertise. In 1908 the city of Staunton, Virginia, hired a city manager to administer local affairs in place of a politically elected mayor. The idea spread slowly at first. But in 1910, again as a consequence of a disastrous flood, Dayton, Ohio, adopted the plan, and eventually it was tried in such larger cities as Cleveland, Kansas City, and Cincinnati. The city manager plan created a new separation of powers. It usually provided for a small city council (elected on a nonpartisan ballot) that would determine general policy and pass ordinances. The council would appoint or hire a city manager (chosen for his administrative and technical skills) who would implement council policies and determine budgets. In some cases the mayor was retained and given mainly titular functions.

City manager plans still exist in many places today, particularly in suburban communities. But larger cities found it difficult at best to keep city managers out of politics and usually abandoned the plan shortly after it had been adopted. Nevertheless the thrust of both commission and city manager reform was clear. In the minds of civic reformers, the boss and his ward-based machine had to be destroyed. As one reformer wrote, "Ward pitted against ward, alderman against alderman, and legislation only effected by 'log-rolling' extravagant measures into operation, mulcting the city, but gratifying the greed of constituents, has too long stung the conscience of decent citizenship."

The efficiency argument also produced another type of structural change—municipal ownership of public utilities. Some reformers believed that regardless of the form of government, bribery and corruption would always fester as long as politicians could collude with big businesses at public expense. These reformers thought they could destroy bosses' financial resources and provide better services by replacing private franchises with publicly owned operations. City-owned water systems had been common since the middle of the nineteenth century. Now, a number of reformers began to advocate public gas, electric, and transportation systems. Although by 1910 several hundred cities, including Cleveland, Detroit, and Chicago, had experimented with forms of municipal ownership, the reform succeeded mainly in smaller cities where profits for private companies were more limited. As Blake McKelvey has noted, public ownership, with its tinge of socialism, frightened many municipal leaders, so that businessmen were not of one mind about this reform. Expeditures on public harbors, roads, docks, and sewers won general acceptance because they stimulated private enterprise. But when advocates of public projects tried to supplant private operations, they frequently met strong opposition. Nevertheless most urban dwellers eventually accepted some form of public regulation of utility rates and services even if public ownership proved unacceptable.

Movements to strengthen existing governmental structures rather than to replace them tended to yield more immediate reform victories, at least in larger cities. During the last third of the nineteenth century many municipal reformers pressed state legislatures to grant cities more legislative and financial independence. Civic groups campaigned for home rule powers that would enable city governments to draft their own charters, pass more of their own ordinances, and determine their own fiscal policies without interference from the state. Agitation by reformers who complained of divided authority and vague responsibilities in local affairs (in 1870 state-appointed boards administered many of New York City's most important departments, including police and health) succeeded in prodding a few states, particularly in the Midwest and West, to reduce control over their municipalities. In 1876 Missouri approved a home rule charter for St. Louis. A provision in the California constitution of 1879 allowed large cities to draft their own charters subject to approval by the state legislature. Washington and Minnesota adopted similar provisions. By 1924 a dozen other states had followed suit.

Civic reformers also urged that mayors assume greater powers. Most new and revised city charters from 1870 onward gave mayors greater veto, appointive, and budgetary prerogatives. Reformers and their allies in state legislatures believed that city councils, often representing disparate interests, had been responsible for fiscal waste. The solution was to centralize power in the executive branch and to allow the mayor to appoint auditors and comptrollers who would watch over the public purse more carefully. In 1882 Brooklyn gave its mayor power to make appointments without council approval, and Boston's charter of 1885 included a similar provision. Part of the home rule and strong mayor arguments contradicted a basic reform attitude. Advocates of greater municipal and executive authority complained in the same breath that bosses were ruining cities by exercising autocratic powers. Yet reformers attempted to resolve the paradox by claiming that their basic aim was to fix responsibility and to make government more sensitive to local needs.

Ironically, structural changes that centralized executive power facilitated the rise of reform bosses, strong leaders who attempted to use government to effect wide-ranging changes. After attaining office reform mayors like Hazen S. Pingree of Detroit, Samuel M. Jones of Toledo, and Thomas L. Johnson of Cleveland moved from eliminating corruption and inefficiency to comprehensive social change that aimed to create greater social and economic equality. Hazen Pingree was the first reformer to build his own political organization and the first politician to work explicitly for social reform. Pingree was a Detroit shoe manufacturer who was drafted into the 1889 mayoral election by the Michigan Club, an influential group of Republican businessmen who wanted to rid Detroit of corruption. Pingree won the election by capitalizing on appeals to the city's ethnic groups. He immediately began to apply business principles of prudence and efficiency to governmental operations, and his success won him reelection in 1891. Pingree's struggles to limit the rates and franchise privileges of the street railway, gas, electric, and telephone companies awakened him to the dangers of such monopolistic enterprises and sharpened his concern for the public who paid for these services. When the depression of 1893–94 brought suffering to tens of thousands of Detroiters, Pingree turned his administration directly toward the welfare of the working classes. He bolstered relief agencies, authorized public works for unemployment relief, and cajoled businessmen to keep prices low and not to lay off workers. Pingree's strong passion for the poor influenced administrations in other cities to assume greater social responsibilities, and his constant battles with utilities companies furnished other reformers with strong arguments for municipal ownership. Although Pingree did succeed in reducing gas rates and in building a publicly owned electric plant, his efforts to bring down streetcar fares were continually frustrated. In 1896 he transferred his crusade to the state level and successfully ran for governor. There his battles with a reactionary legislature afforded him few victories, but he was able to raise issues that eventually became part of progressive reform.

As Melvin Holli has noted, Pingree was one of the few reform mayors to work for more than economy and efficiency in government. During his four terms as mayor he not only ended corruption but also built parks and schools, instituted a more equitable tax structure, established work relief programs for the poor, reduced utility rates, and spoke out for a graduated income tax and for municipal ownership. Moreover, he ignored efforts to impose middle-class Yankee norms on others. He refused to enforce saloon Sunday closing laws, and he tolerated gambling and prostitution. In spite of his radicalism he was a pragmatist, not an idealist. His administration became a model for reform mayors in other cities.

Samuel "Golden Rule" Jones served as mayor of Toledo from 1897 until his death in 1904, and Tom Johnson was mayor of Cleveland from 1901 until a narrow election defeat in 1909. Like Pingree, Jones and Johnson were successful businessmen who became social reformers as politicians. Both actively supported municipal ownership of utilities, and both stressed the need for social justice and equality. Both also included a number of intellectuals in their administrations. Brand Whitlock, novelist and lawyer, was prominent among Jones' advisers and later succeeded him as mayor of Toledo. Frederick C. Howe, Newton Baker, and Edward Bemis were among Johnson's closest associates. Johnson was also influenced by the ideas of Henry George, whose book *Progress and Poverty* (1879) had made considerable impact upon reform thought around the turn of the century. George's proposal to eliminate social inequality by taxing profits that property owners unfairly received from the unearned increment of their land inspired Johnson and others like him to work for social and economic reform. Many of the programs supported by Jones and Johnson bordered on socialism and alienated their business allies. Yet, like Pingree, both mayors and the men who surrounded them sought only to preserve what they believed to be the American tradition, not to change it. Their popular appeal and social welfare projects extended well beyond ordinary economy and efficiency, yet they envisioned their goals as the fulfillment of the American dream. As Brand Whitlock wrote, "The ills from which our cities suffer are not the ills incident to democracy; they are the ills incident to a lack of democracy."

Civic reform produced several other able mayors: Seth Low of Brooklyn and New York, John D. Phelan of San Francisco, Emil Seidel of Milwaukee, Rudolf Blankenburg of Philadelphia, and John Puroy Mitchell of New York. But none of these men—not even Pingree, Jones, and Johnson—could fully reform any large city. The multiplicity of interest groups, the ethnic differences, the complexity and competition militated against unified reform activity. This heterogeneity, according to Robert Wiebe, explains why reformers with limited objectives such as lower taxes or structural changes in government were generally more successful than those who tried to combine several issues into a comprehensive program. In large cities ward organizations often were too strong to destroy. Thus reformers who sought to use politics as a means of effecting change created what Samuel P. Hays has called a "superstructure of social organization," associations existing above ward politics and attempting "to exert political influence from outside municipal government." These groups included Chambers of Commerce, Municipal Research Bureaus, Civic Federations, Good Government Associations (bosses called them "goo-goos"), and Committees of Seventy, One Hundred, or whatever number. Sometimes these people accepted existing political structures. But more often they tried to institute nonpartisan, centralized, citywide activities that would undercut (and control) ward organizations.

Pingree, Jones, and Johnson were the exceptions. Most civic reformers aimed only to "throw the rascals out," and when successful, their "clean governments" fizzled because they could not match the functions performed by political machines. With few positive programs beyond cleansing government and instituting a few structural changes to increase efficiency and economy, reformers had little stamina compared to their rivals, the bosses, who knew how to survive in the political arena. In 1886, four years after it was founded, the New York Reform Club had to suspend its meetings for lack of a quorum. The quick demise of reform administrations in New York and other cities led cynics like Boss George Washington Plunkitt to label reformers as "morning glories" who wilted in the heat of daily politics.

Although civic reform movements became synonymous with honesty and efficiency in government, they rarely mentioned social welfare. Their self-righteousness and obsessive budget cutting failed to touch common needs of jobs, housing, and health. Even their attempts to apply business principles to politics usually revealed insensitivity to the complexities of business and political administration. A reformer, said Mr. Dooley,

> thinks business an' honesty is th' same thing . . . He's got them mixed because they dhress alike. His idea is that all he has to do to make a business administhration is to keep honest men ar-round him. Wrong. I'm not sayin', mind ye, that a man can't do good work an' be honest at th' same time. But whin I hire a la-ad, I find out first whether he is onto his job, an' after a few years I begin to suspect he is honest too. . . . A man ought to be honest to start with an' afther that he ought to be crafty. A pollytician who's on'y honest is jus' th' same as bein' out in a winther storm without anny clothes on.

Thus civic reformers succeeded in improving the general quality of municipal administration by reducing corruption, lowering taxes, and shoring up local control. But their tendency to view urban society only in business and moralistic terms ignored long-term political and social policy and posed no substitute for the welfare functions of political machines.

THE REMEDIES OF SOCIAL REFORM

The liberal creed of the early nineteenth century had been *laissez faire,* the belief that the natural order of things ensured equilibrium. But by the end of the century, that faith had begun to break down. A broad phalanx of reformers, ranging from wide-eyed humanitarians to calculating special interests, marched under a banner of public and private intervention to remove injustices from urban society. This new attitude reflected a belief in what Roy Lubove has called an "organic city." According to this tenet, the modern industrial city depended upon the coordination and cooperation of its specialized parts. Without cooperation, reinforced by a vigilant and well-informed citizenry, competition would run rampant and single interests would gain deleterious power. The counterforce to individual self-interest was community responsibility—the extension of public functions to promote the welfare of all. This was the motivation of social reform. Although this branch of urban reform avoided some of the self-righteousness of civic crusades, its concern with the "public interest" could become confused with an attempt to achieve social control, proving that there was but a short step between "brother's helper" and "brother's keeper."

Like civic reform, social reform grew out of changing economic and social conditions; indeed, some social reformers were also civic reformers. It was based largely in what Robert Wiebe has called the "new middle class." Its membership consisted basically of men and women who were becoming specialists in expanding areas of law, medicine, education, social work, and other professions, as well as new breed professionals in fields of business, labor, and agriculture. Their awakening professional consciousness encouraged them to apply their expertise to their environments. More importantly, it led them to support and to undertake "scientific" investigations of urban problems. From the 1870s onward, a number of different groups, mostly private and voluntary, sponsored examinations of aspects of urban life. These activities included public health and housing surveys, studies of the incidence and location of poverty, and investigations of local corruption. By the turn of the century these procedures had become an institutionalized component of reform strategy.

The emphasis on investigation had two objectives. First, the middle-class reformers were an inquiring generation; they felt a strong urge to know all the facts. Many of them believed they had temporarily lost their ability to understand fast-growing, ever-changing urban society. Only by restoring that understanding could they soothe their sense of crisis and begin to formulate plans that would improve present conditions. Second, and more importantly, reformers from new middle-class ranks had a strong faith in knowledge and conscience as reforming agents. Many believed that if the general public could be kept well informed and if the major problems could be identified and exposed, an enlightened citizenry would rally behind programs to destroy injustice.

A new kind of journalism—the journalism of exposure—became a central vehicle in the drive for information. For nearly a century after the Revolution few city newspapers gave more than a passing glance to local affairs. In the early nineteenth century most newspapers had limited circulations and acted as organs for a political party, focusing mainly on state, national, and international issues. But the decades following the Civil War witnessed an extraordinary popularization and proliferation of newspapers and magazines. The invention of the steam press, which could print copies much faster than old hand presses, and increasing use of paper made of wood pulp instead of rags and linen enabled printers to produce literary materials much more cheaply and voluminously. The telegraph and later the telephone quickened the pace of communications and made information far more accessible than ever before. In order to sell more newspapers publishers began to replace political prose with news and features. Journalists now created news as well as reported it. Circulation-hungry publishers like Joseph Pulitzer, who bought the *New York World* in 1883, and William Randolph Hearst, who acquired the *San Francisco Call* in 1887 and the *New York Journal* in 1896, filled their front pages with screaming headlines, sensational stories, and dramatic photographs. At the same time, the old literary magazines began to give way to more popular, cheaper issues, such as *Cosmopolitan, McClure's,* and *Everybody's,* whose circulations grew to hundreds of thousands.

A large number of newspapers and magazines tried to attract readers by publishing articles that exposed the scandals and injustices of contemporary society. Some articles were lurid and ill informed, but many others were based on careful investigation—a major standard of the new professional journalist—and were designed to alert the middle-class public to the need for reform. A leading spokesman for this kind of appeal was Jacob Riis, a Danish immigrant who worked for twenty years as a police reporter for the *New York Tribune* and later for the *Evening Sun.* Riis rose to national prominence in 1890 with the publication of his *How the Other Half Lives,* an intimate, vivid portrayal of what Riis had seen and learned in the slums of New York during his first twelve years as a journalist. In a tone that was alternately sympathetic and indignant, Riis tried to describe "what the tenements are and how they grew to what they are." The book was illustrated with photographs, most taken by Riis—he was one of the first to use the camera as an instrument of reform. But Riis wanted to do more than describe conditions; his goal was to inform and arouse his readers to the plights of the "other half."

Other journalists stirred public attention with their investigations of political abuses. Probably the most well-known reporter was Lincoln Steffens, whose seven articles on urban corruption originally published by *McClure's* in 1902–1903 were combined in a book titled *The Shame of the Cities,* published in 1904. Steffens was particularly concerned about the unfair privileges that he saw pervading modern American society. Through his exposure of the misrule that he observed in St. Louis, Pittsburgh, Minneapolis, and Philadelphia, and through his review of the partial success of reform in Chicago and New York, Steffens appealed to mass sentiments of responsibility, indignation, and guilt. He carefully constructed his articles to achieve a dramatic impact for the sake of sounding the alarm and enlightening the public. Unlike many of his colleagues, Steffens viewed political bosses with some admiration. He believed that powerful leaders who were intelligent and politically adept could serve society positively. (Later in his life when he became disillusioned with the American system, Steffens transferred his attraction to strong leadership into admiration for the revolutionary dictatorship of Benito Mussolini.) But at the turn of the century, Steffens and other journalists wrote their exposés to arouse the popular will and to revive democracy. As Steffens wrote in his introduction to *The Shame of* the Cities: ". . . these articles, if they have proved nothing else, have demonstrated beyond doubt that we can stand the truth; that there is pride in the character of American citizenship; and that this pride may be a power in the land."

Certainly not all reform-bent journalists—they received the epithet of "muckrakers" from Theodore Roosevelt in 1906—focused exclusively on urban problems. Many writers attacked the malpractices of big business and national politics. Ida Tarbell and Henry Demarest Lloyd exposed the abusive power of the Standard Oil Company. Charles Edward Russell's *Greatest Trust in the World* assaulted the beef industry. Burton J. Hendrick's *Story of Life Insurance* examined the frauds of that business. David Graham Phillips' *The Treason of the Senate,* originally written for *Cosmopolitan,* accused many senators of being servants to big business. Yet because urban problems were so stark and because many middle-class reformers felt threatened and outraged by the problems arising from urbanization, journalists and other writers directed their attention to the cities.

Attempts at reform also pervaded fictional writing. Novelists, in their search for "realism," probed the consequences of urban life on human character. The impersonal quest for power and wealth was depicted by Theodore Dreiser in *The Financier* and by Winston S. Churchill in *Coniston.* Stephen Crane's *Maggie, A Girl of the Streets* and Upton Sinclair's *The Jungle* explored the depths of urban poverty. Sinclair's novel also exposed the loathsome practices of the meatpacking industry and shocked Congress into passing a federal meat inspection law in 1906. The plight of women in the city was poignantly treated by David Graham Phillips in *Susan Lenox, Her Fall and Rise* and by Dreiser in *Sister Carrie* and *Jenny Gerhardt.*

In 1907–1908, investigative social science and journalism combined to produce a six-volume survey that presented the most extensive catalog of modern urban life yet collected. Under the direction of Paul U. Kellogg, a professional social worker, and sponsored by the Russell Sage Foundation, *The Pittsburgh Survey* detailed the economic progress of the city and the social costs of industrialization. It particularly showed how political corruption and irresponsible business practices had contributed to the city's problems of poverty, pollution, and inequitable tax practices. Kellogg and many like him in other cities were almost obsessed with the potential of reason and information as reforming instruments. They invested their strongest faith in what Clark Chambers has termed "the ultimate benevolence of an informed public." This faith reflected the new middle-class reformers' strength and their shortcomings.

The activities of these reformers included a multitude of causes ranging from the religious humanizing of the Social Gospel movement to the "breadbasket" issues of labor organizations. Such a variety of concerns does not fit very well into a generalized interpretation that can categorize every program and personality. From an urban point of view, one of the most salient aspects was the attempt by middle-class individuals and groups to control and mitigate the problems of inner cities, where conditions seemed most menacing. In addition to the concerns with housing and health discussed in Chapter 4, social reformers' efforts in the inner city took four major focuses: moral and religious responsibility for social betterment, epitomized by the Social Gospel; the civic and cultural enlightenment of inner city dwellers sponsored by educational reformers; the settlement house movement's drive to bridge cultural gaps and improve neighborhood life; and the promise of aesthetic invigoration from city planning.

Religious and Moral Reform

During the 1870s and 1880s a few clergymen of older Protestant sects reacted to the social crises and labor struggles resulting from urbanization and industrialization by espousing a new interpretation of their religious mission. The Social Gospel, as this ethic came to be called, turned away from traditional concerns of moral and spiritual dogma and emphasized the social aspects of Christianity. According to the Social Gospel the salvation of society replaced the salvation of an individual soul as the principle religious goal. Before the Civil War Unitarian ministers like William Ellery Channing and Theodore Parker had stressed the duty of good Christians to attend to the needs of the "degenerate" classes. As problems of urbanization heightened after the war, this attitude spread; and leaders of other Protestant sects tried to make their churches instruments of reform.

The leading figure of the Social Gospel movement was Washington Gladden, a Congregationalist minister in Columbus, Ohio. Gladden preached that modern Christians should seek salvation by attempting to realize the Kingdom of God on earth rather than worrying about the afterlife of their individual souls. Gladden and Walter Rauschenbusch, a Baptist minister and professor at the Rochester (New York) Theological Seminary, Josiah Strong, Pastor of the Central Congregational Church of Cincinnati, Shaler Mathews, of the University of Chicago Divinity School, and R. Heber Newton, a New York Episcopalian, stressed the social responsibilities of Christianity through good works and social betterment. Gladden mediated between labor unions and employers, and he supported arbitration as a means of achieving industrial peace. Rauschenbusch worked with Jacob Riis to obtain better living conditions for the poor. Other clergymen sponsored investigations and worked to alleviate poverty and decay in slum districts.

Several socially conscious congregations, with the help of contributions from wealthy members, established institutional churches within the slums. These churches offered programs such as nurseries, kindergartens, clinics and dispensaries, employment agencies, recreation centers, and adult education classes. The goal of all activities was service. As Josiah Strong wrote in *The Challenge of the City*,

> Inasmuch as Christ came not to be ministered unto but to minister, the open and institutional church, filled and moved by his spirit of ministering love, seeks to become the center and source of all benificent and philanthropic effort, and to take the leading part in every movement which has for its end the alleviation of human suffering, the elevation of man, and the betterment of the world.

The Social Gospel was particularly influential in advancing the environmental explanation of urban social ills. Men like Gladden and Rauschenbusch believed that people were not intrinsically bad; rather the conditions in which people lived corrupted them. By reforming the environment Social Gospelers believed they could create a moral, ethical society. Dismayed by the greed and banality of industrial capitalism, they poured their energies into the inner city; and through their investigations, missions, and institutional churches, they awakened a host of sensitive men and women to the needs and methods of social reform. A few Social Gospelers took radical approaches to the solution of urban problems; Boston's W. D. P. Bliss, for example, became a socialist and helped found the Society of Christian Socialists in 1889. But the majority were moderates—clergymen who felt guilty about their own and their churches' neglect of social problems and who reacted by trying to reorient the gospel into a more secular direction. The Social Gospel influenced some Catholics and Jews as well, and it also reached rural areas. But for the most part, it evolved from the impact of urban problems on post–Civil War Protestantism.

One specific crusade that many Social Gospelers joined was the drive to close down saloons. The temperance movement was not new to late nineteenth-century urban America. It had existed since colonial times and had always included a broad spectrum of supporters, ranging from socially conscious reformers to bigoted, antiurban zealots. But after the Civil War the movement gathered fresh momentum, spurred by activists who believed they could improve the conditions of the laboring classes by destroying the centers of vice, immorality, and political corruption. Temperance reformers were convinced that inner-city neighborhoods contained too many saloons. (They may have been right—by the 1890s many city districts had one saloon for every 100 men, women, and children.) Because competition was so keen, reformers theorized, an establishment could survive only by staying open after hours or by offering extra services like gambling and prostitution. Such temptations, plus the addictive effect of liquor, weakened family life and caused men and women to squander their wages. Moreover, saloons were the bunkers of boss politics. Destroy the saloon and you remove the boss's base of operations.

Although temperance and prohibition movements attracted large numbers of rural enthusiasts who feared the evil ways of the big city, much of the leadership and financial support came from urban dwellers, largely native white Protestants who inhabited the outer wards. During the 1880s and 1890s the Anti-Saloon League and Women's Christian Temperance Union organized branches in scores of cities. Some members of these organizations were willing to abandon quests for total prohibition in favor of more pragmatic goals. They worked for enforcement of licensing and closing laws, and they used pamphlets and public school programs to emphasize the dangers of liquor and the virtues of abstinence. In a few cities temperance reformers helped to establish local option rules that permitted individual wards or precincts to vote themselves dry. The greatest successes occurred in Chicago, where by 1908 almost half of the city was dry—mostly in the outer districts.

In the minds of many moral reformers it was a short step from the bottle to other temptations. Thus crusades against the saloons often spread to gambling and prostitution. Most big cities tolerated unofficial segregation of gambling dens and brothels in red light districts. Chicago's "levee," New York's Bowery, and New Orleans' Bourbon Street were well-known centers of vice activity and generally safe from police raids. A few cities, notably Cleveland and St. Louis, experimented with police registration and medical inspection of prostitutes rather than trying to abolish them. But public outcries proved too strong, and a hysteria over the "white slave trade" triggered new efforts to remove the age-old social evil from American cities.

In the early 1900s reformers in several cities established vice commissions to investigate prostitution and gambling and recommend legislation. According to Roy Lubove, the reformers "leveled their attack primarily upon those individuals and institutions which for personal profit advertised vice, stimulated men's demand, and labored to maintain the supply of prostitutes." This meant crackdowns on saloons, bordellos, cheap hotels, dance halls, and red light districts. As remedies, reformers recommended four measures: (1) labor legislation to improve working conditions for women so that they would not be lured by adversity into prostitution; (2) education campaigns to alert the public to the dangers of venereal disease; (3) neighborhood recreational facilities to replace vice centers; and (4) nuisance and abatement laws by which private citizens could obtain court orders to close down offensive establishments. By the 1920s, however, technology enabled vice operators to circumvent most repressive legislation. The automobile enabled gambling and prostitution to flourish in roadhouses outside city borders away from the law, and the telephone created the bookie and the call girl.

Educational Reform

Residents of the outskirts felt a strong need to preserve their conceptions of the American ideal, and they turned to public schools as vehicles of reform. The first problems that reformers faced were those of bringing immigrant and native working class children into the schools. In many cities, seldom more than two-thirds of school-age children attended classes—often because families could not afford to withhold their children from the labor market. At the instigation of urban interests several states enacted compulsory attendance laws in the 1870s and 1880s, and many cities appointed truant officers to enforce the laws. Even then, absenteeism remained a major problem.

Nevertheless increasing populations, coupled with compulsory attendance, swelled enrollments, confronting cities with new problems of inadequate buildings and teacher shortages. New schools accounted for a large proportion of the increased bonded indebtedness in many cities during the last decades of the nineteenth century. Between 1860 and 1880 the number of normal schools training teachers quadrupled, but still could not meet the demand. Significantly, however, increased demands for teachers opened the profession to more women, who now outnumbered men in the common schools. The pressures on public school facilities and personnel would have been worse had it not been for the expansion of parochial education. Responding to the needs of growing numbers of Catholic immigrants, the Third Plenary Council, meeting in Baltimore in 1884, urged that each parish provide schools for its children. By the end of the century nearly a million children were enrolled in Catholic elementary schools, and several dioceses had established parochial high schools.

The larger problems for reformers, however, involved school organization and curriculum choice. Here the reformers manifested two of their most common characteristics: an urge for efficiency and an urge to use public institutions as instruments of social policy. In the case of public education efficiency meant better organization, usually involving the establishment of centralized rather than ward-based school districts and the appointment of professional rather than politically-based administrators. A leader in administrative innovation was William T. Harris, superintendent of St. Louis public schools from 1867 to 1880. Harris believed that urban education should conform to new patterns of economic organization—meaning the factory—, and he constantly stressed the need for regularity in school administration and pupil discipline. He supported reforms such as graded schools, centralized policy making, standardized curricula, and even uniform architecture. This was merely another form of rationalization. In an 1885 report on American urban schools, John Philbrick of Boston wrote, "The history of city systems of schools makes it evident that in the matter of administration the tendency is toward greater centralization and permanence of authority, and that the tendency is in the direction of progress and improvement."

School reformers imported several of their curricular innovations from Europe. During the 1860s urban schools began to implement the teaching methods of the Swiss educator H. H. Pestalozzi who preached that children should be taught through concrete experience instead of learning by rote memorization. Over the next decade many public schools (Harris's St. Louis system and the schools of Quincy, Illinois, for example) added kindergartens, the program of the German educator F. W. A. Froebel. The kindergartens, designed for very young children, stressed the importance of pleasant surroundings, self-activity, and physical training as means to develop learning capacities. Also, physical education for older children, in the form of Swedish gymnastics, was introduced into city school systems by the 1890s.

One of the most important educational innovations directed at inner-city children grew out of the American industrial experience. By the early 1900s scores of cities had established trade schools or vocational education programs to train children in industrial skills. Vocational training combined two major types of educational reform: the arts and crafts movement, which attempted to restore or to preserve handicrafts that had given workers a sense of involvement with the end product of their labor; and industrial trade training, which aimed to provide instruction in marketable skills. As early as the 1870s public schools in Boston and Milwaukee were offering arts and crafts classes. In 1881 Colonel Richard T. Auchmitz opened a manual training school in New York that won wide attention and received a $500,000 endowment from J. P. Morgan in 1892. Other private vocational schools opened in St. Louis, Chicago, Philadelphia, and Cleveland, and a public manual training program was launched in Baltimore in 1883.

Vocational education was originally intended to give society a link to the past and to make schooling more relevant to everyday life. But, as Marvin Lazerson has suggested, it could also be turned into a tool for social control, channeling working-class children into useful but limited occupational functions. The use of manual training to achieve desired social ends entwined two different strains of thought. On one side was Charles Prosser, Deputy Commissioner for Industrial Education in Massachusetts and later Director of the Dinwoody Institute for Vocational Study in Minneapolis. Prosser viewed vocational education as an efficiency device that could enable all children, particularly lower-class children, to aid industrial progress. On the other side stood John Dewey, father of progressive education. Dewey believed that vocational training would restore what industrial progress had eroded. "The invention of machinery," he wrote,

> the institution of the factory system, and the division of labor have changed the home from a workshop into a simple dwelling place . . . While need of the more formal intellectual training in the school has decreased, there arises an urgent demand for the introduction of methods of manual and industrial discipline which shall give the child what he formerly obtained in his home and social life.

Whatever the rationale, supporters of industrial education were able to lobby successfully for their cause. A 1910 survey located industrial education programs in twenty-nine states, mostly in urban schools.

Educational reformers also directed attention specifically to immigrants. In the closing decades of the nineteenth century, many cities established evening schools primarily designed to teach English and civics to immigrant adults. Some schools offered English language instruction in primary grades to immigrant children. These programs sought to Americanize newcomers and to press them into a mold that fit the native middle-class ideal. In a larger sense, educational reform reflected a belief that, according to Robert Wiebe, "the schools would facilitate the arrival of Social Rationality, preparing the nation for a higher civilization." Even those reforms directed at the middle class— the increasing establishment of high schools, for example—revealed a strong belief in formal schooling as the best instrument for shaping American culture and for bringing order to heterogeneous urban society.

Settlements

The settlement house movement was one of the most influential branches of urban reform. The idea originated in England where a group of young intellectuals set up a residence called Toynbee Hall in the London slums in 1884. These men and women sought to improve living conditions for lower-class laborers by bringing them education and appreciation for the arts. At the same time, the residents of Toynbee Hall believed they could learn something about beauty and life from the people they hoped to serve. Their objective was to bridge the gap between classes. Toynbee Hall inspired a number of young Americans who were visiting or studying in England, and several of them organized settlement houses when they returned to the United States. Stanton Coit started the Neighborhood Guild (later renamed University Settlement) in a New York tenement apartment in 1886. Over the next few years Vida Scudder and Lillian Wald started other settlements in New York, Jane Addams and Ellen Gates Starr founded Hull House in Chicago, Graham Taylor opened Chicago Commons in that city, and Robert A. Woods founded Andover House in Boston. By 1897 there were seventy-four settlements in the United States, and by 1910, over four hundred.

Most participants in early settlements were young, middle class, well-educated, religious minded, and idealistic men and women who felt disturbed by the social barriers between classes and frustrated by their own apparent uselessness in a society that cried for reform. As Allen Davis has noted, settlement workers had a strong desire to help, to apply their ideas of service (influenced by the Social Gospel) to the challenges of the city. They also had a strong investigative impulse—an urge to find out for themselves what urban society's problems were like. Moreover, educated women found new opportunities in settlements to apply their knowledge toward the betterment of society. Settlements offered important outlets to women wishing to break away from domestic confinements but barred from male-dominated areas of business and politics.

As residents of the inner city, settlement workers viewed the problems of poverty first hand, and they actively sought to improve living conditions for immigrants and other poor people. The settlement house itself became an instrument of reform, acting as an educational center, information clearing house, and forum for debate. Settlement workers organized English and civics classes, amateur concerts and theatrical productions, and kindergartens. Jane Addams, Robert A. Woods, and Lillian Wald joined other education reformers in lobbying for public adoption of kindergartens, vocational training, school nurses, and playgrounds. Because one of their major goals was revitalization of inner-city neighborhoods, settlement workers strongly backed housing reforms and worked closely with individuals like Jacob Riis, Lawrence Veiller, and Robert W. DeForrest in support of regulatory legislation. In the cause of labor reform settlements offered rooms for union meetings, and Florence Kelly, Mary McDowell, Jane Addams, and Mary Simkhovitch spoke out in support of workers' rights. Inevitably settlement workers were drawn into the politics of reform. They often fought local bosses on the ward level, and they moved into larger arenas of citywide reform in order to achieve their objectives.

The importance of the settlement movement lies in its flexibility and its influence. Although settlement workers were occasionally romantic and naive (one program tried to teach destitute immigrant women how to serve tea from a silver service), their eagerness to learn enabled them to adjust and help the inner city poor. They could not always erase attitudes of condescension and paternalism toward immigrants, and they kept facilities for blacks separate from those for whites from fear of driving whites away. But they also poured energy and compassion into the slums, and they invested faith in a pluralistic, urban society. They believed that immigrants did not have to shed their cultural backgrounds to become good Americans, and that middle-class Americans could learn from the immigrants as well as teach them. Settlements were based, remarked Jane Addams, "on the theory that the dependence of classes on each other is reciprocal."

Eventually the settlement movement succumbed to professionalization. After World War I, the houses lost their attractiveness, and their functions were assumed by trained social workers who brought more expertise to the slums but also more bureaucratic impersonality. As a result the poor came to be viewed as clients rather than as partners in the thrust against poverty and decay. Yet for a full generation, settlements provided hundreds of sensitive women and men with training and experience in social reform.

City Planning

During the middle and late nineteenth century, efforts to create large, landscaped city parks had awakened people to the possibilities of determining the mode and direction of future urban growth. By 1890 landscaping had merged with the new professions of architecture and engineering to create the City Beautiful Movement, an attempt to improve life within cities by enhancing civic design. The City Beautiful blossomed at the World's Columbian Exposition at Chicago in 1893–94. This was the largest of a score of fairs that were held in American cities during the last quarter of the nineteenth century and early years of the twentieth. These extravaganzas became new instruments of boosterism. Heralded as commemorative expositions, they were usually organized to advertise a city's progress and opportunities to the world. The 1893 fair marked the tercentennial of Columbus's voyage to the New World, and Congress had chosen Chicago as the site because the city had made a remarkable recovery from its devastating fire of 1871. The fair's impressive exhibits of agricultural and industrial technology, plus its fantastic entertainments (the Midway offered everything from a Cairo street to a Hawaiian volcano), lured spectators into an idealized future and a romanticized past.

More importantly, the Chicago exposition showed what planners could do if they had the chance. Daniel Burnham, a prominent architect and the fair's supervisor, mustered a battery of notables—including land-scaper Frederick Law Olmsted and maverick architect Louis Sullivan—to plan a totally new city in Jackson Park on Chicago's southern lake-front. Over seven thousand workers (seventeen of whom died in the frenzy of activity to complete the project by opening day) built a "White City," complete with neoclassical buildings, streets, sewers, water system, and other services coordinated to a preconceived master design. The spacious, orderly, monumental character of the exposition in no way resembled gray, smoky, teeming streets of most inner cities. Yet the "White City" captured the imaginations of civic leaders and inspired them to beautify their own communities. Most commonly the City Beautiful was translated into the construction of new public buildings and civic centers. Burnham, Olmsted's son Frederick Jr., Charles M. Robinson (an architect from Rochester whose many publications made him the spokesman of the City Beautiful), and other planners were hired by cities to draw plans for new courthouses, libraries, and government centers.

In a few instances, the City Beautiful movement generated projects that addressed a large segment, rather than part, of a city. In 1900 several of the planners who had been active in the Chicago fair were commissioned to prepare a plan for the beautification of Washington, D.C. Their efforts left the city with a mall between the Capitol and the Potomac River, a number of new monuments, and Rock Creek Park. In 1906 the Commercial Club of Chicago engaged Burnham and his associates to devise a comprehensive plan for the city. Their scheme, submitted in 1909 and accepted by the City Council in 1910, shaped Chicago's development for the next five decades. And it became one of the most influential documents in the history of city planning. The Burnham Plan sought to create a "well-ordered, convenient, and unified city." In practical terms this meant improved transportation, accessible areas for public recreation, and provisions to control subsequent growth. The plan specified a new railroad terminal, an east-west boulevard, a civic center, the development of lakefront parks and beaches along the full length of Chicago's shoreline, and the acquisition of large forest preserves around the city's borders. The plan was expensive, and several schemes had to be abandoned. Yet most of the plan was eventually completed, and its scope and innovation won nationwide fascination.

Burnham's motto was "Make no little plans . . .Make big plans; aim high in hope and work. . . ." Yet few other cities could reproduce Chicago's accomplishments. In most places the City Beautiful represented a

The Aftermath of the Great Chicago Fire, 1871

A View of the World's Columbian Exposition, Chicago, 1893

Although these two photographs do not show the same area of the city, they do contrast the extraordinary destruction that Chicagoans experienced in 1871 with the buoyant optimism that they exhibited in 1893. The Great Fire leveled some 1,700 acres and destroyed $200 million worth of property. The 1893 fair, the epitome of the City Beautiful, cost $19 million to construct and impressed millions of visitors, including novelist Hamlin Garland who wrote his parents on their Dakota farm, "Sell the cook stove if necessary and come. You *must* see this fair." *Both photographs courtesy Chicago Historical Society.*

The San Francisco Earthquake
Ruins of the 1906 disaster still smolder days afterward. The widespread destruction provided planners with an opportunity to initiate projects for renewing the city which otherwise might never have overcome the resistance of private property owners. *U.S. Signal Corps, The National Archives.*

holding action—an attempt to restrain slums and decay from blighting business districts. Anticipating the attempt to "reclaim" the city by urban renewal a half century later, the City Beautiful most often spawned projects to make commercial districts more attractive—and more profitable—for business and government personnel who lived on the urban fringe. The problems of slums and social inequities were seldom addressed. Burnham, Robinson, and others were not oblivious to social problems, but they believed that improvements like parks and sanitation would correct imbalances. A kind of simplistic optimism—plus a faithfulness to the needs of private investment—limited the accomplishments of early planning. As early as the St. Louis Exposition of 1904, the City Beautiful movement began to split, with some people continuing to advocate aesthetics as the answer to civic decay and others beginning to support larger attempts to forestall decay through zoning and regional planning.

Unlike the agrarian reformers, whose crusades against big business, hard money, and the railroads dominated social protest in the 1880s and 1890s, the urban middle-class social reformers accepted, even embraced, the city. They believed that within the city lay the potential for human progress. As Frederick Howe wrote in 1905, "The ready responsiveness of democracy, under the close association which the city involves, forecasts a movement for the improvement of human society more hopeful than anything the world has ever known." But this faith often betrayed a failure to accept the pluralism of modern urban society. Although social reformers felt a responsibility to help the masses, many also wanted to restore traditional values of social deference and cultural purity, however mythical those values might have been in the past. The spirit of service, sacrifice, and love could easily be refashioned into condescension and paternalism. Thus moral idealism allowed some reformers to support prohibition, immigration restriction, and separate and unequal facilities for blacks. Moreover, service-minded middle-class humanitarians often misunderstood human nature. As Mr. Dooley candidly observed,

> . . . (T)is a gr-reat mistake to think that annywan ra-ally wants to rayform. Ye niver heerd of a man rayformin' himself. He'll rayform other people gladly. He likes to do it. But a healthy man'll niver rayform while he has th' strenth. . . . But a rayformer don't see it . . . (He) spinds th' rest iv his life tellin' us where we are wrong. He's good at that. On'y he don't unherstand that people wud rather be wrong an' comfortable thin right in jail.

What was service to some was meddling to others. Yet in spite of their limitations, civic and social reform together brought many changes to urban America. Perhaps more importantly, they provided the foundation for the Progressive Era.

REFORM BECOMES PROGRESSIVE MOVEMENTS

The twentieth century had brought with it the Progressive Era, a period spanning the years between 1900 and 1920, when reform activism spread through almost all facets of American life. Progressivism was not a single movement; it involved shifting coalitions of varied reformers operating on a number of fronts. Some progressive reforms, particularly those involving political structures and railroad regulation, were adopted from the Populist movement of the 1880s and 1890s. Most Populist causes, however, grew out of rural economic distress and were centered in the Midwest and South. In contrast, progressive issues were national in scope and focused on urban problems. In fact the Progressive Era culminated three decades of urban reform. In this respect the issues of the period were not new; they had been the concerns of civic and social reformers for some time. But what was new was the combination of like-minded reformers from different cities into national organizations.

The nationalization of reform was the product of several ingredients. In large part it grew from reformers' basic optimism in their causes. No problem seemed too complex; no geographical area was too large. Failure and frustration on the local level had not dampened reform ardor; they only made national programs more imperative. National organization was also derived from the new middle-class expertise, with its impulse for standardization and professionalization. And certainly faster and easier communications by mail, rail, telegraph, and telephone aided intercity contacts, just as they had facilitated the growth of economic systems that stretched between regions. Whatever their origins, a large number of reformers now carried their particular causes to the national level and provided progressive movements with their intellectual and organizational bases.

One of the earliest of these organizations was the National Municipal League, organized in Philadelphia in 1894 by the First Annual Conference for Good City Government. The League attracted a number of civic reformers and included 180 affiliated societies by 1895. At first members favored the types of elitist reforms that business and professional groups had supported in the 1870s and 1880s—civil service, stronger vice laws, tighter governmental fiscal policies. But, according to David Thelen, the depression of the mid-1890s catalyzed broader concerns about the social and economic problems of urban society and prompted organizations such as the National Municipal League to consider more comprehensive programs for reform. In 1899 the League consolidated its various governmental proposals into a model city charter that provided for home rule, a strong mayor, civil service, and ceilings on taxing and bonding powers. In 1916 members drew a revised model charter that included a commission plan, nonpartisan elections, and shorter ballots. Also, some, though not all, League members became strong advocates of municipally-owned city services. The model charters, support for municipal ownership, and other programs signaled the League's recognition that strong tools were needed to break the bonds between bosses and big business and to reconstruct democratic government. Electing the "best men" and passing "good laws" were no longer enough. Civic reform needed a plan, a plan that could be formulated and supported nationally. Although no city adopted a model charter verbatim, the League's recommendations had considerable influence on local charter committees for the next several decades.

The desire for more coordinated programs also characterized other national reform organizations. The National Civic Federation, founded by business liberals in 1900, organized local branches and enlisted prominent leaders such as Seth Low of New York City and Senator Mark Hanna of Ohio to mediate in labor disputes. The Federation also campaigned nationally for workmen's compensation and for other forms of social insurance. In 1904 Florence Kelly and other middle-class social reformers launched the National Child Labor Committee, which organized campaigns favoring passage and enforcement of laws restricting child labor. Such restrictions had long been the goal of local reformers concerned about the welfare of working-class children and the conditions of tenement sweatshops. The Child Labor Committee also drafted a bill prohibiting child labor, which passed Congress in 1916, only to be overturned by the Supreme Court. The formation of the Federal Council of Churches of Christ in 1905 climaxed the Social Gospel movement. At its first annual conference in 1908, the Council adopted a platform calling for better housing, educational reform, government-sponsored poverty relief, better working conditions in factories, unemployment insurance, minimum wages for manual workers, and equal rights for all.

In 1910 Lawrence Veiller succeeded in combining the various housing reform groups when he convinced the Russell Sage Foundation to finance the organization of the National Housing Association. Settlement workers had helped to found the National Child Labor Committee and the National Playground Association of America, and in 1911 they organized their own National Association of Settlements. In 1909 a number of groups concerned with urban congestion and city planning formed the National Association of City Planning, the forerunner of the American City Planning Institute (today called the American Institute of Planners), founded in 1917. In 1906 the various proponents of vocational training organized the National Society for the Progress of Industrial Education, whose Board of Managers included efficiency expert Frederick W. Taylor, settlement house leaders Jane Addams and Robert A. Woods, the president of American Telephone and Telegraph Company, and the head of the Union of Electrical Workers.

Not all new national organizations centered exclusively around urban issues. The National Farmers Union, the National Womens Trade Union League, and the National Association for the Advancement of Colored People arose out of particular interest group concerns. Nor did all organizations take a liberal tack toward reform. The National Association of Manufacturers, founded in 1895, and the U.S. Chamber of Commerce, organized in 1912, represented the views of conservative urban businessmen. But the formation of large, interregional associations signaled a major shift in urban reform, one which accompanied, and fed, the onset of the Progressive Era.

As a result of nationalization, reform programs by the early twentieth century revealed a detached, pragmatic approach to social and political problems. Their tone was less indignant and less moralistic than that of earlier reformers—the Mugwumps of the 1870s and 1880s. At the same time, the reform character shifted from elitist paternalism—the idea that best men should rule—to bureaucratic control—the idea that experts and specialized agencies should determine social, political, and economic policies. This organizational emphasis was the reform legacy to the modern era.

Most urban progressives believed that trained professionals could best define the public interest and execute proper policies in that interest through specialized, independent agencies. This faith in scientific management blinded reformers to the contradictions between disinterested (nonpolitical and uncorruptible) social engineering and democratic self-determinism. Thus they could advocate more trust in the people and more popular involvement on the one hand while they worked for centralized power and bureaucratic administration on the other. Moreover, they confused the independence of experts and bureaucrats with neutrality, when in fact bureaucracies became as self-serving as the machines that reformers wished to replace. And finally, attempts by progressive reformers to transfer their own achievement-oriented values to all of urban society neglected working-class cultures and institutions as socializing agents. Family life among immigrants and blacks was considerably stronger than educational and humanitarian reformers suspected, and saloons provided more important functions than mere escapism or political connivance. The impersonality of bureaucratic management of social problems and the inability to understand the complexities of urban society with its multiplicity of groups and overlapping interests sometimes limited the progress of urban reform movements. Yet Progressive Era reformers accepted the difficult challenge of grappling with the problems of modern mass society. They realized that the future of American civilization was in its cities, and they tried to prepare for that future while easing the strains of the past and present.

THE RISE OF URBAN LIBERALISM

Although many reform movements evolved from outer-city concerns over conditions in the urban core, the inner regions also organized to improve conditions and to serve working-class interests. Political machines, which were generally inimical to reform, tended to provide inner-city residents with the most available means of protecting their interests. But, as J. Joseph Huthmacher and John D. Buenker have shown, reform included a strong working-class component, and bosses themselves were often responsive to reform goals. In fact immigrant stock working classes, in conjunction with middle-class reformers, provided much of the foundation for the development of "urban liberalism," the ideology of government intervention to ensure the safety and promote the welfare of its citizens.

"(U)rban liberalism," writes Professor Buenker, "was a product of the American urban experience in an industrial age, a growing realization that the power of government could be used to ameliorate the kind of conditions every urban lawmaker had encountered first hand." During the late nineteenth and early twentieth centuries, a number of politicians emerged from immigrant working-class districts to take seats in Congress and in state legislatures. These were men who had worked their way up, usually through the Democratic party, and who were beginning to assume positions of influence by the second decade of the twentieth century. Although their numbers remained too small for them to wield legislative power alone, the urban new stock (immigrant-descended) lawmakers were frequently able to coalesce with reform-minded colleagues to produce some of the Progressive Era's most important measures, involving labor and welfare issues, regulation of big business, home rule, and electoral reform.

From the beginning of the post-Civil War period, urban workingmen had rallied behind legislation promising better conditions in factories and sweatshops. In 1869 Boston laboring groups succeeded in convincing the General Assembly to establish the Massachusetts State Labor Bureau to protect the interests of workers. The Bureau's investigations and statistical reports aided the passage of reform legislation dealing with factory safety and workmen's compensation. These activities set important precedents for the creation of similar bureaus in other states, particularly in the industrialized Northeast. By the end of the century, laboring classes, often led by immigrant-based machine politicians, were pressing for housing and health reforms as well as for breadbasket issues such as higher wages, shorter hours, and more comfortable working conditions.

During the Progressive Era representatives of new stock working classes helped to sponsor reform measures such as widows' pensions, wages and hours legislation, limitations on women's and children's labor, workmen's compensation, factory safety legislation, and tenement regulation. In New York many of these laws grew out of the Factory Investigation Commission hearings instituted after the tragic Triangle Shirtwaist Company fire in New York City in 1911 when 145 young girls were killed. Robert F. Wagner and Alfred E. Smith, graduates of Tammany Hall politics, chaired this commission; and they and their fellow Democrats introduced nearly all of the fifty-six welfare laws passed as a result of the commission's recommendations. In New Jersey Irish American

Democrats from Jersey City and Newark gave strong support to workmen's compensation and factory safety bills in the state legislature. Cleveland's immigrant-based Democrats pushed for welfare legislation in the Ohio legislature. And new stock delegations supported similar issues in other northern and midwestern states. Their efforts were not always fruitful, and they achieved legislative success only when they worked in cooperation with other reform groups sympathetic to workers' concerns. But in each instance, new stock representatives exerted considerable force in guiding the course of reform legislation.

These same lawmakers also backed, though less successfully, measures to strengthen unions, to regulate big business, and to equalize tax burdens. Urban Democratic leaders often rose out of the ranks of organized labor and became strong advocates for the rights of unions to organize, bargain, and strike. In 1911, for example, Boston representatives to the Massachusetts Senate helped pass a bill permitting strikers to picket, although the governor vetoed the act. In business matters, urban lawmakers generally favored government regulation of big business rather than breaking up trusts because workers believed regulation was the surest means of stabilizing economic conditions and ensuring job protection. New stock Democrats particularly favored government control over the rates and services of public utilities, upon which working classes depended. Many of them became strong advocates of municipal ownership of utilities and streetcar companies. For example, Edward F. Dunne, Democratic mayor of Chicago and governor of Illinois in the early twentieth century, backed measures to provide for municipal ownership of several utilities in Chicago. Though he failed, he was able to create a public utilities regulatory commission in 1913. Urban legislators also worked to shift tax burdens to those most able to pay by supporting inheritance taxes, stronger enforcement of intangible property taxes, and, most of all, a graduated federal income tax. In New York, Massachusetts, New Jersey, Ohio, and other states, urban Democrats backed the Sixteenth Amendment to the Constitution establishing Congressional power to levy an income tax because they viewed it, in Robert Wagner's words, as "a tax on plenty instead of necessity. It will lighten the burdens of the poor."

Finally, lawmakers arising out of working-class and immigrant constituencies occasionally promoted political changes that promised to bolster popular control of government. They seldom could agree with most civic reformers, who sought to purify and to centralize government by instituting nonpartisan elections, civil service, short ballots, and at-large candidates; but working-class interests often did favor broadening participation in government by establishing initiative and referendum, recall of appointed officials and judges, woman suffrage, and direct election of U.S. Senators. In Massachusetts and New York, urban delegations strongly supported initiative, referendum, and direct election of senators as a means to temper control of their states by hostile rural representatives. Although urban machines usually opposed giving women the right to vote ("You can't trust these women," asserted Boston's Martin Lomasney. "They are apt to blab everything they know."); by the 1910s, many inner city leaders, including those of Tammany Hall, were backing woman suffrage in hopes of luring women into the Democratic party once they were enfranchised. And new stock working classes also could lend support to measures such as city commissions and direct primaries when it proved politically profitable to do so.

Working classes of inner cities were more than just a social problem; their interests often complemented the goals of progressive reform. Representatives of these interests were not the sole instigators of reform. In fact they often fought key issues of the middle-class drive to improve society, particularly moral reforms such as prohibition, Sunday blue laws, and other attempts to control personal liberty. But such resistance, as Professor Huthmacher has contended, actually fit modern notions of cultural pluralism, the idea that in a heterogeneous society differing groups have a right to maintain their own values. Moreover, the types of measures that new stock urban lawmakers did favor—those directed toward opening up political and economic opportunities and establishing government responsibility for ensuring social welfare—have become the principle components of national reform from the Progressive Era to the present.

BIBLIOGRAPHY

The literature on reform in general and urban reform in particular between 1870 and 1920 is rich and extensive. Some of the best general works include Robert Wiebe, *The Search for Order, 1877–1920* (New York: Hill and Wang, 1967); Richard Hofstadter, *The Age of Reform: From Bryan to F.D.R.* (New York: Knopf, 1955); Samuel P. Hays, *The Response to Industrialism, 1885–1914* (Chicago: University of Chicago Press, 1957); Alfred D. Chandler, Jr., "The Origins of Progressive Leadership," in Elting Morison, ed., *The Letters of Theodore Roosevelt,* Vol. 8 (Cambridge: Harvard University Press, 1954); David P. Thelen, "Social Tensions and the Origins of Progressivism," *Journal of American History,* 56 (September 1969), 323–41; and John G. Sproat, *The Best Men: Liberal Reformers in the Gilded Age* (New York: Oxford University Press, 1968). Studies with particular urban insights include Eric L. McKitrick, "The Study of Corruption," *Political Science Quarterly,* 72 (December 1957), 502–14; J. Joseph Huthmacher, "Urban Liberalism and the Age of Reform," *Journal of American History,* 49 (September 1962), 31–41; John D. Buenker, *Urban Liberalism and Progressive Reform* (New York: Charles Scribner's Sons, 1973); Arthur Mann, *Yankee Reformers in an Urban Age:*

Social Reform in Boston, 1880–1900 (New York: Harper & Row, 1954); Samuel P. Hays, "The Politics of Reform in Municipal Government in the Progressive Era," *Pacific Northwest Quarterly,* 55 (October 1964), 157–69; Blake McKelvey, *The Rise of Urban America, 1860–1915* (New Brunswick, N.J.: Rutgers University Press, 1963); Bayard Still, *Urban America* (Boston: Little, Brown, 1974); Wayne A. Brownell and Warren E. Stickle, *Bosses and Reformers: Urban Politics in America, 1880–1920* (Boston: Houghton Mifflin, 1973); and Bruce M. Stave, *Urban Bosses, Machines, and Progressive Reformers* (Lexington, Mass.: Heath Publishing Co., 1972).

Contemporary works by reformers themselves provide useful insights into the motivations of the period. Especially enlightening are Joseph Lincoln Steffens, *The Shame of the Cities* (New York: McLure, Phillips, & Son, 1904) and *The Autobiography of Lincoln Steffens* (New York: Harcourt Brace, 1931); Jacob Riis, *How the Other Half Lives* (New York: Charles Scribner's Sons, 1890); Jane Addams, *Twenty Years at Hull House* (New York: Macmillan Co., 1910); and Frederic C. Howe, *Confessions of a Reformer* (New York: Charles Scribner's Sons, 1925).

The most notable from a cross section of specialized studies are Alfred D. Chandler, Jr., "The Beginnings of 'Big Business' in American History," *Business History Review,* 33 (Spring 1959), 1–31; Melvin G. Holli, *Reform in Detroit: Hazen S. Pingree and Urban Politics* (New York: Oxford University Press, 1969); Zane Miller, *Boss Cox's Cincinnati: Urban Politics in the Progressive Era* (New York: Oxford University Press, 1968); Allen F. Davis, *Spearheads for Reform: The Social Settlements and the Progressive Movement, 1890–1914* (New York: Oxford University Press, 1967); Roy Lubove, *The Urban Community: Housing and Planning in the Progressive Era* (Englewood Cliffs, N.J.: Prentice-Hall, 1967); Roy Lubove, *Twentieth Century Pittsburgh: Government, Business and Environmental Change* (New York: Wiley, 1969); James H. Timberlake, *Prohibition and the Progressive Movement, 1900–1920* (Cambridge: Harvard University Press, 1963); Henry F. May, *Protestant Churches and Industrial America* (New York: Harper and Row, 1949); Barbara Rosenkrantz, *Public Health and the State: Changing Views in Massachusetts, 1842–1936* (Cambridge: Harvard University Press, 1972); James H. Cassedy, *Charles V. Chapin and the Public Health Movement* (Cambridge: Harvard University Press, 1962); Marvin Lazerson, *Origins of the Urban School: Public Education in Massachusetts, 1870–1915* (Cambridge: Harvard University Press, 1971); Selwyn K. Troen, "Education in the City" in Raymond A. Mohl and James F. Richardson, eds., *The Urban Experience: Themes in American History* (Belmont, Cal.: Wadsworth Publishing Co., 1973), pp. 127–43; Joseph L. Arnold, "City Planning in America," in Mohl and Richardson, *The Urban Experience,* pp. 14–43; Mel Scott, *American City Planning Since 1890* (Berkeley: University of California Press, 1969); Stanley K. Buder, *Pullman: An Experiment in Industrial Order and Community Planning, 1880–1930* (New York: Oxford University Press, 1967); Roy Lubove, "The Progressive and the Prostitute," *The Historian,* 23 (May 1962), 308–30; Jack Tager, *The Intellectual as Reformer: Brand Whitlock and the Progressive Movement* (Cleveland: Press of Case Western Reserve University, 1968); and Louise C. Wade, *Graham Taylor: Pioneer for Social Justice, 1851–1898* (Chicago: University of Chicago Press, 1964).

7

THE EMERGENCE
OF THE URBAN NATION:
THE TWENTIES

NEW URBAN GROWTH

The 1920 federal census marked a milestone in American history—its figures revealed that a majority of the nation's people (51.4 percent) now lived in cities. Of course, this revelation, like other historical watersheds, can be misleading: Massachusetts and Rhode Island had been predominantly urban long before 1920. Moreover in 1920 a city was defined as a place inhabited by at least twenty-five hundred people—hardly a rigorous criterion. Nevertheless the 1920 tallies were symbolically important. In 1890 the Census Bureau had signaled the end of America's youth by announcing that the frontier no longer existed. Now, thirty years later, the figures confirmed that the nation had evolved into a mature, urban society. The city, not the farm, had become the locus of national experience.

The traditional, agrarian way of life, with its slow pace, moral sobriety, and self-help ethic, had been waning ever since urbanization accelerated early in the nineteenth century. To be sure, by the 1920s the demise was far from complete. Several social reform movements and much political rhetoric looked nostalgically backward to the simple virtues of a fancied past. But everywhere signs pointed to an urban-industrial ascendance. A precipitous drop in commodity prices after 1920 spun small farmers into economic distress. Convinced that there was a better life elsewhere, millions gave up the land during the twenties

179

and poured into Atlanta, Memphis, Detroit, Chicago, Denver, and Los Angeles.

Agrarian depression was only part of a broader development. All forms of primary economic activity—mining and other extractive industries as well as agriculture—were receiving a diminishing share of national wealth while tertiary activities—retail and service establishments —were mushrooming. These latter functions created an ever-larger white-collar, urban middle class that became increasingly influential in local and national affairs. At the same time, some critics added a disdain for the rural society to a general cynicism toward social conventions and business. Edgar Lee Masters' *The Spoon River Anthology* (1915), Sherwood Anderson's *Winesburg, Ohio* (1919), Sinclair Lewis' *Main Street* (1920), and Thomas Wolfe's *Look Homeward Angel* (1929) assaulted the drabness of village and small town life. In popular vernacular the term "hick" became a widely used derogatory adjective, equating something clumsy or stupid with the farm. Much of the contempt for rural life represented a larger revolt against what writers called Puritan moralism—a revolt reflected in the popularization of the writings of Austrian psychoanalyst Sigmund Freud. But the debunking of the sturdy yeoman and small town folkways also underscored a cultural shift that accompanied the city's rise to numerical superiority.

During the 1920s urbanization took place on a wider front than ever before. Maturing industrial economies boosted the populations of many areas, particularly steel, oil, and automobile centers such as Pittsburgh, Cleveland, Detroit, Akron, Youngstown, Birmingham, Houston, Tulsa, and Los Angeles. New commercial and service activities primed expansion in regional centers such as Atlanta, Cincinnati, Indianapolis, Kansas City, Minneapolis, Portland, and Seattle. The most exceptional growth, however, occurred in resort cities. Between 1920 and 1930 the population of Miami ballooned from 29,571 to 110,637. As the prime beneficiary of the Florida real estate explosion of the twenties, Miami attracted thousands of land speculators and home builders. A citrus crop failure and two disastrous hurricanes punctured the boom in 1927, but the expansion of warm-climate cities continued—Tampa and San Diego doubled their populations during the twenties.

A new spurt in construction, the biggest since the 1880s, accompanied the urban expansion. Wartime restrictions and high prices for materials had virtually halted construction of new residences between 1917 and 1918. After the war many cities faced acute housing shortages, for workers who had arrived to man the war industries and for returning servicemen looking for employment. By 1919, however, construction costs began to drop while rents and sale values on existing buildings continued to rise. This situation triggered a frenzy of construction that lasted for seven years. New houses and buildings in fast-growing cities could be sold for substantial gains; and many buyers and renters, profiting from the general prosperity of the age and from new forms of credit, could afford the inflation. In the decade after World War I builders erected one hundred thousand bungalows in Chicago and its environs, thousands of two- and three-story apartment houses in outlying neighborhoods, and a string of taller, luxury apartments along the city's north and south lakefronts.

Although the supply of quality housing for low-income residents remained generally inadequate, the notion that government needed to do more to relieve housing problems began to win limited acceptance. Rising rents and prices pushed new housing beyond the reach of most working-class families. Home ownership in the inner cities declined while slum congestion increased. To relieve the housing shortage that occurred during World War I, two federal agencies, the Emergency Fleet Corporation of the U.S. Shipping Board and the Housing Corporation of the U.S. Department of Labor, had built and operated housing units for war workers—the first direct federal program to provide housing. Congress abolished these programs after the war, and although reformers like Clarence Stein, a young architect and former settlement house worker, and Henry Wright, a fellow architect, continued to advocate housing subsidies and government construction, the concept of public housing generated little support. Nevertheless officials in several cities encouraged private, nonprofit groups who sponsored housing construction for workingmen. A 1919 Wisconsin law permitted Milwaukee and other cities to help finance limited dividend cooperative housing companies (that is, companies that would limit profits in order to hold down prices). A few years later New York City received authorization to grant tax exemptions to limited dividend housing projects—although the legislature stifled efforts by Stein and Governor Alfred E. Smith to amend the state constitution to enable creation of a state housing authority that could acquire land and construct public housing.

As in the past most new construction occurred at the edges of cities. As the automobile made outer areas more accessible, speculators started another epidemic of town building, a mania that had spurred urban growth for two and a half centuries. Between 1920 and 1930 suburbs around Los Angeles, Milwaukee, Atlanta, Cleveland, Detroit, and Buffalo doubled and redoubled their populations. Among the most rapidly growing suburbs were Elmwood Park, Berwyn, and Wilmette near Chicago; Beverly Hills and Inglewood near Los Angeles; Grosse Point and Ferndale near Detroit; and Cleveland Heights and Shaker Heights near Cleveland. Charles N. Glaab and A. Theodore Brown have noted that of thirty-eight towns incorporated in Illinois in the 1920s, twenty-six were in the regions of Chicago or St. Louis; of thirty-three incorporations in Michigan, twenty-two were on the outskirts of Detroit; and of fifty-five in Ohio, twenty-nine were Cleveland suburbs. The majority of these were residential communities for the middle class and above; a large number, however, were industrial suburbs, places like East Chicago and Passaic where industries had moved to take advantage of cheaper land and taxes and where factory wage earners comprised a fifth or more of the population.

Occasionally, as in the past, investors overextended themselves; and when the boom broke, they were left with too much vacant land and too many debts. The crash of 1929 transformed Burbank, California, and Skokie, Illinois, into temporary ghost towns, cruel reminders of over-zealous optimism. Usually, however, the middle- and upper middle-class families who populated most new suburbs provided a solid financial base and assured future existence.

The proliferation of urbanization around the fringes of big cities created new attitudes of political independence. Throughout the nine-teenth century suburban areas had eagerly sought to unite with the city nearby in order to receive municipal services such as water, gas, and fire protection. By the turn of the century, however, many people who were fleeing to the suburbs began to balk at paying high city tax rates, espe-cially when they believed their tax money was supporting a corrupt po-litical machine. Thus, although they still needed some of the municipal services, many suburbanites tried to preserve political independence for their communities. In 1910 Oak Park, Illinois residents rejected amalga-mation with Chicago. Thereafter it became increasingly difficult for big cities to annex nearby towns. As one suburban editor reasoned, "Under local government we can absolutely control every objectionable thing that may try to enter our limits—but once annexed we are at the mercy of city hall."

Yet suburbs remained economically dependent upon cities. More than ever before, suburban commuters rode automobiles, trolleys, or the elec-tric interurban railroad to work in the city. And, more than ever before, adjacent towns were satellites of large urban centers connected by ever-expanding transportation and commercial networks.

These networks formed metropolitan districts—regions that included a city and its suburbs. The concept of metropolitanism had been recog-nized as early as 1854, when by an act of the state, the City of Phila-delphia absorbed all Philadelphia County. In 1910 the Census Bureau gave the concept official recognition by identifying twenty-five areas with central city populations of over two hundred thousand as metro-politan districts, and another nineteen with over one hundred thousand in the central city as emerging metropolises. By 1920 the total of metropolitan and near-metropolitan districts had grown to fifty-eight, and together they contained two-thirds of the nations' urban population. By 1930 there were ninety-three cities with populations over one hundred thousand. The rise of urban America had climaxed; the genesis of metropolitan America was underway.

While new towns sprouted around the edges of cities, a new type of building began to dominate the central districts. The decade of the twenties was the age of the skyscraper. Between 1920 and 1926 the value of land in a city with a population above thirty thousand increased to twenty times its original value. Suburban expansion accounted for much of this increase, but also rising rents for offices and stores in central business districts contributed a considerable proportion. Yet the demand for prime locations outran the inflation of rents. This demand, coupled with falling construction costs after 1921 and with technological advances in electrical and structural engineering, prompted builders to erect ever-taller structures. Cities across the country revoked height restrictions, enabling new buildings to protrude above earlier skylines. By 1929 editors of the *American City* could count 377 buildings at least twenty stories tall. Although New York claimed nearly half of them, Syracuse, Memphis, and Tulsa also boasted of their own. These buildings quickly became objects of urban boosterism. Just as lavish hotels and railroad stations had symbolized the prosperity and refinement of nineteenth-century cities, skyscrapers represented progress in twentieth-century cities. Cleveland's fifty-two story Terminal Tower, Chicago's thirty-six story Tribune Tower, and New York's eighty-six story Empire State Building galvanized civic pride and presented a bold image to outsiders.

As business districts expanded horizontally and vertically, the surrounding residential cores began to experience a change of ethnic and racial composition. World War I shut off the flow of foreign immigration that had streamed into cities in earlier years. After the war, a feverish urge for national unity merged with latent prejudices and fears to fuel sentiment for restricting immigration. Support for an end to free immigration had been building since the 1880s among urban reformers as well as unions and nativist conservatives. By 1919 humanitarians who had formerly opposed restriction were willing to admit that the melting pot had not worked and that many immigrants—particularly those from southern and eastern Europe—stubbornly resisted assimilation. Labor leaders, fearful that a new flood of unskilled aliens would depress wages, looked at the high postwar unemployment rates and increased their longstanding support for restriction. At first businessmen opposed the rising clamor out of self-interest; they hoped that a new surge of foreign workers would not only aid industrial expansion but also cut wage rates

The Age of the Skyscraper

A workman sits on the end of a beam and bolts together the framework of the Empire State Building. Completed in 1930, this skyscraper operated with huge financial losses during the first six years of the Depression. *Photograph by Lewis Hine. Work Project Administration, The National Archives.*

and curb unionization. But by 1924 when Congress was debating whether to close the doors more tightly, many industrialists were willing to support restriction because they discovered that mechanization and native migration from farm to city enabled them to prosper without foreign-born labor.

Congressional acts of 1921, 1924, and 1929 successively reduced the numbers of immigrants who could be admitted annually. A system of quotas, ultimately based on the number of descendants from each nationality living in the United States in 1890 severely limited immigrants from southern and eastern Europe, the very groups who had clogged urban cores since 1880. The laws left the doors open only to Western Hemisphere countries. Mexicans now became the largest foreign group entering the country. Many came to work in the fields and vineyards of the Southwest, but others streamed into the region's booming cities. By 1930 Mexicans comprised sizeable segments of the populations of El Paso, Los Angeles, San Antonio, and Tucson. Like the Europeans who preceded them, these "new-new" immigrants were poor and unskilled, and they sought jobs and housing in inner-city districts.

The bulk of new inner-city residents, however, consisted of white and black native Americans, pushed off the farms by hard times and lured to the cities by hope for a more certain existence. During the 1920s rural population in the United States declined by almost a million. In the Midwest scores of thousands of farm families and, particularly, young, single people sought their fortunes in nearby regional centers or headed toward the cities of southern California. (The refrain to a popular song might well have been revised to read, "How ya gonna keep 'em down on the farm after they've seen Des Moines?") Larger movements occurred in and out from the South. Many whites moved northward to work in the automobile plants around Detroit, in the steel mills of Pittsburgh, and in various industries in New York, Chicago, and Cincinnati. Many more whites pushed into nearby cities in the south. After lagging behind the rest of the nation for nearly a century, the South now became the most rapidly urbanizing section in terms of proportionate population growth. Memphis, Atlanta, Birmingham, and Chattanooga experienced extraordinary expansion. Smaller cities, many of them created by textile companies who had left New England to take advantage of cheap southern labor, also helped boost the urban population of the South to thirteen million by 1930.

The most visible contingents of native migrants from World War I onward were the millions of blacks who moved into northern and southern cities. Pushed off their tenant farms by failures in the cotton fields and lured by jobs in labor-scarce cities, hundreds of thousands of black families packed up and boarded the trains for Memphis, New Orleans, Chicago, Detroit, Cleveland, and New York. When the war cut off the influx of cheap foreign labor, some companies began to hire blacks, sending recruiters south to promise instant wealth to potential migrants in much the same way that railroads and industries had recruited laborers in Europe a generation or two earlier. By 1920 four-fifths of the country's blacks residing outside the South lived in cities. During World War I Chicago's black population increased by fifty thousand, almost doubling in two years—in 1920 only one of every seven blacks in Chicago had been born in Illinois.

Like other migrants who preceded them, blacks squeezed into low-rent districts of the inner city. In many places blacks had earlier resided in unofficially delimited districts, embryonic ghettos recognized and accepted by both races. New York's Harlem, on the other hand, was formerly a middle-class district transformed after 1900 into a slum by property owners, including black realtor Philip Payton, Jr., who tried to profit from demand by packing three or four black families into quarters originally designed for just one. In some places, notably where blacks comprised only a minute fraction of the total population, they lived scattered among several neighborhoods. After the war, however, huge numbers of newcomers overflowed old districts and pressed against white neighborhoods. Racial prejudice and fear sizzled along the edges of expanding ghettos where whites either fled or desperately tried to protect homes and neighborhoods acquired after long struggles to escape the slums.

Hostility exploded in 1919. That year, housing shortages, strikes, fears of radicalism, inflation, and unemployment fanned racial hatreds and ignited riots in twenty-six cities. Although the majority of incidents were in the South, a new wave of violence struck cities of the North. The worst riot occurred in Chicago where both races terrorized each other for nearly a month. When the violence finally ceased, thirty-eight people had been killed (twenty-three blacks and fifteen whites), 520 were injured (342 black and 178 white), and 1,000 black families were left homeless by arsonists and vandals. Over the "red summer" of 1919 race riots also erupted in Omaha, Knoxville, Charleston, and Washington, D.C. Racial antagonisms did not account for all mob violence that year; on May Day antisocialist riots broke out in Boston, New York, and Chicago. But the race riots overshadowed the others. Blacks were emerging as an urban group to be reckoned with.

The Chicago experience suggests that urbanization for blacks had catalyzed self-respect and racial cohesiveness that sparked impulses toward self-protection. Black poet Claude McKay expressed this resoluteness when he wrote

> If we must die, O let us nobly die,
> So that our precious blood may not be shed
> In vain; then even the monsters we defy
> Shall be constrained to honor us though dead.

As migrations continued during the 1920s, new militancy plus increasing numbers of blacks in cities, particularly in large cities, may well have diffused open white hostilities, for the epidemic of riots did not return. By the end of the decade, New York's black population had increased from 152,000 to 328,000; Chicago's from 109,000 to 234,000; Philadelphia's from 134,000 to 220,000; Detroit's from 41,000 to 120,000; and Cleveland's from 34,000 to 72,000. Blacks now comprised between 5 and 10 percent of the populations of each of these places.

Meanwhile the ghetto matured as a cultural, as well as physical, embodiment of black urban experience. Like other migrant groups, Afro-Americans grappled with the problems of self-identification in pluralistic urban society. But more so than for other newcomers, group consciousness had been forced upon blacks. Jim Crow (segregation) laws, slanderous stereotypes, and white racist violence constantly reminded blacks of their inferior status. The ghettos, physically isolated and racially uniform, reinforced black segregation and inequality.

Since its founding in 1910, the National Association for the Advancement of Colored People (NAACP) had been working to achieve political equality and educational opportunities which would break the bonds of prejudice and injustice by creating an integrated society. By the 1920s, however, many blacks had become skeptical of integration and were searching for a way to translate their imposed separation into racial pride and cultural expression. Part of this search was aided (and in some ways deflated) by white patronage. As jazz music, uniquely a black creation, spread from New Orleans northward to Memphis, St. Louis, Kansas City, Chicago, and New York, it drew middle-class whites into black night clubs to hear the unrestrained rhythms of the Mississippi Delta. Intellectuals now accepted jazz as a legitimate form of American music, although it only became "respectable" when white musicians like Bix Beiderbecke and Paul Whiteman began to copy jazz styles. African art and artifacts also became fashionable among urban middle-class circles of both races in the twenties.

Yet for blacks themselves, the quest for cultural roots went beyond aspects of entertainment and fashion. In Harlem, a "Negro Mecca" in the twenties, a literary renaissance developed as Langston Hughes, Countee Cullen, Claude McKay, and James Weldon Johnson struggled with the dilemma of whether they were spokesmen for an oppressed race or for universal art. Harlem also bred the Universal Negro Improvement Association, a militant black nationalist movement. Led by Marcus Garvey, a fiery, flamboyant Jamaican, the U.N.I.A. attracted over a million followers in Chicago, Detroit, and other cities as well as New York. Most members were lower-class blacks inspired by the promise that removal from white society would uplift them from hopelessness. Garveyism declined by the mid-twenties, but not until it had raised new feelings of militancy born out of poverty and discrimination in the cities. For some whites, the ghetto had become a place of fascination and entertainment. For most blacks it remained a breeding ground for frustration and discontent.

THE AUTOMOBILE AGE

The end of World War I marked the emergence of the United States as a mature industrial power. Changes in business organization and in technology multiplied industrial output while enabling tremendous savings in the costs of production. As corporate profits soared, investors looked for new areas of expansion by investing abroad and by creating new markets and new products at home. The maturing national economy created thousands of new white-collar jobs in business and government bureaucracies and in booming service activities. Rising productivity and technological innovation gave wage earners more leisure time. In 1920 the six-day, sixty-hour work week had been common. By 1929 most people worked only five and a half days and forty-eight to fifty-four hours. Although corporate profits and investment returns rose much faster than industrial wages, the prospering economy nevertheless gave a large number of Americans time and money for movies, sports, radios, and phonographs.

As in previous eras cities stood in the center of economic change. Urban populations, now comprising a majority, more than ever provided workers and consumers for expanding industry and related services. Following population patterns the urban economy now became a metropolitan economy, a system of interdependence between an urban nucleus and its contiguous regions. Industry began to decentralize. Mechanization and assembly line production reduced the number of workers needed to manufacture an item but also increased the desirability for deploying production on one floor rather than in multistory lofts, common in the nineteenth century. Thus, beginning before 1900 but accelerating in the 1920s, some factories moved from urban cores to suburbs where large tracts of land were cheaper. At the same time, a separation of production from management was underway. A number of firms retained or acquired offices in central business districts while building factories farther away in suburbs or even in other cities. Transportation between offices and factories via streetcars or highways and communications over the telephone made this separation possible.

Retailing also followed a pattern of centrifugal dispersion, particularly in the larger cities. Outlying secondary business centers around major intersections and streetcar transfer points grew rapidly during the twenties. Neighborhood banks, movie theaters, office buildings, branches of major department stores, and chain stores such as Woolworths, Kresge's, A&P, and Walgreen's, brought the amenities of downtown to the periphery and suburbs. In Chicago, corners at Lincoln and Belmont Avenues, Lawrence and Halsted, Sixty-third and Halsted, and West Madison and Crawford Streets became bustling business centers where land values reached ten thousand dollars per front foot by 1928.

The twenties witnessed the birth of the country's suburban shopping centers. In 1922 Jesse C. Nichols, a Kansan well-versed in land economics, built the Country Club Plaza Shopping Center as the commercial hub of his huge real estate development in Kansas City. A few years later, Sears Roebuck and Company began to build stores in outlying districts to reap sales from growing suburban populations. The major proliferation of shopping centers occurred after World War II, but decentralization was well underway in the 1920s. Doctors, saloonkeepers, restauranteurs, and independent merchants followed clients and customers into expanding residential areas until business districts speckled every quadrant of a city's map. Downtown was still the focus of activity, but in many places its eclipse was imminent.

The proliferation of commercial and service establishments in the cities reflected the rise of a mass consumer economy on a national level. American industrialists during the twenties utilized mass production techniques to market commodities that practically any family could afford. Aided by advertising and by new forms of consumer credit, producers and promoters created a democratized materialism. A dizzying array of comforts and luxuries now dangled within reach of most consumers—washing machines, vacuum cleaners, refrigerators, radios, canned goods, lamps, cigarettes, and automobiles. Installment buying ("a dollar down and a dollar forever") made acquisition possible. And advertising— an expanding professional service—made acquisition desirable by celebrating consumerism in the popular media—newspapers, pulp magazines, radio, billboards, and motion pictures. "You have to *create* a demand for a product," lectured one advertising man. "Make the public want what you have to sell. Make 'em pant for it."

Most advertising campaigns were directed at urban consumers, particularly at the expanding middle class, because these were the people who had money to buy new products—or at least to make a down payment. Between 1920 and 1929 farmers' share of the national income dropped from 16 to 9 percent while industrial and service incomes, most of which went to urban households, mushroomed. Moreover the proportion of urban dwellings wired for electricity rose from 10 percent in 1920 to over 50 percent in 1930, while even at the later date very few farmhouses had electricity. Thus most household appliances, vanguards of the new materialism, could be sold mainly to urban families.

Women of the urban middle classes became the particular objects of the new consumerism. Many new products were designed for use in the home, changing women's functions but not their stations. Refrigerators, toasters, washing machines, canned goods, nylon stockings, and ready-made clothing transformed wives and mothers from domestic producers into domestic consumers. But even as chief consumers, women were economically dependent on men. The nineteenth-century perception of women as moral protectresses and guardians of the home proved quite adaptable to the twentieth-century economy of mass consumption.

Opportunities for women to work outside the home accompanied changes on the urban scene. Between 1900 and 1930 a host of new clerical and sales jobs were created by expanding bureaucratic and service functions, most of which were located in the cities. By 1930, according to William Chafe, "almost 2 million women were employed as secretaries, typists, and file clerks, and another 700,000 worked as salesgirls in department stores." Yet, as before, most women held jobs in the cities only as temporary expedients while they awaited marriage, or as supplements to family incomes. Domestic service, clothing production, and canning factories employed over half of all working women, and wages remained far below those paid to men. The flapper may have symbolized moral independence for a small number of urban middle-class women, but the more common type was the working girl, unglamorous and economically dependent upon a male income.

Another type of consumption basically supported by urban dwellers was the expanding range of leisure activities. A mania for sports, movies, radio, and fads gripped every city in the nation. In 1923, 300,000 fans attended the six-game World Series of baseball between the New York Yankees and the New York Giants. In 1926 the attendance of 130,000 at the first Jack Dempsey-Gene Tunney heavyweight championship prize fight in Philadelphia broke all records. But the return bout the next year shattered the newly set marks: 145,000 spectators jammed Soldier Field in Chicago, paying $2,650,000 to see the contest—even though many seats were so far from the ring that thousands were unable to see Tunney win.

Spectator sports were only half the attraction. Each week millions of enthusiasts filled tennis courts, golf links, and beaches. During banner years between 1927 and 1929, weekly movie attendance reached an estimated 110 million people (a number almost equal to the nation's total population). Many moviegoers were country folk who streamed into the Bijou on Main Street in a thousand towns and villages. But many more were urban dwellers who stood in line for one of the six thousand seats in Roxy's in New York or to sit in the luxury of one of the Balaban and Katz movie palaces in Chicago. In 1922 three million homes had radios; in 1930, twelve million. By the latter date radio production had become a billion dollar industry. Stations sprouted in hundreds of cities and became sources of community pride. To prevent chaotic expansion the federal government in 1927 created the Federal Radio Commission, which distributed broadcasting licenses and frequencies among 412 cities. A dizzying succession of games and other fancies passed through the cities. During 1922 and 1923 the Chinese game of mah jong was the rage. A new fad, the crossword puzzle, rose in 1924. Newspapers boosted sales by printing daily puzzles, and crossword puzzle books broke into the best seller lists. At the end of the decade fun seekers were adopting miniature golf. By 1930, thirty thousand courses had filled empty lots in scores of towns and cities.

New Leisure Time for Urban Dwellers
Crowds of bathers jam a Lake Michigan beach in Chicago, ca. 1925. *U.S. Office of War Information, The National Archives.*

But all the new products, services, and entertainments paled when placed beside the automobile—the economic and social wonder of the age. Invented in Europe, the gas-powered horseless carriage was a curiosity on American streets through the early 1900s. Then, in 1908 Henry Ford introduced the Model T, an inexpensive, durable motor car, built by an assembly line of machines and workers. This manufacturing process, according to Ford, applied "the principles of power, accuracy, economy, system, continuity, speed, and repetition." By atomizing production into a smoothly flowing stream of simple, repetitive tasks, Ford was able to fashion more cars for cheaper costs, while raising the wages of his workers. He had democratized the automobile.

Between 1920 and 1930 automobile registrations in this country nearly tripled, from eight to twenty-three million. The effects on the economy were extraordinary. By the mid-twenties the automobile industry used 20 percent of the nation's steel output, 80 percent of the rubber, and 75 percent of the plate glass. It revamped the petroleum industry from one of illumination and lubrication to one of propulsion. It created a vast new service network of filling stations, repair shops, and parts and accessories dealers. Unlike their European counterparts who viewed the automobile as an item of luxury, American manufacturers, such as Ransom E. Olds and Henry Ford, intended their product for a mass market. Like other new products, the automobile's demand had to be created: the

The Palatial Urban Movie House

First-nighters crowd the sidewalk in front of the opulent Warners' Theatre in New York, August 6, 1926, for the opening of "Don Juan" starring John Barrymore. Note the lavish use of electricity—for lighting as well as for air conditioning. *U.S. Office of War Information, The National Archives.*

horseless carriage became a major subject of advertising and financing operations. The passenger car was becoming the vehicle of the common man. By the end of the decade there was one registered motor vehicle for every five Americans. (During the mid-twenties a Ford Model T sold for under three hundred dollars; a Chevrolet Coupe sold for seven hundred dollars.) A 1933 report on changes in contemporary American life said of the automobile, "It is probable that no invention of such far reaching importance was ever diffused with such rapidity or so quickly exerted influences that ramified through national culture, transforming even habits of thought and language. . . ."

The automobile also transformed cities. It revised patterns of settlement by enabling homebuilders to fill in vacant land between streetcar routes. It catalyzed much of the suburban expansion, encouraging speculators to plot new subdivisions in districts neglected in previous eras. In the mid-twenties over eight hundred thousand houses were built a year, most of them on the urban fringe. Urban sprawl had burst the restraints of accessibility to mass transit. Automobiles brought the country and the city closer to each other. On weekends thousands of cars permeated the countryside, carrying picnicking and sightseeing families. Long-distance travel became more convenient as service stations, restaurants, and hotels sprouted along new highways. Cars further broke down rural isolation, giving farm families ready access to urban stores and services. It is sometimes believed that automobiles encouraged Americans to move from one place to another more frequently than ever before. This belief is inaccurate because Americans had been a people on the move long before the horseless carriage appeared. Nevertheless the motor car quickened travel speed, extended distances that could be traversed easily, and blurred distinctions between city and country.

Automobiles forced changes in habits of urban life. By giving new meaning to the riding habit, they undercut the popularity of mass transit. Streetcars, once the marvels of progress, now seemed uncomfortable and unaccommodating when compared to the freedom and luxury of motor cars. Automobiles did not cause congestion; vehicular and human traffic had clogged city streets since colonial times, and autos merely confounded the problem. But the car's speed and threat to life and limb prompted new regulations. Cities passed speed limits and established other measures of traffic control. In 1924 the General Electric Company began to produce timed electric traffic lights, and almost immediately several cities installed the devices on busy corners. Many cities also began to prohibit parking and standing along well-traveled thoroughfares.

The automobile also influenced social attitudes. Contemporaries believed the '20s to be an age of revolt, when youths snubbed traditional manners and morals. Moral critics believed motor cars were contributing to this revolt, especially in the cities. In 1919 one in ten cars had closed tops; by 1927 five of every six were covered, giving the inside of autos new secrecy. Although alarmists probably exaggerated the extent of misdeed by youths who parked in darkened lanes away from adult eyes, the car provided a new source for parental anxiety. More importantly, for many families the automobile symbolized social freedom and self-respect. Historian John B. Rae has noted that in 1906 Woodrow Wilson expressed fear that possession of a motor car would bring on socialism because it would provoke envy of the rich. Instead, says Rae, it incited the common man to "desire to own an automobile, not to change the social system." In urban-industrial America the car, inexpensive and available, became a badge of equality, the ultimate expression of mobility. As one writer suggested in 1924, "It is hard to convince Steve Popovich, or Antonio Branca, or plain John Smith that he is being ground into the dust by Capital when at will he may drive the same highways, view the same scenery and get as much enjoyment from his trip as the modern Midas." Yet while an auto symbolized family pride, it also reflected financial priorities. As a social and economic necessity, it forced many families to endure sacrifice and financial worry.

The mushrooming growth of automobile travel would not have been possible without a burst of highway and road construction. Many cities poured heavy sums into street construction and maintenance. Planners in Detroit proposed to widen and extend several of the city's main streets. The project, accepted instead of a subway system, created several multi-lane arteries and boosted suburban growth in the Detroit area. But most road building schemes only encouraged heavier reliance on automobile transportation, which in turn overloaded streets and throughways as soon as they were built.

Increasing long-distance travel made highways a state and national concern. Although cities were unable to secure much direct assistance from state capitols or from Washington in meeting local traffic needs during the twenties, urban interests were successful in influencing the evolution of national highway policy. As early as the first years of the twentieth century, urban merchants and industrialists had supported the Good Roads Movement because they believed that more and better highways would aid business. But among the most influential advocates of federal assistance were agrarian interests, such as the National Grange Association, which wanted to improve transportation between farm and market. The first attempt to initiate federal aid to highway construction reflected this rural base. In 1902 Congress considered, but did not pass, a bill that would have created a Bureau of Public Roads within the Department of Agriculture and would have provided $20 million in matching funds to states wishing to construct rural roads. The bill prohibited cities from receiving any appropriations.

It was not long, however, before metropolitan interests helped to swing federal highway policy to an urban axis. By 1915 increasing truck traffic gave urban businessmen stronger arguments for the construction of arteries to aid freight transportation between cities rather than to help farmers bring their crops to market. The Federal Roads Aid Act of 1916, the first legislation to create federal responsibility for highway improvement, revealed an ambivalence between support for arterial commerce between cities and aid for farm-to-market routes. The act authorized the Secretary of Agriculture to make matching grants to state highway departments (thereby forcing states to create their own highway departments) for the improvement of post roads. World War I intervened before most projects could begin. But the war demonstrated the nation's need for trunk highways, especially after the railroads became overburdened and the Council for National Defense was forced to use trucks to relieve rail congestion. As a result, Congress passed the Federal Highway Act of 1921, providing federal aid to primary state roads that would contribute to a connected system of interstate highways. More importantly, the act also created the Bureau of Public Roads, which by 1923 was planning a national highway system to connect all cities of fifty thousand or more inhabitants. Although it was not until the 1930s that federal funds were designated for road construction within cities, the new highway system reflected the emerging dominance of metropolitan interests in national affairs.

The road, the car, the new goods and services, and the construction boom infused cities with an expansionist spirit during the 1920s. But by mid-decade dark clouds were gathering. Speculation in securities was draining private capital from mortgage markets and pushing the costs of home ownership beyond the reach of many families. Housing construction ebbed in the inner cities and the outskirts. As prices for land and buildings soared, real estate operators used inflated paper profits as security on loans obtained for stock market speculation. Moreover advertising and consumer credit had created huge new demands for products, but demands themselves could not raise buying power. To be sure, the new prosperity had lifted the wages and living standards of urban workers, but a rising proportion of private incomes was spent on interest payments for installment purchases, instead of on goods and services. The economy of the urban nation was teetering on a weakening base—a base that crumbled in 1929.

SOCIAL FUNDAMENTALISM

The era between World War I and the Great Depression has often been characterized by its Fords, flappers, and fancies. But it also was a period of fanatics and fundamentalists. Many of the dominant social issues were provoked by reactionaries—moralists and bigots who battled desperately to restore a lost past. The triumph of national prohibition and the rebirth of the Ku Klux Klan seemed to be last gasps of fading rural resistance to urban civilization. Yet cities were not mere passive objects of crusades for moral and racial purity. They contributed to the initial successes of these campaigns and to their ultimate failure.

In 1917 Congress capped a long drive for prohibition by proposing the Eighteenth Amendment to the Constitution. The measure prohibited the manufacture, sale, and importation of intoxicating liquors. One year later a sufficient number of states had ratified, and at the end of 1919 Congress passed the Volstead Act, which enforced the amendment. Although rural groups, particularly small-town Methodists and Baptists, had been in the vanguard of the dry crusade, a number of urban interests were also attached to the Great Cause. Middle-class Protestants in the cities (with the exception of Episcopalians and Lutherans), mostly residents of peripheral and suburban districts, supported prohibition as a reform instrument. They linked liquor with poverty, vice, and corruption. And they believed that enforced abstinence would improve worker efficiency, fortify family life, and blunt the power of political machines.

It is probable that national prohibition would not have passed without support from urban groups. On the other hand, urban dwellers were also instrumental in crippling the crusade. Prohibition simply could not prohibit. Large numbers of people refused to renounce the bottle. Although enforcement of the law worked well at first, smuggling and illegal distilling were increasing rapidly by the mid-twenties. The Volstead Act forged new contacts between local police and federal agents in the attack against bootlegging. But it was impossible to dry up the cities. Not only were local efforts less than energetic; federal enforcement was sporadic, undermanned, and inept.

The results are well known. Speak-easies blossomed in cities across the country, and crime became a big business. Yet organized crime was certainly not unique to cities in the 1920s. Gangs of thieves, pickpockets, and extortionists had plagued American cities since the eighteenth century. Long before prohibition, gangsters and vice operators supervised elaborate and profitable crime syndicates that found ready customers for gambling, prostitution, and stolen goods among all classes of society. Among the most notorious of the nineteenth century were Rufus Minor, described by police as "one of the smartest bank sneaks in America," who directed a string of robberies which stretched from Boston to Cleveland to Augusta; Walter Sheridan, whose forgery ring bilked banks and stockbrokers in New York, Philadelphia, and Washington; the nationally known pickpocketing team of Christene "Kid Glove Rosey" Mayer and "Black Lena" Kleinschmidt; and Terrence "Poodle" Murphy, leader of New York's largest petty larceny gang.

By the early twentieth century these operations had adopted business techniques that utilized payrolls, modern communications, and coordinated management. But the public desire to evade prohibition gave organized crime new opportunities and dimensions in the twenties. As Mark Haller has remarked regarding Chicago, "Because bootlegging provided such resources in money and organization, an unprecedented consolidation and centralization or organized crime occurred." Like other twentieth century businesses, crime had been rationalized. In New York, Chicago, Detroit, Cleveland, Kansas City, Buffalo, and other cities, big time criminals expanded from illegal activities into labor racketeering and into control of small businesses, such as barbershops and dry cleaners.

The most notorious feature of organized crime in the 1920s was the use of violent extortion and wholesale murder to win customers and eliminate competition. Merchants who refused to accept gang-controlled business, such as slot machines or bootleg beer, or who refused to pay protection money, were beaten and their property was destroyed. Between 1925 and 1928 over four hundred gang-related bombings of business establishments occurred in Chicago alone. Rivals who contested a gang leader's will were assassinated, and their bodies, with feet encased in cement slippers, were dumped into nearby rivers and harbors. In Chicago a dispute over the bulk of illegal liquor traffic burst into a violent war when henchmen of crime boss Johnny Torrio murdered arch rival Dion O'Banion in O'Banion's florist shop in 1924. Torrio and his lieutenant, Al Capone, were considerate enough to send a basket of flowers to O'Banion's lavish funeral, but the gesture failed to console the florist's gang, now led by Hymie Weiss. The gang went on a bullet-filled rampage, driving Torrio into retirement, and Capone assumed full control of Torrio's legions. Combat raged for more than four years, climaxing on St. Valentine's Day, 1929, when Capone's agents, posing as policemen, trapped seven members of the O'Banion gang in a North Side garage and executed them with submachine guns. By this time Capone ruled the Chicago suburb of Cicero and had spread his influence from bootlegging into a huge network of rackets that included ninety-one trade unions. He was earning over $100 million a year, and his flamboyant habits made him as famous as Charles Lindbergh and Babe Ruth. He was not yet thirty-two years old.

During the twenties Chicago, New York, Kansas City, and Detroit witnessed hundreds of gangland killings, almost all of which went unsolved. These were only the most grisly features of what had become a big business. Other factors besides prohibition contributed to the rise of big-time crime. Trucks and automobiles gave criminals and illegal commerce new mobility. Submachine guns and other weapons inherited from World War I made crime more threatening. And the times themselves had given birth to an indiscriminate worship of swagger. But also, crime itself—long a fact of life for inner-city residents—had come to serve important functions. Crime provided a ladder of social mobility, a means of "making it" for immigrants and other downtrodden groups forced to live on the margins of society. Some social analysts believed that the criminal underworld was professionalized by Italian and Sicilian immigrants who transferred such outlaw institutions as the Black Hand and Mafia to America. Yet Italians did not monopolize the underworld. A 1930 report of 108 crime leaders in Chicago revealed that 32 were Italian, 31 Irish, 22 Jewish, and 13 black. Barred from many legitimate paths to success, some immigrants and blacks found profits in illicit activity. Crime, like politics, furnished opportunities to inner-city youths whose ambitions might otherwise have been blocked.

The important point, however, is that in the early decades of the twentieth century, those with blocked ambitions did not invent organized crime as a way out of poverty. The distribution and sale of illegal goods and services has had a long history in urban America because there has always been a wide gap between the moral ideals that legislators have embodied in statutes and the extent of legal enforcement that the citizenry will accept. By the 1920s prohibition and the cultural diversity created by immigration widened this gap and tangled respect for the law with the ideology of personal liberty more than ever before. By supplying liquor, gambling facilities, and prostitutes, organized crime served real needs of a consuming public. Thus Al Capone, who amassed a huge fortune by ignoring the law, saw himself as an ordinary businessman. "Prohibition is a business," he once remarked. "All I do is to supply a public demand. I do it in the best and least harmful way I can."

By 1933 Capone was in jail, and prohibition was repealed. The return of legal liquor swept away most of the bootlegging but left behind more sinister underworld activities that had accompanied the growth of organized crime in the twenties—extortion, racketeering, narcotics (activities in which gangsters created demand far more than they served existing needs). These areas gave the underworld its future.

Another major issue of the decade was the reemergence of the Ku Klux Klan. Revived in 1915 by a Georgian, William J. Simmons, the Klan grew very slowly until 1920 when Simmons hired two public relations experts, Edward Clarke and Elizabeth Tyler, to recruit members. By sending agents into Masonic Lodges and other organizations, Clarke and Tyler were able to build membership to a figure between two and four million by 1924. For a time the Klan wielded frightening power in Arkansas, California, Indiana, Ohio, Oklahoma, Oregon, and Texas. Although, like its ancestor in the 1860s and '70s the new Klan avowed "to maintain forever white supremacy," its constitution also pledged Klansmen "to conserve, protect, and maintain the distinctive institutions, rights, privileges, principles, traditions, and ideals of a pure Americanism." Feeding on the fears and hatreds spawned by post-World War I disillusion and reaction, the Klan added antiimmigrant, anti-Catholic, and anti-Jewish venom to its racist poison. From 1921 onward Klansmen paraded, harangued, and assaulted in the name of Protestant morality and Anglo-Saxon purity.

Although the Klan flourished in rural districts and small towns of the West and South—areas where people feared and distrusted the city— it also enjoyed considerable success in metropolitan areas. Kenneth T.

Jackson has estimated that half the Klan's membership lived in cities of over fifty thousand people. Detroit, Atlanta, Indianapolis, Memphis, Philadelphia, Portland, and Denver had sizeable contingents. Chicago, with an estimated fifty thousand Klansmen, contained the largest single operation in the country. In many cities the urban Klan thrived in the Zone of Emergence—the belt of modest neighborhoods that separated the inner core from the periphery. Here, working-class and lower middle-class white Protestants, one step removed from the slums, grew increasingly apprehensive over nearby inner districts that were bulging with black and foreign migrants. As blacks, Catholics, and Jews began to spill into Zone neighborhoods and to press upon housing markets, many white families, still on the lower rungs of the socioeconomic ladder, grasped for some means of soothing their anxieties and reinforcing their identification with "100 percent Americanism." The Ku Klux Klan, with its ceremony, secrecy, and emotionalism, served this need.

In the rural countryside the Klans' activities included parades, cross burnings, and lynchings. In the cities Klansmen often turned to politics rather than using violence and display to achieve their goals. Usually operating within one of the two major parties rather than independently, the KKK was partially successful in influencing local elections: it helped to elect a Republican mayor of Indianapolis, and Democratic mayors in Denver and Atlanta. But after 1924, racked by scandals and dissidence, the "Invisible Empire" swiftly declined. The Klan waned locally because its political machinations failed to bring substantive results. Politics provided the only avenue where nativists could translate 100 percent Americanism into policy, but even the election victories produced only short-term effects. The Klan never offered a positive alternative; moreover by the mid-twenties Catholics and Jews, along with liberal Protestants, could outvote it. As Professor Jackson has written, "The Ku Klux Klan provided a focus for the fears of alienated native Americans whose world was being disrupted. In the city the Invisible Empire found its greatest challenge, and in the city it met its ultimate defeat." By 1930 the Klan had resubmerged into the current of intolerance that has flowed beneath the stream of American history, but racism and nativism in the twenties opened new sores that still have not healed today.

Cities not only fed such rural-based movements as prohibition and the Ku Klux Klan, but they also endowed new impulses to religious fundamentalism, another striking social issue of the 1920s. The most famous religious clash of the decade occurred in Dayton, Tennessee, in July, 1925. Here, at the trial of John Thomas Scopes, a high school biology instructor arrested for teaching the theory of evolution, the issue was joined between fundamentalists and modernists, the unquestioning religion of the country and the scientific "higher criticism" of the city. The battle lines sharpened when the prosecution enlisted the counsel of William Jennings Bryan—self-proclaimed defender of the faith—and the defense obtained the assistance of big-city lawyers Clarence Darrow, Arthur Garfield Hays, and Dudley Field Malone. Although the jury found Scopes guilty of breaking Tennessee law prohibiting instructors in state-supported schools from teaching that man had descended from some lower order of animal, it was a Pyrrhic victory for the fundamentalists. Scores of newspaper reporters conveyed the circuslike event to a national audience and made the trial an object of ridicule, especially after Darrow cross-examined Bryan and bared all the ambiguities of literal interpretation of the Bible. Afterward humorist Will Rogers remarked, "I see you can't say that man descended from the ape. At least that's the law in Tennessee. But do they have a law to keep a man from making a jackass of himself?"

It appeared, then, that cosmopolitan urban culture could shrug off the challenge of rural old-time religon. Yet at the same time, pietistic fundamentalism, with its "holiness," "pentecostal," and storefront churches, was surging dramatically in cities across the country. In part this upswing accompanied the move of Black Americans to northern and southern cities in the twenties. Blacks transplanted their churches from the rural countryside and looked to them for solace, adjustment, and identification. The majority of urban fundamentalists were white, however. Urban fundamentalist churches, like the Ku Klux Klan, drew much of their membership from groups caught between the middle and lower class. "Insecure, frustrated, feeling inferior and different," William G. McLoughlin, Jr., has written, "most of them were struggling not so much to get into a higher social bracket as to keep from sinking into a lower one." Many were rural migrants attracted by the friendliness, lack of dogma, and closeness to God that the various storefront churches and gospel tabernacles promised.

Most leaders of these churches were professional evangelists, charismatic figures who operated outside of the regular Prostestant denominations. Using the ballyhoo and pageantry of the new advertising age, they attracted huge followings and stirred up a revivalistic fervor. In Los Angeles, Aimee Semple MacPherson, the widow of a missionary, established the Four Square Gospel Temple where she produced extravaganzas of religious vaudeville. Sister Aimee's sumptuous services, flowing gowns, and moving sermons captivated thousands of newly arrived Midwesterners and Southerners. Her Sunday evening "shows for the Lord" were broadcast by her own radio station, KFSG, throughout southern California each week. Similar cults, founded by evangelists and graduates of Bible institutes, appeared in a host of other cities. They included Clinton H. Churchill's Evangelistic Tabernacle in Buffalo, Paul Rader's

Chicago Gospel Tabernacle, Katherine Kuhlman's Denver Revival Tabernacle, E. J. Rolling's Detroit Metropolitan Tabernacle, T. H. Elsner's Philadelphia Gospel Tabernacle, Karl Wittman's Tabernacle in Toledo, and Luke Rader's River Lake Gospel Tabernacle in Minneapolis. Most of these churches had their own radio programs or stations, their own newspapers, Bible camps, and foreign missionaries.

Yet fundamentalist churches, along with Prohibition and the Klan, were not unique responses by native Protestants who were trying to infuse their urban experiences with ideals of a romanticized past. Rather, these institutions were part of a larger organizational impulse that pervaded all urban society. City populations were too large and diverse to sustain a unified sense of community that many believed once existed in small towns and villages—even though the belief was often mythical. In a fragmented society, people turned to new forms of association that revolved around interest group identities. Membership rolls of middle-class organizations such as Rotary, Kiwanis, Lions, Elks, and women's clubs swelled during the twenties. Football, baseball, and basketball games brought people together in new forms of community identification. Community chests, public campaigns for support of local welfare projects, increased in number from 12 in 1919 to 363 in 1930. Each of these activities reflected a kind of social adjustment to the new urban society where tight and tiny communities no longer existed and where people tried to bring order to the complexities of group and personal loyalties. The impulses of group organization had always been characteristic of the city, but the tensions and self-consciousness of the decade between World War I and the Depression heightened the search for identity.

NEW INITIATIVE AND NEW POLITICS

On March 4, 1921, an ashen Woodrow Wilson left the White House to accompany Warren G. Harding to the latter's inauguration as twenty-ninth President of the United States. The event signaled the end of an era. Wilson, the progressive governor of New Jersey and self-righteous president who had rallied the nation to the defense of democracy, was now a beaten, sick, and bitter man. Harding, the dapper, backslapping politician from Ohio, shunned all reformist zeal. He was "a regular fellow, . . . just plain folks." His successor to the presidency, Calvin Coolidge (nicknamed the Yankee Sphinx by Washington newsmen) was equally plain and uninspiring. The fads and yahooism of the twenties seemed symptomatic of an emptiness that now permeated American politics.

Yet on the local level, the normalcy of the age failed to suffocate the initiative that had been growing for several decades. Although war, disillusion, and successful achievement of reform goals weakened the structure of national progressivism, the urban foundations remained. A number of movements that had originated a quarter of a century or more earlier extended through the 1920s. Urban research and planning were two areas that hummed with activity. In addition the seeds of new partnerships, also planted in the late nineteenth century, began to bear fruit that would increasingly dominate the urban scene. These hybrids included unions between bosses and reformers and unions between city and federal governments.

Perhaps the strongest progressive impulses surviving into the 1920s were the systematic identification of urban problems and professional management of urban affairs. Like the muckrakers, settlement workers, and other reformers of a generation earlier, concerned individuals in the twenties tried to make sense out of cities by examining them with the finest tools. Many believed such analysis was prerequisite to the solution of urban problems. Nowhere was the passion for identifying urban patterns stronger than at the University of Chicago, where a school of sociology, launched by Robert E. Park and Ernest W. Burgess during World War I, trained scholars who combed Chicago with analytical rigor and spread their techniques to colleagues in other cities. The Chicago school's methods involved drawing relations between people and their environment in much the same way that biologists examined interactions between plants and animals and their surroundings. This approach to the city was known as human ecology, and it was a natural outgrowth of the progressive concept of an organic city with interrelated parts.

Human ecology was a technique and a theory. Its emphasis on relationships between people and their environment spurred students to pay particular attention to data—numbers, characteristics, maps, and ratios. The data then formed part of the general theory that neighborhood communities had become the cores of individual and group life in the city and that these communities held the keys to the adjustment of people to urban society. These ideas were central to such studies as Burgess' concentric ring thesis, which depicted urban growth in terms of a series of concentric zones radiating outward from the urban core; Harvey W. Zorbaugh's *The Gold Coast and the Slum*, which outlined the life patterns of contrasting neighborhoods; Louis Wirth's *The Ghetto*, which probed the development of a single residential type; Frederick Thrasher's *The Gang*; and Roderick D. McKenzie's *The Metropolitan Community*. These works furnished city planners, economists, and officials with background for the formulation of policy. Although the community concept contained distortions—critics have since charged, for example, that the emphasis on neighborhoods looked nostalgically backward to the preurban village—, it has exerted a strong influence on twentieth-century urban thought.

Professional city planners of the 1920s tried to make sense out of unwieldy cities. Planners generally were split, however, between those who considered sweeping schemes to bring order to huge and unmanageable "dinosaur cities" and metropolitan regions and those who specialized in narrow problems such as zoning and traffic control. Members of the first group, particularly the Regional Planning Association of American (RPAA), included among its leaders architect-planners Clarence Stein and Henry Wright and intellectuals Lewis Mumford and Benton McKaye. Although not overlooking specific planning concerns such as housing, streets, water supplies, and transportation, the RPAA believed that the physical totality of a city and its surrounding environs should form the basis for the solution of modern problems. Wright and Stein asserted that uncontrolled urban expansion was causing unnecessary congestion and that decentralization would relieve the pressures of housing and traffic. Following the English model of Ebenezer Howard's Garden Cities—new, planned communities with limited populations and surrounded by open land—many regional planners hoped to secure a more rational pattern of settlement. The RPAA tried to prove the merits of decentralization by planning two projects near New York. In 1924 it sponsored Sunnyside, a limited-dividend housing corporation in Queens planned by Wright and Stein and intended for low-income residents. Radburn, New Jersey, a genuine garden city, was begun in 1928 on a large tract seventeen miles from New York. Although Sunnyside and Radburn won much publicity for their advanced design, both proved to be too costly for low-income occupants. Nevertheless they provided important antecedents to housing schemes and new town developments that followed later in the century.

The regional movement also prompted consolidation of comprehensive planning for metropolitan areas. The most notable scheme was the one drawn for New York City and its surrounding counties during the '20s and presented in 1931. Initiated by planning advocate Charles D. Norton, financed by the Russell Sage Foundation, and directed by planner Thomas Adams, the New York Regional Plan consisted of eight volumes of survey material and two volumes of proposals. It was the most extensive planning project yet attempted. Its recognition of the interrelationships between the different regions and different functions of a metropolis influenced similar projects envisioned in other cities. But also the plan's acceptance of growth as inevitable and its celebration of the automobile as the best means of transportation meant that it underemphasized possibilities for controlled growth and gave highways precedence over mass transit. Other surveys were taken for the metropolitan areas of Philadelphia, Chicago, Boston, San Francisco, and Cleveland. Although civic leaders held conferences and appointed commissions to discuss regional problems of highways, land use, and water supplies, political rivalries and economic jealousies prevented substantive consolidation of cities with their surrounding territories. Schemes to combine city and county governments of Cleveland, St. Louis, and Seattle were defeated, and efforts to integrate planning in Cook County, Illinois (Chicago region), were tabled.

A much more successful form of city planning during the 1920s was zoning. Originally intended as a means of confinement, zoning became a tool of exclusion that still governs land use patterns today. Copied from Germany and elsewhere abroad, zoning is a type of local police power that restricts certain types of building or land use to certain districts of the city. The earliest comprehensive zoning ordinance was passed by New York in 1916 to prevent skyscrapers and high-rise garment industry lofts from encroaching on the fashionable Fifth Avenue retail district. By 1924 every major city, plus hundreds of smaller cities, had established zoning regulations. Although loopholes left room for easy circumvention, the laws generally controlled areas and heights of buildings, determined boundaries of commercial and residential zones, and fixed density limitations. Zoning laws aimed to establish stability in existing districts and orderly growth in newer regions, but they also protected the interests of real estate developers and owners of commercial property by insuring that residential or commercial zones would not be invaded by unwanted features. Later, zoning would commonly be used to exclude "undesirable" people from the suburbs. In the 1920s zoning became the principal activity of the scores of planning commissions established in cities across the country. Planning staffs spent much of their time drawing maps that identified patterns of land use, traffic, health, lighting, utilities, and other aspects of the urban environment. Such projects proved very helpful in systematizing policy planning, but they mainly ratified the status quo. Zoning maps could not erase slums, abolish want and crime, or improve the quality of life for all urban dwellers.

The scope of public initiative in cities expanded broadly during the twenties. In addition to traffic signals and electric fire alarms, most cities began to purchase police cars and to equip them with radio-receivers. Local governments bought snowplows, garbage trucks, and school buses. Pittsburgh, Chicago, Cincinnati, Cleveland, St. Louis, Denver, and Rochester took steps (seldom successful) to control smoke pollution. As air transportation became a reality, several cities began to construct facilities for the airlines. By mid-decade, Philadelphia, Detroit, Boston, Kansas City, and Cleveland had municipal airfields. Cities literally roared with the sound of public construction as projects planned before and postponed during World War I began to reach completion—government offices, parks, beltways, libraries, stadiums, and terminals.

Behind the flurry of activity urban politics were readjusting to new conditions. To be sure, bosses and reformers still contested for the reins of power, but now both had to be more sensitive to each other's presence as well as to changing patterns within the electorate. For one thing the curtailment of European immigration, by World War I and later by legal restriction, shut off one important source of urban population growth, but other sources remained. Newcomers by the hundreds of thousands still poured into many cities, but they were often of a different sort than those who had preceded them. Many, as before were poor rural southerners, black and white, while others were dark-skinned Latin Americans from Mexico and the Caribbean who brought new languages, customs, and pressures to old neighborhoods and schools. At the same time, the children of those who came during the peak immigration years of the early 1900s were reaching the voting age. In 1907, the year of heaviest foreign influx, two-thirds of all school-age children in the nation's thirty-one largest cities had foreign-born fathers. During the twenties these children became adults—voters, workers, parents. Their impact upon urban politics and society now bore considerable weight.

From the 1880s onward bossism and reform had sometimes intertwined in the cities as politicians responded to the needs and votes of new stock, working-class constituents. Bosses such as George B. Cox of Cincinnati, Abe Ruef of San Francisco, Martin Lomasney of Boston, and Charles F. Murphy of New York had been willing to accept reform measures; and reformers such as Hazen Pingree of Detroit and Tom Johnson of Cleveland had built machine-like organizations. Although these blends were often awkard and uncomfortable, they reflected demands by an increasingly complex society and an increasingly influential electorate. In the 1910s and early 1920s it was usually the Democratic party, already established as the party of new stock voters, that recognized the potential of these trends and that made efforts, often unconsciously, to narrow the gap between boss and reformer.

The first politician to bridge the gap substantially was New York's Alfred E. Smith—legislator, governor, and the nation's first Catholic presidential candidate. Smith's early career almost duplicated the backgrounds of the Tammany bosses who ruled the city during his youth. Born in a lower East Side tenement, Smith left school at an early age to support his widowed mother. His toughness and ambition led him into Tammany Hall, where he rose rapidly within the organization and within the Democratic party. In 1903 he won a seat in the State Assembly and attracted attention for his legislative acumen. As a lawmaker Smith managed to satisfy Tammany chieftains while at the same time allying with prominent progressive reformers such as Robert F. Wagner and Frances Perkins. His vice-chairmanship of a committee that investigated New York City's Triangle Shirtwaist Company fire in 1911 heightened his social awareness, and he continually supported welfare and labor reform legislation. In 1918 Smith successfully ran for governor of New York and served from 1919 to 1921 and from 1923 to 1928.

Smith's political success and broad appeal made him a logical presidential candidate. His attempt to win the Democratic nomination in 1924 failed, but in 1928 he could not be denied. His campaign against Republican Herbert Hoover, although provincial and impolitic, was vigorous and boisterous, stressing labor reform and an end to Prohibition. Although both candidates tried to avoid religious issues, bigots managed to hurl some malicious barbs at Smith's Catholicism. But prosperity was the major issue, and in 1928 the country was still prosperous. Hoover and his party readily accepted credit for the good times, and Smith was badly beaten at the polls. Nevertheless the voting returns revealed some suggestive results. In almost every major city Smith drew a significantly higher proportion of the total vote than had any other Democratic presidential candidate for the past generation. For the first time since 1892 the Democrats carried several large cities in the presidential election. Hoover and the Republicans managed to retain large majorities in places like Indianapolis, Akron, Kansas City, and Portland where native white Protestants still predominated, but Smith carried immigrant cities as diverse as Providence, Jersey City, Milwaukee, and St. Paul.

Though he lost the election, the "Happy Warrior" had ratified a new political situation, which had been evolving for over a generation. His Catholicism, his Irish immigrant ancestry (somewhat exaggerated by Smith himself), and his rise from the slums provided urban immigrants and their children with what students of politics call a "vicarious identification." He gave urban ethnic voters a symbol and pulled them into national politics. In 1924 just over half of those eligible to vote did so; in 1928 over two-thirds voted. Much of the increased turnout occurred in cities. In heavily Catholic Boston, for example, 44 percent more people voted in 1928 than in 1924. Although successes of Democratic candidates for national office in off-year elections were not consistent enough in the cities to justify calling 1928 the year of the "Smith Revolution," his candidacy nevertheless signaled the emergence of urban America as a strong factor in presidential politics, a factor that reinforced the census returns.

The growing importance of the city on the national scene was also reflected in the expanding relationships between municipal functions and the federal government. Many of these relationships dated from the latter half of the nineteenth century. For example, the federal government had the constitutional responsibility for such activities as maintaining a postal service and for improving waterways and harbors, and cities had always sought federal assistance in these areas. Congress extended these responsibilities during and after World War I when it pumped funds into the construction of highways, airports, and even some housing. Increasingly federal contracts and payrolls sustained a share of urban work forces—although the proportions were still small and many of the funds were filtered to the cities through the states. At the same time, several metropolitan areas had grown so large and complex that they rivaled the states of which they were parts for influence in the federal system. New York, Chicago, Philadelphia, Los Angeles, and Detroit—each with a population over one million by 1930—were rising above the screen of state government, which had formerly intervened between municipalities and Washington. These metropolises and the thirty-two others whose 1930 populations ranged between one-quarter and one million, were economically and politically powerful enough to comprise a third, urban partner to traditional federal-state relationships. When the economic crash of 1929 and its ensuing depression wiped away urban self-sufficiency, the lines of assistance and communications that had been stretched between cities and the federal government in the 1920s became the framework for the structure of government activities that was built in the 1930s.

BIBLIOGRAPHY

The history of urban America from World War I to the Great Depression begins to merge closely with national history, so that a number of general works offer insights into urban developments. The best single–volume study of the 1920s in America is William E. Leuchtenburg, *The Perils of Prosperity, 1914–1932* (Chicago: University of Chicago Press, 1958). Other broad works useful for urban trends include John Higham, *Strangers in the Land: Patterns of American Nativisim, 1860–1925* (New Brunswick, N. J.: Rutgers University Press, 1955); Richard Hofstadter and Michael Wallace, eds., *American Violence: A Documentary History* (New York: Knopf, 1971); Thomas C. Cochran and William Miller, *The Age of Enterprise: A Social History of Industrial America* (New York: Harper, revised ed., 1961); Daniel J. Boorstin, *The Americans: The Democratic Experience* (New York: Knopf, 1973); Frederick Lewis Allen, *Only Yesterday: An Informal History of the 1920's* (New York: Harper, 1932); and George E. Mowry, *The Urban Nation, 1920–1960* (New York: Hill and Wang, 1965). The first two chapters of Blake McKelvey, *The Emergence of Metropolitan America, 1915–1966* (New Brunswick, N. J.: Rutgers University Press, 1968) detail many of the developments pertinent to this era. See also the compilation on *The City* edited by Robert E. Park, Ernest W. Burgess, and Roderick D. McKenzie (Chicago: University of Chicago Press, 1925).

Specialized studies for the period cover a wide spectrum of topics. For urban land values, land management, annexation, and architecture, see Homer Hoyt, *One Hundred Years of Land Values in Chicago* (Chicago: University of Chicago Press, 1933); Kenneth T. Jackson, "Metropolitan Government Versus Political Autonomy: Politics on the Crabgrass Frontier" in Kenneth T. Jackson and Stanley K. Schultz, eds., *Cities in American History* (New York: Knopf, 1972), pp. 442–62; Sam Bass Warner, Jr., *The Urban Wilderness* (New York: Harper and Row, 1973); and Christopher Tunnard and Henry Hope Reed, *The American Skyline: The Growth and Form of Our Cities and Towns* (Boston: Houghton Mifflin, 1955). Studies of racial patterns include Alan Spear, *Black Chicago: The Making of a Negro Ghetto, 1890–1920* (Chicago: University of Chicago Press, 1967); Gilbert Osofsky, *Harlem: The Making of a Ghetto* (New York: Harper and Row, 1966); William Tuttle, *Race Riot: Chicago in the Red Summer of 1919* (New York: Atheneum, 1970); John Hope Franklin, *From Slavery to Freedom: A History of American Negroes* (New York: Knopf, 3rd ed., 1967); and Nathan Irwin Huggins, *Harlem Renaissance* (New York: Oxford University Press, 1971). The rebirth of the Ku Klux Klan is best treated by Kenneth T. Jackson, *The Ku Klux Klan in the City, 1915–1930* (New York: Oxford University Press, 1967), and religious responses to urbanization are traced in William G. McLoughlin, Jr., *Modern Revivalism: Charles Grandison Finney to Billy Graham* (New York: Ronald Press, 1959). John Rae's two studies, *The American Automobile:A Brief History* (Chicago: University of Chicago Press, 1965) and *The Road and the Car in American Life* (Cambridge: M.I.T. Press, 1971) provide excellent analyses of the automobile's social and economic effects. William H. Chafe's *The American Woman: Her Changing Social, Economic, and Political Roles, 1920–1970* (New York: Oxford University Press, 1972) offers important insights into urban women, particularly their work patterns. The adjustments of small town America to the new urban age are treated in Robert S. and Helen Merrell Lynd's classic *Middletown, A Study of Modern American Culture* (New York: Harcourt, Brace, and World, 1929).

The problems of temperance and prohibition have been treated by James H. Timberlake, *Prohibition and the Progressive Movement: 1900–1920* (Cambridge: Harvard University Press, 1963); and Joseph R. Gusfield, *Symbolic Crusade: Status Politics and the American Temperance Movement* (Urbana: University of Illinois Press, 1963). For the development and effects of urban crime, see Mark H. Haller, "Urban Crime and Criminal Justice: The Chicago Model," *Journal of American History*, 57 (December 1970), 619–35; Haller, "Organized Crime in Urban Society: Chicago in the Twentieth Century," *Journal of Social History*, 5 (Winter 1971), 21–34; and Humbert J. Nelli, "European Immigrants and Urban America," in Raymond A. Mohl and James F. Richardson, eds., *The Urban Experience: Themes in American History* (Belmont, Cal.: Wadsworth Publishing Co., 1972), pp. 61–78. For patterns of urban politics, see Samuel Lubell, *The Future of American Politics* (Garden City: Doubleday, 1951), particularly pp. 29–60; John D. Buenker, *Urban Liberalism and Progressive Reform* (New York: Charles Scribner's Sons, 1973); Oscar Handlin, *Al Smith and His America* (Boston: Little, Brown, 1958); Arthur Mann, *LaGuardia: A Fighter Against His Times* (Philadelphia: Lippincott, 1959); David Burner, *The Politics of Provincialism* (New York: Knopf, 1968); and Jerome M. Clubb and Howard W. Allen, "The Cities and the Election of 1928: Partisan Realignment?" *American Historical Review*, 74 (April 1969), 1205–20.

8

ECONOMIC CRISIS AND
THE RISE OF A
FEDERAL-CITY PARTNERSHIP

THE COLLAPSE OF URBAN INITIATIVE

After nearly a decade of optimistic economic expansion, something very uncharacteristic happened to the American nation in the autumn of 1929: a wildly plummeting stock market dissolved $30 billion worth of fortunes and pushed the country into a decade of sacrifice and deprivation. In retrospect the signs of imminent decline seem clear. Farmers had been suffering long before 1929. The construction industry had weakened after 1926. Automobile manufacturers and related industries had overextended production relative to the buying power of the general public. Unbridled speculation, encouraged by irresponsible banking practices, had created huge paper profits that perverted the economy's productivity. The stock market crash bared these weaknesses, and during the last weeks of October an era of expansion gave way to an era of depression. In spite of considerable trauma, American cities survived the ensuing decade; but economic collapse pulled them and the federal government into a new alliance, one in which Washington became the dominant partner. It was during the 1930s that urban problems became national problems.

Just as (or perhaps because) prosperity in the 1920s had been most visible in the cities, economic crisis struck urban dwellers with particular severity. The effects came slowly, however. At first the depression seemed far away, a temporary setback that had bankrupted a few New York investors. Workingmen in Minneapolis and Houston joked about frantic stockbrokers jumping out of hotel windows, and advertisers in Atlanta and Los Angeles continued to celebrate the virtues of credit and consumerism. But the crash generated a brutal recession that gradually deepened in every city. Factories and stores cut back their payrolls. Families were forced to consume less. Private loans and IOUs circulated widely. In Chicago, Cleveland, Milwaukee, and Grand Rapids, public school teachers went without paychecks for months. In New York the International Apple Shippers Association sold crates of surplus apples to six thousand unemployed workers, who then peddled the fruit at five cents apiece. Relief rolls in the automobile capital of Detroit swelled while assembly lines slowed to a snail's pace. Everywhere savings accounts dwindled, insurance policies lapsed, and mortgage payments fell delinquent.

The major source of hardship was unemployment. The Depression spun a vicious cycle: the more the business community contracted production in order to economize, the more people it threw out of work, and the more it diminished the nation's purchasing power. By 1932 between 12 and 15 million Americans were jobless. The figures were astronomical in big cities: 1 million unemployed in New York; 600,000 in Chicago; 298,000 in Philadelphia; 178,000 in Pittsburgh, and 53,000 in Cincinnati. The weight of unemployment fell most heavily on the unskilled, the young, and the black. Employers laid off those who were needed least, and many factory owners downgraded skilled workers so they could fill unskilled jobs. Local surveys revealed that joblessness among people in their late teens and early twenties ran twice as high as among other age groups. Much of the unemployment resulted from the fact that young people entering the job market for the first time simply could find no work. Although blacks were able to retain jobs in some industries—meat packing, for example—the aphorism "last hired and first fired" rang true in the depression. A census of unemployment in 1931 found that in fourteen of sixteen northern and western cities, the percentages of blacks out of work were much higher than those for whites. In Chicago, Pittsburgh, and Philadelphia rates of joblessness among employable blacks reached 50 percent and higher.

The displacements of the Depression saddled local governments with unprecedented responsibilities. President Hoover believed that the crisis should be attacked at the local as well as the national level. On November 15, 1929, he began a series of meetings with business leaders in which he urged more construction and plant expansion in order to maintain wage rates and employment. A week later he sent out a flood of telegrams calling upon governors and mayors to initiate public works projects to provide jobs for the unemployed. In 1930 Hoover appointed an Emergency Committee for Employment, reorganized in 1931 as the Organization on Unemployment Relief, to encourage local communities to care for their jobless citizens. But at the same time, he also emphasized the need for balanced budgets that he believed would stabilize all levels of the economy.

Municipal governments responded quickly to the economic challenge. Even before the stock market crash, Cincinnati's City Manager C. O. Sherrill, partly influenced by the local Citizens' party, organized a committee to survey possibilities for public works, job training and placement, and other aspects of employment. After the onset of the Depression, other cities copied the Cincinnati model. According to Blake McKelvey, the city of Rochester appropriated $800,000 for work relief in 1930, and its city manager requested $1 million for 1931. By the end of 1930 the 75 largest cities were spending $420 million annually on public works projects. Yet even the most generous efforts failed to keep people out of bread lines and off the relief rolls. In 1929 Detroit spent $2.4 million on relief; in 1931 it spent $14.9 million. Over those same two years relief expenditures rose from $620,000 to $2.9 million in Milwaukee, and from $582,000 to $3.5 million in Philadelphia.

The problem for cities was basically a financial one, but underneath it lay serious political and ideological issues. The Depression caught municipalities between two millstones. On one side, the need for services hiked costs of government operations, while on the other side, unemployment and falling business reduced municipal revenues. One of the most universal problems was property tax delinquency. In 1930 among the 145 cities with 50,000 or more inhabitants, nearly 11 percent of local taxes went unpaid. By 1933 the rate had reached 25.2 percent. In order to collect more revenue, some cities, such as Dayton and Des Moines, agreed to accept late payments without penalizing the delinquents. But conservatives charged that such breaks only encouraged irresponsibility among taxpayers. Other cities drew and spent budgets on anticipation of full collection of tax revenues or borrowed against uncollected revenues, thereby falling deeper into debt. In an attempt to increase their incomes some municipalities levied a sales tax. Introduced in West Virginia in 1921, the sales tax won few advocates during the good times of the twenties. But between 1930 and 1935 twenty-one states and several cities, including New York and New Orleans, began taxing the sale of certain goods, mainly luxury items. By 1940 New York City's 3 percent sales tax was raising $60 million annually.

On top of revenue problems lay financial burdens inherited from the past. During the expansion years of the early 1900s, and especially during the 1920s, cities had floated large bond issues that came due in the 1930s. Unable to make payments on either principal or interest, many cities defaulted. Others were able to meet their obligations only by depleting their sinking funds—emergency monies set aside to be used to relieve debt only in the last resort. As a result the prices for municipal bonds plunged. By 1933 bond issues of Detroit and of Greensboro, North Carolina, were worth forty cents on the dollar. In Los Angeles debt charges (that is, interest payments and retirement of principal) accounted for 78 percent of the 1934–35 budget. Local officials were quick to point out that rates of default by municipal governments were much lower than those by private corporations; nevertheless the financial problems of cities affected a greater number of people. Some governments were forced to take drastic steps in reaction to the fiscal plights of local businesses. In 1932, during the depths of the Depression, many people became distrustful of failing banks and hoarded currency to such an extent that the amount in circulation declined precipitously. The shortage became so acute in the South that a few cities—Richmond, Knoxville, and Atlanta, for example—began to print their own scrip to pay public employees and relief recipients.

The cities' failure to meet their debt obligations raised cries for state control of local finances that echoed charges of irresponsibility that reformers had leveled at boss-ridden city governments in the 1870s and 1880s. Now, a half-century later, conservatives revived proposals that state officials intervene in local affairs and insure fiscal stability by reviewing budgets, limiting debts, and supervising tax levies. The real tug, however, was less between city and state than between those who advocated prudence and those who favored more debt and liberal public spending. Many civic leaders, such as Milwaukee's socialist mayor, Daniel W. Hoan, and the members of the International City Managers Association, believed that public funds should be conserved to protect the solvency of local governments. They adopted a pay-as-you-go policy toward relief projects, approving only those that would not drain the public till. Others, like mayors Frank Murphy of Detroit and later Fiorello LaGuardia of New York, preferred to expend whatever money was available and borrow more for relief, even if it meant paring budgets of other municipal services. Both policies—economizing and spending for relief—severely limited the activities of those departments deemed nonessential. Planning boards, underfinanced even during the 1920s, shrank to skeletons in the early years of the Depression. In 1933, 57 percent of the nation's 739 city planning boards received no appropriations, and 25 percent received less than $1,000. Between 1929 and 1933 total expenditures by parks and recreation departments in 795 cities and towns decreased by 50 percent. Public parks programs in Fall River, New Bedford, Providence, and San Antonio were completely eliminated and saved only by private donations.

In some respects the drive for economy produced beneficial results by consolidating departments whose functions duplicated or overlapped each other. For example, to conserve funds, Fresno, California, and New Haven, Connecticut, combined previously separate parks and recreation departments. More importantly, city and county departments were merged to create more centralized administration and a more regional recognition of metropolitan needs. The Chicago Park District, created by the Illinois state legislature in 1933, consolidated the nineteen independent park districts of the Chicago area under one board. Cincinnati's welfare responsibilities were absorbed by Hamilton County, and in New Jersey and New Hampshire, state agencies assumed welfare functions formally handled by their various cities. In other places city and county healthy departments were combined. Local officials recognized that they could not drop services that had gradually expanded for a half-century or more and that to preserve them meant questioning and rearranging administrative structures.

Whether or not public leaders favored belt tightening or more spending, the rampant epidemic of hardship brought intense pressures for the relief of hunger and unemployment. Public and private agencies everywhere struggled through the early years of the Depression groping for ways to help. During the fall of 1931, the National Association of Community Chests and Councils, following President Hoover's suggestion, sponsored a drive that raised $85 million for relief in cities and towns throughout the nation. The sum, according to Blake McKelvey, was hopelessly inadequate. In Milwaukee all municipal salaries were reduced by 10 percent, freeing a million dollars for temporary job relief in 1932. The next year, however, the city voted a drastic tax reduction, eliminating a large portion of public revenues and forcing money saved by salary cuts to be used to support essential services. Through coordinated efforts by public and private organizations, Cincinnati and Minneapolis, among other cities, were able to forestall severe destitution during the winter of 1931–32. But the Depression continued to deepen, and many families who had teetered on the margins of subsistence for two or three years succumbed and applied for relief. Faced with mounting hardship and shriveling tax revenues, even the most resourceful municipalities began to run out of funds. (Per capita government expenditures in cities with over 100,000 people dropped from $78 in 1929 to $67 in 1933, while per capita expenditures on relief rose from $0.90 to $2.94.)

Inevitably cities looked to Washington for help. In May, 1932, at the invitation of Mayor Murphy, twenty-six mayors met in Detroit and appealed to the federal government for $5 billion to finance public construction projects. President Hoover rejected the mayors' request but did approve the Reconstruction Finance Corporation (RFC), an agency that was to loan money to banks, railroads, and other big businesses in hopes that by stabilizing these institutions, recovery would filter down to the rest of society. Later the RFC was authorized to make loans to local government agencies for self-liquidating projects. Money trickled into the cities at a very slow pace, however, and the bankers who increasingly assumed control as cities defaulted on debt payments could offer little help except to institute further retrenchment. Moreover the RFC failed to bring relief to the unemployed, who needed it most. Hoover vehemently opposed direct assistance and squelched Congressional proposals for public works projects designed as unemployment relief. Instead, he continued to push voluntaristic efforts.

Mayors, city managers, and other civic leaders were not uniformly in favor of greater assistance from the federal government. A number of these men were longtime Republicans, supporters of Hoover's policies who accepted the RFC as a meaningful reform. Yet, as their local economies and services continued to collapse by fall of 1932, many civic leaders began to ponder what would happen if the Democratic presidential candidate, New York's governor Franklin D. Roosevelt, should win and carry out his promise for a new deal. When Roosevelt did win cities were quick to revive their pleas, and the new government was quick to respond.

THE NEW DEAL IN THE CITIES

In his acceptance speech at the Democratic National Convention in the summer of 1932, Franklin Roosevelt had proclaimed, "I pledge you, I pledge myself to a new deal for the American people." In time *a* new deal became *the* New Deal—the legislative and administrative measures generated by Roosevelt and his advisers to bring about relief, recovery, and reform. Once in office the new president galvanized his programs quickly. Within one hundred days he had instituted measures affecting banking, agriculture, industry, and conservation. These and other measures like them affected cities only indirectly, if at all. In fact several New Deal measures revealed a bias against cities. FDR was a lover of nature, and he responded favorably to programs aiming to revive small, rural communities. A back-to-the-land intent was clearly part of the Subsistence Homestead Division, a program inaugurated in 1933 to remove slum dwellers to some one hundred government-sponsored rural communities, and of the Tennessee Valley Authority, the government experiment in regional reconstruction.

Yet the New Deal policy makers did accept the fact that large-scale cities had become the principal centers of the national experience. To be sure, concern was directed not so much at urban life itself as toward the ways in which urban problems existed as part of the national economic crisis. Still many of the bills passed and agencies created grew out of the urban experience, where thrift, self-help, and rugged individualism had always shared the stage with mutual benefit and public responsibility. The effect, if not the intent, of the New Deal was to meet traditional needs of urban dwellers. It touched cities directly in three areas: relief and welfare, housing, and planning.

Relief and Welfare

Unemployment loomed as one of the most serious problems facing FDR when he assumed office. Its impact upon cities had been devastating: Hoover's programs had not reached the urban masses. By 1933 unemployment rates were 40 percent in Chicago, 30 percent in New York, and 26 percent in Cincinnati. As one newspaper remarked, "What this relief business needs is less RFC and more PDQ." Roosevelt responded first by proposing the Federal Emergency Relief Administration (FERA). Created by Congress in May, 1933, the FERA distributed $500 million to the states for direct relief. Although the program was not explicitly designed to aid urban dwellers, 42 percent of the 1933 appropriations were spent in five heavily urbanized northern states. Relief administrator Harry Hopkins, a former social worker, suggested that the money be used for cash payments to the poor, but shortly thereafter proposed that the funds support work relief projects, which would make welfare less demeaning. Hopkins' career as a social worker in New York City had given him an earnest sympathy for victims of economic calamity. As the director of federal relief he grew impatient with conservatives who warned against reckless spending and who advised that conditions of the poor would improve in the long run. "People don't eat in the long run," Hopkins sneered. "They eat every day."

The import of the FERA on the local level was that it braced up municipal relief programs and convinced many families that accepting aid did not mean loss of dignity. To be sure, a number of people sponged off the public purse and made no attempt to get off the relief rolls. Also, local administrators faced the predicament of whether or not to assist needy families who had migrated to the city merely to take advantage of larger and readier handouts. Still the numbers of chiselers were small, and the FERA helped convince the populace that the federal government now cared about their troubles. Relief had been institutionalized as a government function.

By the winter of 1933–34, almost eight million families (comprising twenty-eight million individuals) were receiving federal relief. The heads of nearly half of these households were enrolled in work relief projects sponsored by the Civil Works Administration, an agency created in November, 1933, to give jobs to the unemployed. Also directed by Harry Hopkins, the CWA paid minimum wages for work on road and school repair, park and playground maintenance, pest control, educational programs, and other projects. Unlike the FERA it directly administered works projects, putting employees on the federal payroll. Although critics charged that most jobs were wasteful boondoggling (one worker complained, "We dig ditches and fill them up again."), the CWA served a needed function. Before it was dismantled and absorbed by the FERA in April, 1934, it had pumped a billion dollars into the economy and had carried millions of people through the winter. The CWA, like the FERA, was meant to apply to the entire nation. But many of its 400,000 projects were located in, and directly benefited, cities. CWA workers built 500 airports and improved that many more. Many of the 50,000 teachers employed by Hopkins offered adult education classes in city schools. Millions of construction workers developed city parks, dug city swimming pools, and laid city sewer lines. Moreover wages paid for CWA jobs were spent in business-starved city establishments—barber shops, shoe stores, drugstores, and clothiers.

The rapid action taken by the CWA contrasted with the sluggishness of a similar work-relief agency, the Public Works Administration (PWA), directed by Interior Secretary Harold Ickes. Created in May, 1933, as

Working for Uncle Sam

These CWA workers are refurbishing the dome of the Colorado State Capitol in Denver in 1934. This was one of the thousands of projects devised to relieve unemployed laborers. *U.S. Information Agency, The National Archives.*

part of the National Industrial Recovery Act (NIRA), the PWA was supposed to sponsor a comprehensive system of public works, ranging from the rebuilding of submarines to slum clearance. Ickes, however, was a more cautious administrator than was Hopkins. He had learned about politics in the wards of Chicago, and he feared that local politicians would only waste federal money on useless projects. Agreeing with Lewis Mumford that public works required careful planning, Ickes was determined that projects receiving PWA funds should have strong merit. Thus he moved slowly. Eventually, however, PWA proved very beneficial, especially to cities. It built a new water supply system in Denver, a municipal auditorium in Kansas City, and thousands of new schools and hospitals across the country.

In 1935 the Roosevelt administration responded more radically to continued cries for more jobs and security. Early that year the President asked Congress to turn over care of unemployables to the states and localities while retaining federal responsibility for providing work relief to needy employables. As a result Congress created the Works Progress Administration (WPA) to finance public projects, many of which were located in municipalities. Although it never employed as many as the CWA, the WPA included over two and a half million workers on its payrolls by 1936. Under the guidance of Harry Hopkins the WPA sought to fill needs that had been neglected or postponed by private enterprise and civic initiative. Between 1936 and 1941 almost one-fifth of the nation's work force was employed by the WPA at one time or another. WPA workers built almost 600 airports and landing fields, 500,000 miles of roads and streets, 100,000 bridges and viaducts, 500,000 sewerage connections, and 110,000 libraries, schools, auditoriums, stadiums, and other public structures. Like the FERA and CWA, many of the WPA projects pumped new life into civic improvement. Indeed the U.S. Conference of Mayors, headed by New York's Fiorello LaGuardia, strongly influenced the size of WPA appropriations by pressing urban needs before the White House. The costs were heavy. Over $10 billion in federal funds flowed through the WPA, and opponents chided the agency by circulating jokes like the one about the WPA worker who was injured when the shovel he was leaning on gave way. In spite of its shortcomings, however, the WPA sustained a significant number of families until revival of the national economy could put them back on their feet.

The Social Security Act, passed in August, 1935, had a more permanent impact than did the relief agencies. The act created programs of old age insurance, unemployment insurance, and federal assistance to the blind, the disabled, and dependent children. The consequences of these programs were not felt at the time, but the Social Security Act set a momentous precedent for the nation and its cities. Care of the aged and the distressed was now accepted as a national rather than a local concern, and the path had been broken for a long line of antipoverty programs that would follow. Collective responsibility for the relief and prevention of poverty, long a major issue of urban growth, had been nationalized. Critics often charged that relief programs and Social Security benefits fostered only indolence and encouraged spongers to expect something for nothing. Yet almost every New Deal relief measure was tied to the traditional work ethic. New Dealers tried hard to avoid charges that the federal government was handing out doles, and Social Security insurance programs were to apply only to those who were, or had once been, employed. Although mutual assistance had won the day, the old distinction between deserving and undeserving poor lingered.

Housing

Between 1929 and 1935 the volume of new housing construction in this country shriveled to almost nothing. In 1932 the editors of *Fortune* magazine wrote that "at least half of America's 30,000,000 families are not even decently housed." And the specter of eviction threatened millions of homeowners. Between 1926 and 1933 the number of annual mortgage failures quadrupled, and by the latter date home mortgages were being foreclosed at the rate of one thousand per day. These plights made housing an early concern of the New Deal. The Roosevelt administration adopted a two-pronged approach: an insurance program to stabilize financial conditions for homeowners and for mortgage lenders, and publicly sponsored construction and slum clearance projects to improve housing conditions for the poor and boost employment in the building trades. Both programs set the pattern for subsequent urban growth. Mortgage insurance made possible a new and massive wave of suburbanization after World War II. Public housing and slum clearance brought the federal government into the urban core.

During the whirlwind of activity in its first one hundred days, the New Deal Congress created the Home Owner's Loan Corporation (HOLC) to bail out endangered homeowners and stabilize mortgage markets. The HOLC was established almost exclusively to serve urban interests—the Emergency Farm Mortgage Act passed almost a month earlier was designed to relieve rural foreclosures. The HOLC was empowered to refinance private loans with government money carrying interest of 5 percent and fifteen years to repay. The loans were to enable homeowners to escape foreclosure, to pay taxes, and to make needed repairs. The HOLC did not reduce a person's debt, but it did save millions from defaulting. In its three years of lending the HOLC granted $3 billion in loans to one-fifth of the nation's nonfarm households and held about one-sixth of all urban home mortgage debt.

Mortgage relief was only a stopgap measure; it did little to relieve either the construction industry or the housing market. Thus at FDR's instigation, in June, 1934, Congress passed the National Housing Act, which created the Federal Housing Authority (FHA), an agency to insure loans made by private lending institutions to families wishing to renovate or build homes. Over the next six years the agency underwrote $4.25 billion for the modernization of 3 million existing units and the construction of over 600,000 private homes and 600 rental units. The FHA drastically revised the nature of mortgage lending and by doing so triggered a new housing trend in metropolitan areas. Because the FHA would guarantee a borrower's mortgage (the borrower had to pay only a small fee for the guarantee), lending banks could reduce the interest rates to as low as 4 percent and could stretch out loans over twenty-five to thirty years. These new terms broke sharply with the five to seven year loans with interest rates of 6 to 12 percent that had been common in the preceding half-century. Applicants for FHA insurance had to demonstrate their ability to afford a new home; nevertheless long-term, federally insured mortgages made homebuilding and homeowning much easier than in the past. Now the middle-income classes could join the flight to the suburbs.

But HOLC and FHA had little effect upon the one-third of the nation whom President Roosevelt described as "ill-housed, ill-clad, ill-nourished." The plight of these groups raised to national dimensions the specter that had haunted urban reformers for a century: the slum. By amplifying local decay the Depression alerted even the most economy-minded leaders to the costs of physical deterioration. Early 1930s' studies of conditions in Cleveland and Boston revealed that maintenance of city services in slum areas was much more expensive than in other districts. Such studies galvanized new efforts to abolish blight and provide low-income groups with adequate housing. These had been long-standing reform goals, but the new component was the increasing belief that projects should be financed with public funds. As one official admitted in 1934, "If housing costs the taxpayers something, in the long run it probably saves them more." For decades most Americans had cast only a cursory glance at the impressive public renewal projects in European cities, such as Paris, Glasgow, Vienna, Berlin. By the 1930s however, many civic leaders were able to view fiscal and physical decay as part of the same problem, and they paid more attention to European precedents.

Early in the summer of 1933 an Emergency Housing Division was attached to the PWA. This agency financed local projects for slum clearance or for construction of low-cost modern housing. Although the work was done by private contractors, the projects were intended to provide work relief for people on PWA rolls. In four years the PWA Housing Division received about five hundred loan applications, fifty of which were financed. The first was in Atlanta where workers leveled eleven slum blocks and replaced them with Techwood Homes, a group of low-rent apartments. Other slum-conversion projects included Lakeview Terrace in Cleveland, Jane Addams Houses in Chicago, and Williamsburg Houses in Brooklyn. PWA funds financed the construction of some twenty-two thousand dwelling units. Yet most projects failed to help those in need of better housing. Rents averaged twenty-six dollars per month, still too high for the many working-class families whose incomes were under a thousand dollars a year. Clearance programs only pushed these people into other slums. The first wide-scale federal participation in housing reform resulted in the demolition of some of the worst urban eyesores and the construction of better facilities for some lower middle-class groups. But because it placed its major emphasis on work relief and self-liquidating projects, it failed to address the most acute problems.

The obstacles to housing programs were political. As in the past public officials were reluctant to lead government, whether local or national, into the hallowed region of housing construction and maintenance. Even President Roosevelt preferred that Congress should support private, rather than public housing. Opposition to direct federal participation won the upper hand in 1935 when a U.S. District Court, in the Louisville Lands Case, ruled that the federal government could not condemn private property for low-cost housing. Although the decision was later reversed, the original ruling had the effect of steering federal programs away from direct supervision and toward indirect grants-in-aid or loans to municipalities that could use funds at their own discretion.

This, in effect, was the strategy adopted by the U.S. Housing Authority (USHA), created as an agency of the Department of Interior by the Wagner-Steagall Housing Bill of 1937. Passed by Congress only after Senator Robert F. Wagner of New York, long a champion of public housing, had secured the reluctant support of President Roosevelt, the bill authorized $500 million for loans and grants to state and local authorities for slum clearance and housing developments. The law stipulated that tenants in USHA units be in the lowest income third of the population, and it particularly benefited blacks. Some 47,500 federally financed, low-cost dwelling units, nearly a third of those built in northern and southern cities, were occupied by black families. Critics charged that USHA-sponsored public housing was undermining the private market, but most accusations were false. Without the aid of public funds, private enterprise was unable and unwilling to clear slums and construct

Black Housing During the 1930s
These shanties in a black neighborhood of Atlanta typified the quarters that the U.S. Housing Authority attempted to replace. *Courtesy of the Library of Congress.*

modern low-cost housing. Units built under the USHA averaged $2,720 in cost, about 25 percent less than costs for privately erected housing. Yet the USHA was more important for its precedent than for its accomplishments. It cleared more slums than had any other program in the previous half-century; but it only dented the problem, and it left millions of families still without decent housing.

Planning

New Deal relief and housing programs brought the federal government into the local arena more than ever before. They also revitalized the city planning movement that had withered during the Depression. The administration of FDR gave new meaning to the term, plan. Public works requisites under the FERA, PWA, and WPA challenged planners and officials to organize projects for the use of federal funds on local improvements. The Wagner-Steagall Housing Act gave city planners, reformers, and architects federal support for the amelioration of slum conditions. Agencies like the National Resources Planning Board and the Tennessee Valley Authority merged urban and rural planning into regional coordination.

But in what was perhaps its most daring and ambitious planning activity, the construction of experimental greenbelt towns, the New Deal bypassed a federal-city partnership and attempted to defuse urban problems by diffusing them into the suburbs. This policy summed up a whole century of ambivalence toward the city, and it reflected a nostalgia for the small community of the rural past and a faith in the beneficial effects of modern suburbanization.

The intent of the policy was previewed in 1935 by Rexford G. Tugwell, a member of Roosevelt's brain trust and a leading exponent of large-scale planning, who wrote, "My idea is to go just outside centers of population, pick up cheap land, build a whole community and entice people into it. Then go back into the city and tear down whole slums and make parks of them." This was an extension of the attitudes taken by many sociologists and regional planners of the 1920s who indicted unplanned urban sprawl and had predicted that ever larger urban populations would produce only further disorder and depersonalization. As head of the Resettlement Administration, Tugwell attempted to transfer Ebenezer Howard's garden city concept to America and to succeed where the planners of Radburn and Sunnyside had failed. Tugwell determined from a careful study of population trends that suburbs offered the best opportunity for future planning, and he envisioned a network of three thousand planned communities dotting the country. These greenbelt cities were to be of limited size (about ten thousand people), located on the outskirts of metropolitan centers, surrounded by farms and open land, built with federal funds, and leased to cooperatives of local residents. By locating these towns in pleasant surroundings near employment opportunities and constructing the towns with federal assistance, Tugwell believed that the government could relieve slum congestion, provide low-cost housing, and rebuild community cohesion. Here were the advantages of the city and the country combined—and they were to be offered to low-income families.

With President Roosevelt's approval the greenbelt program got underway late in 1935. Although Tugwell initially had plans for twenty-five greenbelt towns, only three were built: Greenbelt, on the Maryland countryside north of Washington, D.C.; Greenhills, on farmland near Cincinnati; and Greendale, three miles southwest of Milwaukee. Each town was totally planned, with a physical layout focusing around neighborhood units of apartments and single dwellings. Each town contained a community center (usually the school), a shopping center (including a consumer's cooperative), and separate traffic routes for vehicles and pedestrians. Also each was built by unemployed workers hired as a means of giving them relief. Tenants began moving into Greenbelt, the first town to be completed, in September, 1937, and by the end of 1938 most dwellings in all three towns were occupied. By this time millions of

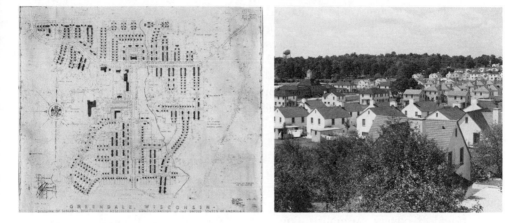

A Greenbelt Town

Left, A plan of Greendale, Wisconsin, preparaed in 1936 by the Division of Suburban Resettlement of the U.S. Resettlement Administration. *Right*, A photograph taken of Greendale in September 1939. The view is looking southwest toward the Administration Building with the water tower in the background. *Both photographs courtesy of the Library of Congress.*

visitors from all over the world had already come to view the new town experiment.

Tugwell's scheme had been grandiose; but Congress held the purse strings, and private interests made certain that those strings were pulled tightly. Critics frequently complained (often justifiably) that greenbelt dwellings were ugly and costly. Some charged that the projects smacked of socialism. But behind these complaints lay the fear of private developers that government-sponsored planned communities would infiltrate prime suburban land with undesirable (meaning lower-class) people who in turn would deflate real estate values and ruin the suburban dream. In Milwaukee, for example, the building and loan associations sued to prevent Greendale from being built. Many politicians sympathized with this fear. In spite of the hopes of a number of city planners Congress neither expanded the greenbelt program nor encouraged private builders to adopt any of the program's innovations. After the three original greenbelt towns were completed in 1938, the Resettlement Administration was abolished. Thereafter the towns' affairs were bounced about between several agencies. After World War II Congress authorized sale of greenbelt land and buildings to nonprofit organizations. Federally initiated community planning dissolved into a fog of apathy.

New Deal experiments in housing and planning taught federal officials a lesson in politics. Tugwell and his supporters sensed that the new

American dream would be lodged in the suburbs, but their attempts to initiate government planning in order to make the suburbs accessible to less affluent citizens chafed against the twin totems of local independence and private enterprise. Middle-class suburbanites wanted to select—or to exclude—their neighbors without interference from federal programs of misguided philanthropy, and real estate developers resented federal intrusion into their domains of land speculation and housing construction. Consequently government policies provided for "safe" programs—mortgage insurance for those who could afford the suburbs, and second-class housing, like the PWA projects, which confined the poor to the inner city. These two priorities fixed the course of federal housing policy for the next third of a century.

The New Deal etched its mark on cities in many other ways. The National Recovery Administration (NRA) mustered local producers and consumers behind industrial codes of fair trade and price limits, and it also boosted local labor organization by guaranteeing collective bargaining. The Wagner National Labor Relations Act, passed in 1935 after the Supreme Court had dissolved the NRA, rescued and reiterated the NRA labor provisions. The NRA, the Wagner labor bill, and the Fair Labor Standards Act of 1938 were not aimed at cities, but they did implement some of the goals of a half-century of urban reform: minimum wages, maximum hours, an end to child labor and the sweatshops, and licensing of business (NRA codes even covered the burlesque industry; in New York, "Izzy" Herk, executive secretary of Code 348, limited each show to just four strip-teases.). In addition the WPA Writers' Project, a relief program for unemployed journalists, novelists, and other people of letters, made important contributions to urban history by compiling statistical guides for scores of cities and states. The WPA's Historical Records Survey, begun in 1936, employed relief workers to take inventories of, and to preserve, local public records. Finally federal action prodded many cities to institute independent efforts to meet their problems. By 1940, there were over eleven hundred local planning boards, double the peak number of the 1920s. Some of these agencies had begun to think more seriously about regional planning, and they created a few metropolitan district authorities to administer special services, such as sanitation and parks. By 1940 most cities had reduced tax delinquency and had constructed sounder fiscal bases. Some supplemented state and federal relief programs with innovations of their own. In 1939, for example, Rochester implemented a food stamp program that enabled poor people to purchase staples for two-thirds market price. Over the next year and a half the program spread to over one hundred cities.

In its largest sense the New Deal nationalized the communal action that had been a part of urban life for three centuries. For most urban dwellers the Depression had dissolved the vestiges of nineteenth-century individualism, and national crisis had bared the need for social service and collective action. The requisites of urban life had become those of the nation.

SOCIAL CONTINUITIES AND CHANGES

Picture for a moment a few hypothetical scenes from urban society, say Chicago, on a spring night in 1936. In a middle-class home on the outskirts, a cocktail party is underway: the conversations center on whether or not Chicago will ever be able to have a skyscraper as tall as New York's new Empire State Building. Next door, the house is dark; the couple has gone to the movies. In spite of hard times, films are attracting eighty-five million viewers per week, and in 1935 Cinema Queen Mae West earned half a million dollars. Across the street two couples are engrossed in a tense hand of bridge. Around the corner a family clusters around a game of Monopoly while the radio fills the room with mellow tones from Benny Goodman's clarinet. A few miles away in a working-man's bar, two men debate the imponderables of the new baseball season. At issue is whether the Cubs can win the National League pennant again this year. In an apartment house down the street, the workers' wives speculate about what will happen next on the popular radio soap opera, "One Man's Family."

The same debates, movies, games, and interests circulated through the villages and towns as well, but the significance of these activities lies in the cities. Just as in the 1920s—indeed as in almost all previous eras—the city continued to be the seat of style. To be sure, poverty and joblessness cast a gloom over the whole nation and prompted intellectuals to look pessimistically at their society through treatises, novels, and plays that explored themes of economic exploitation and class conflict. But even the Depression did not alter the technological, consumer society that had accompanied the rise of cities and had given urban dwellers a variety of pastimes. Rural Americans had always enjoyed a number of entertainments, but they had often considered mass diversions a waste of time. The emergence of a national urban culture, however, gave positive value to sports and other leisure activities. Cut loose from nature, urban dwellers took on an almost undiscriminating view of the pursuit of happiness. Not even extreme deprivation and fiscal collapse could block the march of mass culture; indeed they often encouraged the search for escape.

Urban consumers dictated popular tastes across the country. Big city tabloid newspapers tripled their circulations during the thirties, mostly by dramatizing public interest stories, such as the kidnapping of the son of Mr. and Mrs. Charles A. Lindbergh, the birth of the Dionne quintuplets, and the killing of bank robber John Dillinger, "public enemy number one." Downtown and neighborhood movie houses teemed with people anxious to escape into places like the high seas, as in "Mutiny on the Bounty" (1936), the Old South, as in "Gone With the Wind" (1939), the realm of horror as in "The Bride of Frankenstein" (1935), or the dreams of fantasy, as in "Snow White and the Seven Dwarfs" (1937). To offset the Depression, many movie theaters offered reduced prices, ladies nights, sneak preview, and bank nights (raffles). Attendance at baseball and football games, which had dropped between 1930 and 1935, revived later in the decade. Even during the depths of the Depression, however, the World Series averaged forty thousand fans per game. Although urban dwellers witnessed relief lines, angry radicals, and labor rallies on the streets, most could return home to read about Joe Louis or Shirley Temple and turn on the radio to Fred Allen, Guy Lombardo, or The Green Hornet.

Yet beneath the frivolity, social changes were underway. A major reason for the expansion of popular culture was that Americans, particularly those in cities, had more time for it. Depressed conditions of industry plus ceilings on hours set by the NRA shortened the work week more dramatically than had any previous combination of events and reforms. By the late thirties the forty-hour, five-day week had become the rule, and Saturday closings were common in most cities. In many cases this situation meant underemployment or layoffs, especially for those on the lower rungs of the work force. Industrial laborers faced plant closings, and young men entering the labor force found limited openings.

For some men the Depression seems to have blocked even the most ordinary paths of upward mobility. Stephan Thernstrom's study of Boston has revealed that during the 1930s far fewer manual laborers were able to attain nonmanual occupations than in any other period since 1880. Bostonians in low white-collar occupations—clerks, semiprofessionals, and petty proprietors—fell into manual laboring ranks in greater proportions than in previous eras. The same patterns of reduced opportunities and more frequent downward mobility occurred in Norristown, Pennsylvania, a much smaller city. Although in Boston economic recovery of the 1940s enabled some men to climb back up the occupational ladder, as Thernstrom notes, the unemployment and insecurity of the thirties "left scares on men . . . that continued to handicap them long after. . . ."

The situation of women was somewhat different. The stock market crash and its aftermath forced hundreds of thousands of women off payrolls and back into the homes. Many of the jobs that had opened within expanding private and government bureaucracies as a result of urban and industrial expansion in the twenties now evaporated. In the thirties the proportion of women in professional occupations fell from 14.2 to 12.3 percent. As jobs became scarce, some employers gave preference to men, maintaining that in hard times women should remain in the home while their husbands exercised their traditional roles as breadwinners. Early in the Depression many cities prohibited the hiring of married women as civil servants, and some school systems fired female teachers when they married. Yet economic necessity forced wives and mothers to seek part-time and marginal employment to help support their families. Women dropped out of the work force more slowly than did men, and they also reentered it more slowly. In many cities industrial laborers (mostly men) were laid off faster than store clerks, file clerks, and secretaries (mostly women). Thus in 1931 unemployment among women was 18.9 percent compared to 26.1 percent among men. But as New Deal relief projects put men back to work, by 1938 the proportions were reversed—22.1 percent of women and 14.3 percent for men.

The impact of these patterns on urban family life has yet to be measured. It seems reasonable to assume that unemployment and insecurity jumbled traditional relationships. What happened when a wife, rather than the husband, became the principal wage earner? Did women in these circumstances replace men at the command of household finances? What happened when children who had left their families to seek their fortunes returned home jobless and disillusioned? Did city apartments become more crowded from families who joined together to economize their resources? Did adversity reinforce the sense of communal welfare that critics believed urbanization to have destroyed? Or did tensions resulting from insecurity heighten the traumas of urban life and tear apart families? Was family life in the thirties more or less resilient on the farms than in the cities? Clear answers to these and to a host of related questions remain obscure, but they may hold the key to real effects of the Depression on the urban social fabric.

Beneath the outer layers of popular culture and the adjustments of family life in the city during the 1930s sores were beginning to fester. Just as prosperity during the twenties had not reached all segments of society equally, hard times struck some more fiercely than others. More than one hundred thousand Puerto Ricans left the destitution of their island only to discover discrimination in New York. Blacks particularly bore the brunt of calamity. Life in the rural South had always been difficult for blacks, but to those who clustered in northern and southern cities the depression had a shattering effect. Unemployment was two or three times greater among urban blacks than among whites. In 1933 a third of black families in New York, Chicago, Philadelphia, and Detroit were on relief, and the percentages were even higher in smaller cities.

As purchasing power disappeared, the small black middle class of merchants and professionals began to wither. Working-class families were forced to seek cheaper living quarters, sometimes by necessity and occasionally by do-good government slum clearance.

The New Deal, particularly through the WPA and USHA, made some attempts to ease the hardships, but blacks responded in their own ways. Their most notable activities included religious mysticism and social protest. Both were related, and both grew out of the urban experience. Unorthodox religious cults, organized by charismatic leaders and offering emotional experiences, proliferated in several big cities after World War I. In many ways the cults resembled the urban holiness churches that had sprung up to serve the needs of rural whites transplanted to the city. The black cults shunned doctrine and emphasized personal and communal ritual as a relief to mundane misery. During the Depression these churches assumed an increasingly important function for blacks caught in the web of unemployment and deprivation. In Harlem, Father Divine, who called himself "the true and living God," amassed a huge following by ministering to both spiritual and material needs. Other cults included Daddy Grace's United House of Prayer for All in Washington, D.C., Prophet Kiwah Costenie's Church of the Almighty God in Brooklyn, and Noble Drew Ali's Moorish Science Temple of America in Chicago and other cities.

Several cults fostered a social and political militancy among blacks that was echoed outside the churches. A few blacks attempted to form cooperatives to prevent money from flowing out of the ghetto into white men's pockets, but successes were minimal. In industrial cities a small number of blacks were allowed into unions of the newly formed Congress of Industrial Organizations (CIO), but most were either barred from joining or were afraid of losing precious jobs by unionizing. In New York and a few other cities, blacks picketed and boycotted stores that would hire only whites. These actions, too, were futile. In Harlem hopelessness and bitterness burst open on March 19, 1935, in a riot that left 100 people injured and damaged $2 million of property. It was a frenzy of looting in which, according to poet Claude McKay, "crowds went crazy like the remnants of a defeated, abandoned, and hungry army." This was the first time blacks had initiated violence on such a scale. It was a ghetto riot, not a race riot. Looters pillaged food and clothing stores owned by both races and fought the police but did not attack whites. Afterward a commission appointed by Mayor LaGuardia blamed the riot on discrimination, unemployment, and police brutality and predicted that riots would recur if these conditions were not improved. The alarm bell had been rung, but few people wished to hear it.

The Depression did not disrupt continuity. The urban poor had always been poor. Nonwhites continued to face segregation and discrimination. The march of popular culture was too far advanced to change course. But changes were beginning to surface. There were new doubts about the promise of American life and new dissatisfactions with life as it was. Perhaps most importantly for cities, a new political situation was emerging.

THE EMERGENCE OF A NATIONAL URBAN POLICY

"This election," Herbert Hoover predicted in 1932, "is not a mere shift from the ins to the outs. It means deciding the direction our nation will take over a century to come." In many ways he was right. Franklin Roosevelt's New Deal has been called, "the third American Revolution" because it blanketed so many areas of American society with government protection. Yet on the local level, the federal government in the 1930s was doing little that leaders, elected or adopted, had not been doing a generation earlier. What was new, though not necessarily intended, was the way in which government programs formed the nucleus of the country's first national urban policy.

The New Deal, as confusing and contradictory as it was, provided jobs, security, and hope by imposing the federal government on the national economy. In many ways urban dwellers were more attuned to such imposition than were rural types. By the mid-thirties, two-thirds of the populations of the eleven cities with over a million inhabitants were first or second generation immigrants, most of whom had few loyalties to rugged individualism and few scruples about state interference. These were the same people who had come to expect positive assistance in times of need from their leaders and who had exerted a strong influence on the development of an urban liberalism. Roosevelt responded to these new stock urban dwellers more than had any previous national leader. During Roosevelt's early career in New York politics, Boss "Big Tim" Sullivan had told him, "The people who had come over in steerage . . . knew in their hearts and lives the difference between being despised and being accepted and liked." As President, FDR remembered this advice. He exuded a warmhearted personality, and his New Deal agencies offered direct relief with a minimum of questions. Thus support flowed to FDR because the effects of many of his national programs resembled what bosses and machines traditionally had done on the local level.

But New Deal support in the cities was more than another kind of boss constituency; it included a coalition between new stock, working-class interests and elements of social and economic reform, a coalition that had begun to form in the late-nineteenth century. The various regulatory agencies, relief programs, labor laws, and social security measures implemented many of the goals that had been part of reform crusades for half a century. Important New Deal personalities such as Rexford Tugwell, Harry Hopkins, Frances Perkins, Robert F. Wagner, and Harold Ickes had backgrounds in urban reform, and they helped shape federal programs into the framework of a national urban policy during the thirties.

Urban voters voiced their reactions to the New Deal in the presidential election of 1936, when Roosevelt won a resounding victory by carrying every state but Maine and Vermont. Support for FDR was particularly strong in the cities. The nation's ten largest cities contributed one-third of Roosevelt's eleven million vote margin over Alfred M. Landon. Smaller places, many of them traditionally Republican, also piled up huge majorities for the Democratic president. Duluth, Gary, Scranton, Canton, Youngstown and others, which had supported Hoover in 1932, gave nearly three-fourths of their votes to FDR. In 1936 six million more voters went to the polls than in 1932, and it has been estimated that Roosevelt attracted five million of them. Immigrants and their children, who had responded to Al Smith's candidacy in 1928 and to other Democrats earlier in the 1920s, moved solidly behind FDR. A new dimension, urban black voters, joined the Democratic fold. Although the New Deal in many ways was insensitive to racial problems, it had at least dispensed relief with less discrimination than had any other previous government effort. The effect on blacks was to break their ties with the party of Abraham Lincoln and to draw them into FDR's camp. Ghetto districts in Chicago, Cleveland, Detroit, and Philadelphia, which had given majorities to Hoover in 1932, now swung to the Democrats and became ever-important fixtures of the party's national base.

If the federal government now began to assume the positive functions of machine politics—relief, jobs, and security—, what now happened to the boss? Certainly bossism did not wither away. Some of the most powerful urban leaders survived and flourished during the New Deal: Crump of Memphis, Hague of Jersey City, Pendergast of Kansas City, and Kelly of Chicago. Although a number of bosses originally supported Al Smith for the Democratic nomination in 1932, almost all accepted Roosevelt by the time of the election. FDR maintained good relations with these men, and they often turned to the president for assistance. Yet the New Deal did alter the nature of boss politics in several important ways.

Most fundamentally, the New Deal diluted some of the boss' personalized services while embellishing his function as a broker between ordinary citizens and their government. Political machines could not handle the traumas of depression. The Christmas turkeys, burial money, summer outings, and free shoes for school children no longer sufficed. As the federal government assumed responsibilities for offering relief and insuring security, it scaled down the boss' power. To be sure, many New Deal benefits were filtered to the needy through local politicians, but the recipients knew the jobs and cash were coming from Washington. Equally important, by fostering a huge expansion of organized labor, the New Deal indirectly gnawed away at several functions of bossism. In the past most unionization had been confined to skilled laborers, many of whom actively excluded assmbly line workers. The unskilled—and most immigrants were unskilled—had to depend on political leaders for welfare and protection. Now, however, Section 7a of the NIRA and the Wagner Labor Act encouraged unskilled, industrial workers to organize. Under the CIO and other unions more laborers than ever before had access to jobs, protection on the job, and unemployment compensation. Moreover union halls offered new social centers to workingmen, sometimes replacing saloons, and union leaders organized picnics, speeches, and other affairs that had previously been the prerogative of political machines. Because the labor vote became an increasingly important political force, the craft and industrial unions commanded the attention of city halls, state capitals, and Washington. Thus bosses now had to share their role as spokesmen for the working classes.

On the other hand, the New Deal gave some bosses unprecedented opportunities. By spreading its influence over local affairs, the federal government created new sources of patronage jobs, paid with federal money but controlled by local leaders. Particularly in cities where ward and precinct divisions had remained (that is, where district representation had not been replaced by city councils or city commissions elected at large), such as Pittsburgh and Chicago, the reinvigorated Democratic party offered employment possibilities to many men. In Pittsburgh, as Bruce Stave has shown, the New Deal helped the Democrats oust the Republicans from power and install David Lawrence as a powerful boss. As bosses adjusted to the increased powers of the federal government their intermediary functions became more important. They not only acted as information agents, telling constituents where and how to obtain services now offered by the federal government, but also built political bridges, increasingly supporting reform projects like schools, culture centers, and better housing. These issues often brought bosses into the camps of their traditional enemies, businessmen and social reformers. But only those bosses who recognized the need for new flexibility could survive after the New Deal. They could still control patronage, nominations for political office, and elections, but to do so meant acquiring a broader image.

At the mayoral level the depression and New Deal further blurred the distinction between machine politician and social reformer. Since the end of the nineteenth century reform "bosses" like Hazen Pingree of Detroit, Tom Johnson of Cleveland, and Samuel Jones of Toledo, plus boss-reformers like Charles Francis Murphy of New York and Edward F. Dunne of Chicago had moved closer together in their concern for new stock, working classes. Now, with prolonged hard times facing them, all mayors had to deal with pressing needs for money and jobs. Those who were most successful were the ones who could combine reform qualities of professional expertise with a boss's display of personal concern.

The epitome of this merger and the best-known mayor of the New Deal era was Fiorello LaGuardia of New York, a former insurgent Congressman who could outduel any machine politician in popular appeal. LaGuardia was born in the Lower East Side of New York, but he spent his youth in Arizona, where his Italian immigrant father was a bandmaster for the U.S. Army; and he spent his young manhood in southeastern Europe, where he worked for the U.S. Consulate. In 1906 he became an interpreter on Ellis Island, the famous entry station for immigrants coming to the New York port. Here young LaGuardia acquired firsthand experience with the plight of newcomers to the American city. He attended New York University Law School at night and then entered politics. Squeezing his way up through the Republican party, he won a seat in Congress in 1916 where he quickly gained notoriety as a peoples' advocate. He then made some frustrated attempts to unseat Tammany Hall from power in New York City and finally was elected mayor on a Fusion-Republican ticket in 1933, after Jimmy Walker, the scandal-tainted Democratic mayor, had been removed from office. LaGuardia immediately became a national spokesman for the urban cause. Along with Mayor Murphy of Detroit, he took a leading role in the newly formed U.S. Conference of Mayors, an organization that, throughout the 1930s, lobbied forcefully for federal assistance to cities. In New York LaGuardia's fiery, dynamic personality won him great affection, particularly from the city's many ethnic groups. As one observer wrote,

> LaGuardia *is* melting-pot America—first-generation Italian-American, with a Jewish great-great grandparent. . . . The Mayor is adept in all branches of political fanfaronade: he can lead the Fire Department Band, he can dress up in a sand-hog's helmet to inspect new tunnels, he can step into the pitcher's box on opening day at the Yankee Stadium and cut loose with a high hard one in the general direction of home plate.

As mayor, LaGuardia not only succeeded in obtaining large shares of PWA and other federal relief funds but also started a local program of public works and slum clearance, restored the city's credit, improved public facilities, obtained a new city charter, and initiated low-rent public housing. He was reelected twice, serving until 1945.

By the end of the 1930s the rising prominence of cities in national affairs prompted new initiative on the local and metropolitan levels. Planning commissions revived surveys and projects postponed by the depression. Responding to new pressures from automobile traffic, New York, Los Angeles, Detroit, Pittsburgh, and Cleveland planned or constructed belt highways and freeways, often with the aid of federal funds. Studies by sociologists, economists, geographers, and political scientists examined a host of issues ranging from urban land values to mental illness.

Still, however, the efforts of local planners, builders, and scholars paled beside the activity of the federal government. The New Deal had tightened the federal-city knot, and local officials were reluctant to loosen the bonds—especially since state governments maintained their traditional hostilities toward their cities. Skeptics like Harold Buttenheim, editor of *The American City,* warned that Uncle Sam was becoming "Boss Sam," but most urban leaders accepted federal programs and appropriations without fear of interference by Washington in local affairs.

It is significant that at this time the federal government sponsored the first national study of urban life. In 1937 the National Resources Committee, a branch of the Department of the Interior, published a report entitled *Our Cities: Their Role in the National Economy.* This study, headed by Clarence Dykstra, former city manager of Cincinnati, was intended as a complement to the report of the Country Life Commission, which had examined rural society for President Theodore Roosevelt three decades earlier. In its foreword the National Resources Committee clearly recognized the central themes of the evolution of America as an urban nation:

> The city has seemed at times the despair of America but at others to be the Nation's hope, the battleground of democracy. Surely in the long run, the Nation's destiny will be profoundly affected by the cities which have two-thirds of its population and its wealth. . . . The failures of our cities are not those of decadence and impending decline, but of exuberant vitality crowding its way forward under tremendous pressure—the flood rather than the drought.

The report urged the federal government to pay more attention to the needs of urban dwellers; and after a brief outline of the process of urbanization in the United States, it catalogued the nation's unsolved urban problems (no less than thirty-six) and presented a list of recommendations. The solutions proposed nothing new. They included public housing for low-income groups, more planning, increased and more equitable welfare services, abolition of slums, streamlined local governments, and more research. But the fact that these suggestions were now being offered by the federal government itself presaged a new era in the country's urban history.

By the outbreak of World War II that era seemed to have arrived. In 1941 the National Resources Planning Board, an agency created during the Depression to develop long-range plans for conserving the nation's land, water, and forests, turned directly to the problems of American cities. Under the guidance of Frederic A. Delano, FDR's uncle and one of the nation's most experienced veterans of city and regional planning, the NRPB fashioned a series of experimental programs enabling the federal government to assist urban redevelopment once the war was over. According to Philip J. Funigiello, the goal of these programs was "to attain a new level of sophistication in urban planning by treating the city not simply as an artifact but by integrating social, economic, and cultural factors into the planning process." This objective was attempted in *Action for Cities: A Guide for Community Planning*, a manual prepared by the board to familiarize planners and elected officials with progressive procedures in the physical, social, and economic aspects of urban redevelopment. Here was the embryo of an explicit, national urban policy.

Although the NRPB succeeded in convincing over one hundred cities to establish their own planning councils, the ultimate influence of its urban policy fell far short of expectations. The NRPB devised new models for federal aid to cities by proposing to furnish human, technical, and financial resources, but it overlooked basic problems of the poor. Moreover its concern with social control of urban land use frightened fiscal conservatives and private real estate interests whose allies in Congress managed to eliminate the NRPB in 1943.

The Roosevelt administration, in spite of its biases against cities, had rescued urban America during the depths of the Depression. Through the Report of the National Resources Commission in 1937 and the activities of the National Resources Planning Board between 1941 and 1943, the federal government made a direct commitment to extend its rescue efforts to plans for permanent improvement. Significantly these agencies identified cities' basic problems to be the exodus of productive middle classes to the suburbs and the unhealthy division between the inner and outer parts of the metropolis, a division aggravated by continued dependence upon the real property tax as the major source for local revenues. Failure by the federal government to sustain an urban policy toward these problems has left a much greater task for the present generation than otherwise might have been.

BIBLIOGRAPHY

The most useful surveys of the New Deal Period are William E. Leuchtenburg, *Franklin D. Roosevelt and the New Deal, 1932–1940* (New York: Harper and Row, 1963); Dixon Wector, *The Age of the Great Depression, 1929–1941* (New York: Macmillan, 1948); and Arthur M. Schlesinger, Jr., *The Crisis of the Old Order* (Boston: Houghton Mifflin, 1957), *The Coming of the New Deal* (Boston: Houghton Mifflin, 1959), and *The Politics of Upheaval* (Boston: Houghton Mifflin, 1960). An indispensible urban perspective is presented in Blake McKelvey, *The Emergence of Metropolitan America, 1915–1966* (New Brunswick, N. J.: Rutgers University Press, 1968). Also important are Clarence Eugene Ridley and Orin Frederyc Nolting, eds., *What the Depression Has Done to Cities* (Chicago: International City Managers Association, 1935); Raymond L. Koch, "Politics and Relief in Minneapolis During the 1930's," *Minnesota History* 41 (Winter 1968), 153–70; Bonnie Fox Schwartz, "Unemployment Relief in Philadelphia, 1930–1932," *Pennsylvania Magazine of History and Biography*, 92 (January 1969), 86–108; and Sam Bass Warner, Jr., *The Private City: Philadelphia in Three Stages of Its Growth* (Philadelphia: University of Pennsylvania Press, 1969), Part 3.

For insight into general social issues of the era, see Caroline F. Bird, *The Invisible Scar* (New York: D. McKay Co., 1966); Frederick Lewis Allen, *Since Yesterday: The Nineteen Thirties in America* (New York: Harper & Brothers, 1940); Studs Terkel, *Hard Times: An Oral History of the Great Depression* (New York: Pantheon, 1970); and Robert S. and Helen Merrell Lynd, *Middletown in Transition: A Study in Cultural Conflicts* (New York: Harcourt, Brace and Co., 1937). For more focused social and economic studies see Stephan Thernstrom, *The Other Bostonians: Poverty and Progress in the American Metropolis, 1880–1970* (Cambridge: Harvard University Press, 1973); William H. Chafe, *The American Woman: Her Changing Social, Economic, and Political Roles, 1920–1970* (New York: Oxford University Press, 1972); and Hollis Lynch, ed., *The Black Urban Condition: A Documentary History, 1866–1971* (New York: Crowell, 1973). Excellent analyses of New Deal planning and greenbelt towns are presented by Paul Conkin, *Tomorrow a New World: The New Deal Community Program* (Ithaca, N.Y.: Cornell University Press, 1959); and Joseph L. Arnold, *The New Deal in the Suburbs: A History of the Greenbelt Town Program, 1935–1954* (Columbus: Ohio State University Press, 1971).

Studies pertinent to urban politics include Samuel Lubell, *The Future of American Politics* (New York: Harper, 1965); Arthur Mann, *LaGuardia Comes to Power, 1933* (Chicago: University of Chicago Press, 1965); John D. Buenker, *Urban Liberalism and Progressive Reform* (New York: Charles Scribner's Sons, 1973); Bruce M. Stave, *The New Deal and the Last Hurrah: Pittsburgh Machine Politics* (Pittsburgh: University of Pittsburgh Press, 1970); Rita Werner Gordon, "The Change in the Political Alignment of Chicago's Negroes During the New Deal," *Journal of American History*, 56 (December 1969), 584–603; and John L. Shover, "The Emergence of a Two-Party System in Republican Philadelphia, 1924–1936," *Journal of American History*, 60 (March 1974), 985–1003. For glimpses of important personalities of the period, see John Chamberlain, "Mayor LaGuardia," *Yale Review*, 29 (September 1939), 11–27; "The Kelly–Nash Political Machine," *Fortune*, 14 (August 1936), 47–52 and 114–30; and J. Joseph Huthmacher, *Senator Robert F. Wagner and the Rise of Urban Liberalism* (New York: Atheneum, 1968). See also James Michael Curley's engaging personal reminiscences, *I'd Do It Again* (Englewood Cliffs, N.J.: Prentice-Hall, 1957). The development of federal urban policy during the New Deal and into World War II is best covered by the Urbanism Committee to the National Resources Committee, *Our Cities: Their Role in the National Economy* (Washington: Government Printing Office, 1937) and by Philip J. Funigiello, "City Planning in World War II: The Experience of the National Resources Planning Board,'" *Social Science Quarterly*, 52 (June 1972), 91–104.

9

URBAN AMERICA IN THE MODERN AGE, 1945-1975

THE SUBURBAN NATION

Americans' faith in their cities peaked in 1940 when a U.S. senator proclaimed, "With God's help we will lift Shanghai up and up, ever up— until it is just like Kansas City!" Since then the nation has experienced the onset of an urban crisis, certainly not the first in American history, but possibly the most serious. For three centuries cities had been able to generate the social and economic opportunities that mitigated the problems resulting when large, heterogeneous populations pressed together in relatively small spaces. But by the middle of the twentieth century, many of these opportunities seemed to have dissolved. The United States had evolved into a postindustrial society in which services demanding specialized skills were replacing long-established manufacturing activities as principal sources of employment. Automation and modern transportation enabled many companies to leave big cities where land was expensive, labor was militant, and taxes were high. In addition the eternal quest for a dream house pulled more middle- and upper-class families out of cities and into suburbs. The cities left behind faced problems they had always faced—poverty, crime, pollution, unemployment, social tension—only now, as never before, these conditions rested upon decaying physical plants and revenue bases that were not growing as rapidly as needs required. Over the past three decades the nation has heard a myriad of schemes, private and governmental, to save and improve cities. But the vast majority of these plans have reflected an ambiguity that has pervaded our urban past: the belief, on one hand, that cities need to be saved, the nostalgia, on the other hand, to return to the small, autonomous, preurban community.

In large part this ambiguity has survived because more than ever before popular thought—and much official policy—divides urban America into inner and outer parts. The urban and rural distinctions that characterized American society for so long no longer hold. Because three-fourths of the nation's population now live in what the Census Bureau defines as urban areas—districts containing fifty thousand or more people plus contiguous or nearby regions with population densities above one thousand people per square mile—, the terms *urban* and *suburban* have become the most accurate characterizations of living experiences. These distinctions represent the culmination of historical process, for they simply translate the inner city-outer city dichotomy of the last half of the nineteenth century into new political divisions.

In 1970 urbanization in the United States reached a new milestone, as symbolic as the mark passed in 1920 when urban dwellers became a majority of the population. The 1970 census revealed that more Americans now lived in suburbs than in cities. Of two hundred million people, seventy-six million lived in areas around but not inside cities, sixty-four million in cities themselves. The suburban totals represented an extraordinary increase: in 1950, thirty million had lived in suburbs, fifty million lived in suburbs in 1960. The centrifugal dynamics of urban sprawl, created in the 1850s, had become the predominating force of population movement.

Suburbanization is not new to American history. Throughout the nineteenth century towns just outside the borders of Philadelphia, Boston, New York, and Chicago increased in population more rapidly than did the big city nearby. Ferries, trolleys, and railroads made outlying areas more accessible, and crowding, social tension, and crime within the old walking cities made the suburban dream more desirable. As early as 1848, landscape architect Andrew Jackson Downing wrote, "Hundreds of thousands, formerly obliged to live in the crowded streets of cities, now find themselves able to enjoy a country cottage, . . . and these suburban cottages enable the busy citizen to breathe freely, and keep alive his love for nature. . . ." During the last decades of the century cities were able to annex settled regions on their borders and absorb suburban populations, but in the twentieth century contiguous towns resisted consolidation so that today suburbanites outnumber urban dwellers.

Not surprisingly, the 1970 census also disclosed that suburbs contained more housing units than did cities. After World War II, FHA mortgage insurance and liberal loans from Veterans Administration programs helped pull aspiring middle-class families toward the suburbs and

The Postwar Housing Explosion
Signs in an undeveloped section outside San Diego advertise the types of housing and government support that invigorated suburbanization after World War II. *Courtesy of the Library of Congress.*

encouraged thousands of new real estate developments. By guaranteeing home loans the federal government virtually eliminated down payments, enabling lower middle class and even some working-class families to buy or build in the urban outskirts. The ease of credit and acceleration of general prosperity by the late 1940s triggered a massive construction boom that lasted for nearly a decade. In 1950 alone almost a million single-family houses were begun, the vast majority of which sprouted in outlying or suburban districts. The postwar decade witnesses the flowering of bedroom suburbs—the Levittowns and Park Forests—across the country.

Much of this expansion was possible because highway construction opened up previously unsettled land. After World War II a huge increase in the number of automobiles pressed existing roads within and between cities beyond their capacities. Between 1945 and 1950 automobile registrations rose from twenty-five million to over forty million, and they were approaching sixty million by the mid-fifties. Traffic, parking, and air pollution—problems with long histories in urban areas—began to receive special attention as local and federal governments sought ways to accommodate the proliferation of cars and trucks. As roadbuilding became an increasingly costly venture (relief of congestion now required four- and six-lane superhighways and expressways), cities began to look to the federal government for assistance. In 1947 Congress authorized a 37,000-mile national highway network and designated funds for the construction of nearly 3,000 miles of roads in or near 182 large

The Highway and the City
This complex of highways, photographed in 1946, provides access from Long Island to New York City and has made possible explosive suburban growth along its arterial paths. *U.S. State Department, The National Archives.*

cities. By 1949 the federal government was spending $2 billion a year on highways. The annual appropriations had doubled by 1956 when President Eisenhower signed the Interstate Highway Act, initiating a 42,500-mile, $60 billion highway system (the costs eventually reached far beyond estimates) to streamline national defense. The new road network was to be anchored by every major city in the country.

Like the railroad and trolley lines a century earlier, new highway systems accelerated urban sprawl. From the 1930s onward highway planners conceived of urban road networks in terms of a hub (the downtown) and a wheel (radial arteries fanning out from the center and beltways circling the city on the outskirts). The interstate system followed this analogue except in places like Los Angeles, which were already too dispersed to have a single central business district. Los Angeles' highways were to follow a giant grid. Whatever the pattern, real estate developers bought up (and are still buying) huge tracts of open land along proposed interstate routes around urban outskirts and began offering lots and building homes for prospective suburbanites. Capitalizing on transportation connections, developers reinvigorated the city-building process that had so long been a preoccupation of American expansionists. Outside Los Angeles, for example, the town of Anaheim, location of Disneyland and beneficiary of the Santa Ana Freeway, mushroomed from 17,267 people in 1952 to 91,100 in 1959.

Businesses naturally followed the residential expansion—although in some instances they located ahead of actual settlement in outlying districts—and formed secondary commercial centers near principal highway interchanges. This, too, was not new to urban expansion. Since the mid-nineteenth century, business districts had been growing around elevated railway stations and intersections of transit routes. As early as the 1920s this process foreshadowed the decline of downtown. Now in the mid-twentieth century the planting of these business districts began to take on a more formalized character. Shopping centers, complete with closed arcades of shops, large anchor department stores, and sprawling parking lots became major retail marketplaces for the metropolis. As population radiated outward, it became increasingly convenient for a family to fill its material needs in shopping centers rather than in old central business districts. The various malls and plazas could boast of every service the middle-class consumer might desire: specialty shops, department stores, drug stores, groceries, movie theaters, restaurants, cocktail lounges, insurance offices, and, best of all, free parking. A New Mexico shopping center built in the early 1960s even intended to double as a bomb shelter in case of atomic attack, and it advertised that it could accommodate eight thousand people underground for up to two weeks. For a prepaid fee of $250, customers were guaranteed "organized schools, movies, games, and survival . . . to minimize panic and depression." As one researcher predicted in 1962, "It's not far-fetched to say that the shopping centers will become downtown areas." The centers themselves, their size (many now cover over one hundred acres) and their glitter became new objects of boosterism as each year chauvinists from a different community boasted that they had the biggest shopping mall in the state/region/country/world.

Thus outward movement energized a new multiplier effect. Access to highways attracted residents, who in turn lured businesses who then brought jobs and more enticement for residential development. Industry also entered the cycle. New and rapidly growing firms in areas such as research and development, electronics, aerospace, and chemicals did not depend upon locations near raw materials or near rail hubs. Like retail businesses, these industries took advantage of highway accessibility and built plants outside of big cities (along the Route 128 belt around Boston and the beltways circling Baltimore and Washington for example). During the fifties and sixties some communities developed industrial parks, special outlying tracts zoned exclusively for light industry. For cities that had annexed vacant land on their perimeters, industrial parks provided a means of maintaining tax revenues by keeping "footloose" industries within city borders. Usually, however, the benefit went to suburbs.

From a social perspective, suburbanization in the decades after World War II repeated the process that had been underway for a century. As Herbert Gans discovered in his study of Levittown, New Jersey, most people who moved to suburbia were seeking more space. They wanted a free-standing house, with large closets, a den or recreation room, and a yard. Of the people interviewed by Gans, nearly 60 percent cited house-related factors as the principal reason for moving to Levittown. As one observer wrote, "Most Levittowners acquired their houses for one or both of two reasons: (1) a Levitt house is a bargain in well-equipped shelter; (2) the community is spacious enough to give every kid an opportunity to grow up with grass stains on his pants." To a lesser extent, people moved because of dissatisfactions (poor schools, shabby neighborhoods, racial fears) with their former residences. These were the same push and pull forces that had always governed residential change within metropolitan areas.

In addition, like all urban neighborhoods of the past, in- and out-migration kept suburbs in constant flux. The average Levittowner had moved once every two and a half years since his or her marriage. In Park Forest, Illinois, a third of the apartments and one-fifth of the houses changed occupants each year in the early 1950s. Of all the people who moved to Levittown in the late fifties, nearly half (45 percent) had previously lived in another suburb—dampening the notion that most suburbanites were disaffected urbanites who had fled the city. As Daniel Boorstin observed,

> A small town was a place where a man settled. A suburb was a place to or from which a person moved. . . . (S)uburbanites did not think of building their town for their children or their grandchildren. They expected their children to live elsewhere. And even before their children grew up they themselves hoped to have moved to a more "exclusive" suburb.

Certainly all of the thousands of suburbs that now ring cities did not fit the model of Levittown and Park Forest. Cicero, Illinois, and Hamtramck, Michigan, both heavily ethnic and working class in composition, are much different varieties. Still the public image was set by quick-grown, transient, middle-class communities that sprouted after the war.

This image, however, has been a distorted one because it has reflected expectations that could never be fulfilled. Since the 1950s intellectual critics and sociologists have leveled a barrage of accusations at what they have considered to be emptiness and artificiality in suburban life styles.

The titles of books and articles reveal the nature of prevailing sentiment: "Trouble in the Suburbs"; *The Crack in the Picture Window; The Split Level Trap;* and "The Crabgrass Roots of Suburbia." Novelists appropriated these themes to blast contemporary society. In David Karp's novel, *Leave Me Alone* (1965), the hero snarls at his fellow suburbanites,

> You are probably the most dreary collection of slack-jawed yahoos it has ever been my bad luck to meet. I don't know what sins against the human spirit and the intellect can be excused on the grounds of neighborliness and civic pride, but however many there are, I've gone over my quota tonight. Those of you who aren't cowards are bigots, and those of you who aren't bigots are sheep, and some of you are both.

And Hollywood was quick to join the parade. Moviemakers analyzed the suburban malaise, as in the filmed version of Sloan Wilson's novel, *The Man in the Gray Flannel Suit,* and exploited the theme in lurid works such as *Sin in the Suburbs,* an "art film" that Scott Donaldson described as unfolding.

> 'The whole scandalous story . . .': the faithless wives abandoned too long by husbands who had to catch 'that damned 7:21,' the workmen who dropped in on hot-eyed suburban wives for an hour of pleasure, the younger set made up of boy rapists and girl lesbians, the sex club members who played musical beds on Tuesday and Thursday evenings.

To some extent suburbs deserved the contempt. In the race for profits after World War II, developers bulldozed away natural beauty, created ticky tacky houses, and reserved prime land along feeder highways for motels, gas stations, and fast food franchises. But the critics failed to admit that poor land use planning had been a major failure of all urban growth for two and a half centuries. Private real estate and commercial interests have always determined the nature of urban *and* suburban expansion. Moreover critics often overlooked the broad variety of suburbs. As early as 1925, scholar and theologian Harlan Paul Douglass confessed that he was unable "to furnish a satisfying list of the types of suburbs which surround American cities." Today, a half-century later, an attempted classification would bewilder the most careful cataloger. The range of suburbs not only stretches from residential to industrial, poor to rich, black to white, but also contains innumerable hybrids. Even the most widely recognized characteristic of suburban life, commuting, has little relevance. Today many suburbanites live near their work, and many city dwellers reverse commute to factories, offices, and shops in the suburbs. Moreover transportation studies have revealed that only a minority of workers, even suburbanites, live more than thirty minutes from their jobs.

Most importantly, as Kenneth T. Jackson has observed, ". . . for all the criticism, . . . suburbs have grown and doubtless will continue to grow because they satisfy the needs of those who live there better than any currently available alternative." Suburban life has generally reinforced, not disrupted, traditional institutions of family and community. Gans observed that suburbs solidified family ties by focusing activities on the house and yard. The image of a fragmented family in which the commuting father is only a martini-guzzling weekend visitor while the mother acts as a harried chauffeur for pampered children may apply to modern middle-class society, but not to suburbs alone. Gans also asserted that suburbs encouraged community contact and social organization, though often unintentionally, by combining people of similar age, status, and stage in life cycle. "Most new suburbanites," Gans concluded, "are pleased with the community that develops; they enjoy the house and outdoor living and take pleasure from the large supply of compatible people, without experiencing the boredom or malaise ascribed to suburban homogeneity."

A number of writers linked the women's liberation movement of the 1960s and early 1970s with the suburban malaise. Betty Friedan's *The Feminine Mystique* (1963), which sounded the clarion call for a feminist revival, seemed to be aimed directly at middle-class suburban housewives who were trapped in domestic "concentration camps," smothered by gadgets and child-rearing responsibilities, and blocked from full realization of individual potential. The book sold over a million copies and undoubtedly raised the consciousness of thousands of suburban women to the ways in which they were manipulated in a male-dominated society.

But the feminists' quest for greater equality and opportunity resulted from forces larger than suburban or middle-class boredom that Friedan and others identified. In part, these forces involve economic and demographic change. The proportions of women working, which had dropped after their World War II peaks, began to climb again in the 1950s; and by the late 1960s, 40 percent of American women held jobs. Almost half of mothers with school-age children worked. These rates have risen because in modern urban society women no longer need or want to remain at home tending children for as long as their mothers and grandmothers did. Today the average urban (and suburban) woman marries a few months before her twenty-first birthday, has her first child when she is twenty-two or twenty-three, ends child-bearing at thirty, is left without children at home when she is forty-six, and can expect to live to seventy-four. Having experienced independence and broad social contacts in college or work before marriage, many modern women (particularly of the middle class) have reached the stage where they desire activities in addition to motherhood after or even during the eight or ten years when requirements of child nurture are most pressing. Thus in the postwar era, women have increasingly entered the job market, and when neo-feminists blasted the restrictiveness of the traditional female sphere, they spoke from a base of rising expectations. Moreover, the climate of the 1960s, which fostered movements to attain equal rights for racial minorities, alerted women to the nature of economic and social discrimination and prodded women to attempt to transcend their circumscribed roles. Suburban women, mostly affluent and educated, along with their urban counterparts have had the time and resources to participate actively in the quest for women's rights, but the movement has roots in changes affecting all of metropolitan America.

Much of the intellectual disaffection with suburbs erupted during the 1950s when liberals blamed the rise of Eisenhower Republicanism on suburban materialism. Critics theorized that Democrats from the city acquired different attitudes in the suburbs—success, symbolized by moving to a suburb, made people more conservative in their politics. "Whatever the cause," wrote William H. Whyte, Jr., in 1956, "it is true that something does seem to happen to Democrats when they get to suburbia." The "something" was that they became Republicans. The proof was that Democratic percentages in the cities were declining while Republican totals in the suburbs were climbing. In 1952 suburban areas contributed 52 percent of Eisenhower's vote, and in 1956 the Republican vote outside of big cities such as Philadelphia, New York, Chicago, St. Louis, and San Francisco was large enough to supersede the Democratic majorities inside. Although political analysts contended that suburbanization, rather than converting Democrats to Republicans, simply transplanted lifelong Republicans, the trend seemed clear. As Jacob Arvey, a Democratic boss in Chicago, moaned in 1952, "The suburbs beat us."

But the political pendulum swung the other way in 1960. That year the Democratic candidate, John F. Kennedy, won 49 percent of the total suburban vote; his opponent, Richard M. Nixon, won just over 47 percent. The Republican ascendancy in the fifties had been attached mainly to Eisenhower. By 1960 two-party competition for the suburban presidential vote had returned to a relative draw. In 1964, however, Lyndon Johnson's national landslide swept through suburbia, creating a new imbalance. In that election the Republican nominee, Senator Barry Goldwater, captured under 34 percent of the suburban vote, an extraordinary decline from Eisenhower's 60 percent share in 1956.

The 1968 and 1972 results were even more confusing. Although Richard Nixon generally carried the suburbs, political analysts uncovered a wide incidence of party instability in Congressional and local elections. As Americans as a whole and suburbanites in particular became better

TABLE 5

Central City, Black, and Metropolitan Populations for Selected American Cities, 1940 and 1970

City	1940 Central City	1940 Blacks	1940 Metro Area	1970 Central City	1970 Blacks	1970 Metro Area
Atlanta	302,288	104,533	558,842	496,973	255,051	1,390,164
Baltimore	859,100	165,843	1,139,529	905,759	420,210	2,070,670
Boston	770,816	23,679	2,209,608	641,071	104,707	2,753,700
Buffalo	506,775	17,694	958,487	462,768	94,329	1,349,211
Chicago	3,396,808	277,731	4,569,643	3,366,957	1,102,620	6,978,947
Cincinnati	455,610	55,593	787,044	452,524	125,000	1,384,851
Cleveland	878,336	84,504	1,267,270	750,903	287,841	2,064,194
Dallas	294,734	50,407	527,145	844,401	210,238	1,555,950
Denver	322,412	7,836	445,206	514,678	47,011	1,227,529
Detroit	1,623,452	149,119	2,377,329	1,511,482	660,428	4,199,931
Houston	384,514	86,302	528,961	1,232,802	316,551	1,985,031
Indianapolis	386,972	51,142	460,926	743,155	134,320	1,109,882
Kansas City (Mo.)	399,178	41,574	686,643	507,409	112,005	1,256,649
Los Angeles	1,504,277	63,774	2,916,403	2,816,061	503,606	7,032,075
Louisville	319,077	47,158	451,473	361,472	86,040	826,553
Memphis	292,942	121,498	358,250	623,530	242,513	770,120
Miami	172,172	36,857	267,739	334,859	76,156	1,267,792
Milwaukee	587,472	8,821	829,629	717,099	105,088	1,403,688
Minneapolis	492,370	4,646	967,367	434,400	19,005	1,813,647
Nashville	167,402	47,318	257,267	447,877	87,876	541,108
New Orleans	494,537	149,034	552,244	593,471	267,308	1,046,470
New York	7,454,995	458,444	8,706,917	7,894,862	1,668,115	11,571,899
Newark	429,760	74,965	1,291,416	382,417	207,458	1,856,556
Philadelphia	1,931,334	250,880	3,199,637	1,948,609	653,791	4,817,914
Pittsburgh	671,659	62,216	2,082,556	520,117	104,904	2,401,245
Portland (Ore.)	305,394	1,931	501,275	382,619	21,572	1,009,129
Providence	253,504	6,388	695,253	179,213	15,875	789,186
Rochester	324,975	3,262	438,230	296,233	49,647	882,667
St. Louis	816,048	108,765	1,464,111	622,236	254,191	2,363,017
Salt Lake City	149,934	694	211,623	175,885	2,135	557,635
San Francisco	634,536	4,846	1,461,804	715,674	96,078	3,109,519
Seattle	368,302	3,789	593,734	538,831	37,868	1,421,869
Washington, D.C.	663,091	187,266	967,985	756,510	537,712	2,861,123

educated and more affluent, party identification, became less secure; and more voters declared themselves to be independents.

Political fluctuations signify that middle-class white suburbanites really have several kinds of loyalties. On the one hand, they are pursuing an Old American dream: security in private surroundings, a flirtation with nature, small-community political autonomy, and escape from the disorganization and complexities of crowded cities. These have been the ideals of the ambitious, aggressive family and have been attached, during this century, to the ideology of the Republican party. On the other hand, many of the families now populating middle-class suburbs are second and third generation immigrants only once removed from the inner city. They have brought with them remnants of urban liberalism, that bundle of welfare and labor goals traditionally attached to the Democratic Party. Yet the new suburbanites have sought to protect their stake in the middle-class dream by strongly supporting measures to keep out "undesirables": blacks, Chicanos, and other minority groups. (In 1970 only 5 percent of the nation's black population lived in suburbs.) And finally, suburbs, particularly those closest to the city, have begun to experience the problems of urban life that suburbanites originally sought to escape—soaring taxes, crowding, creeping decay, pollution, and crime. The growth of these problems has forced many suburban officials to abandon a self-help stance and to seek aid from metropolitan, state, and federal agencies. Thus in order to protect their interests, suburbanites have become issue-oriented, not party-oriented. And they have protected these interests at the expense of others.

THE DILEMMA OF THE GHETTO

Since World War II the division between cities and suburbs has assumed a racial dimension—whites on the outside, blacks on the inside. Between 1950 and 1966, 70 percent of the increase in the nation's white population occurred in suburbs, while 86 percent of the increase in the black population took place in central cities. The opening of jobs in war industries during the 1940s, and postwar prosperity of the fifties and sixties pulled four million blacks off farms and into cities. By 1970 about three-quarters of blacks in the United States lived in cities, compared to about 64 percent of whites. In the North, 93 percent of all blacks were urban. By the mid-1970s, six major cities—Washington, D.C., Newark, New Orleans, Baltimore, Atlanta, and Gary—were over 50 percent black. Some demographers predict that over the next decade blacks will constitute majorities in Cleveland, St. Louis, Detroit, Philadelphia, Oakland, and Chicago.

In addition several cities have experienced huge increases of migrants from Mexico, Puerto Rico, and Cuba. These Spanish-speaking peoples have been the newest of new immigrants, and like the foreigners who preceded them, the Latins and Chicanos have crowded into central cities. During the 1920s, Puerto Ricans had begun to enter New York and Mexicans had moved into new cities of the Southwest, and after World War II the numbers of these groups rapidly swelled. In 1970 there were over 800,000 Puerto Ricans in New York City, over 100,000 Mexicans in Los Angeles, and over 100,000 Cubans in Miami. Unlike earlier immigrants, but like native blacks, the Spanish-Americans arrived when demand for unskilled labor was declining. Moreover their dark skins often made them victims of racial discrimination.

The changing economy and unchanging racism combined to separate residential and economic experiences of the new urban dwellers from those of all white groups. As the National Advisory Commission on Civil Disorders (Kerner Commission) reported in 1968 regarding blacks, "The nation is rapidly moving toward two increasingly separate Americas . . . a white society principally located in suburbs, in smaller central cities, and in peripheral parts of large central cities; and a Negro society largely concentrated within large central cities." These divisions have become a major dilemma of the urban nation.

The Kerner Commission also warned that, "What white Americans have never fully understood—but what the Negro can never forget—is that white society is deeply implicated in the ghetto. White institutions created it, white institutions maintain it, and white society condones it." The ghetto—a place of confined, decayed residence from which escape is difficult at best—has been the central fact of black urban experience in the twentieth century. In part it was created by the process of urban growth, the process that had begun in the middle of the nineteenth century. As affluent whites dispersed into more comfortable regions of the periphery, they loaded central cities with severe burdens. Residential sprawl pulled with it commercial and service establishments, leaving behind the lowest jobs, cheapest housing, and poorest educational and health facilities. These were conditions that all migrants, poor and unskilled, faced when they arrived in central cities.

Most groups had been able to improve their situations by escaping from run-down inner districts into better neighborhoods, often within a generation after arriving in the city. But not blacks. Unlike residential districts of all white migrant groups, black ghettos expanded, rather than dissolved. As black families tried to move outward, whites fled. The walls of the ghetto were extended, but the confinement remained. By the middle of the twentieth century huge ghettos, consisting almost totally of black inhabitants, covered core areas of big cities—the South and

West Sides in Chicago, Harlem in New York, Hough in Cleveland, Watts in Los Angeles. Racial segregation, not just residential but in jobs, schools, and public accommodations as well, has made permanent for blacks what was temporary for other migrant groups. Only Puerto Ricans, Mexicans, and Indians, isolated in their own ghettos and barrios, have shared inferior opportunities with blacks.

The past century has witnessed a rising curve of black struggle against discrimination. This curve reached its peak during the past quarter-century in large part because urbanization has brought blacks into direct exposure to the promises and frustrations of mass consumer society and the myth of opportunity. On tenant farms blacks felt the sting of poverty and discrimination, but the range of choices was narrow. White society, with all its comforts, was distant, almost unattainable. In the cities, however, blacks acquired more cash to spend on magazines, radios, television, and movies—all that celebrated the materialism of white, middle-class, urban (and suburban) culture. Here the harder blacks tried to join consumer society, the more they discovered they were shut out. Not only did they receive inferior jobs, housing, schooling, and health care; but they were also excluded from white-owned motels and restaurants, forced into separate sections of bus stations and airports, and subjected to usurious credit arrangements. Segregation and inferior services had always haunted blacks, but by the 1950s these conditions aroused new angers about discrimination.

The angers often stemmed from rising expectations. During and after the war, the economic situation of blacks in this country improved, especially in the cities. Most blacks were still relegated to menial jobs, but a significant urban minority was climbing into skilled and white-collar employment levels. In Boston the proportions of blacks in middle-status jobs rose steadily between 1940 and 1970. The proportions of blacks in menial jobs declined steadily while those in skilled and white-collar jobs doubled. The problem, however, was that at almost all levels black incomes were only 70 percent of those for whites. Moreover the ghetto, with its inferior housing and inferior schools, remained. The city, which had kindled expectations and thwarted opportunities, had primed blacks to push for a more equitable share of the American promise.

The most momentous events early in the campaign occurred in Southern cities, for it was here that social forces laid bare the conflicts between equal rights and local autonomy. For half a century civil rights groups, such as the NAACP and the Urban League, had been working to eradicate the separate but equal doctrine, which the U.S. Supreme Court had upheld in 1896 as justification for Jim Crow segregation laws passed by southern cities and states after Reconstruction. Using the courts, these organizations began to weaken the barriers. The breakthrough came in

1954 when the Supreme Court, in *Brown* v. *Board of Education,* stated that, "in the field of public education the doctrine of 'separate but equal' has no place." The Court ordered an end to legislated school segregation to proceed "with all deliberate speed," but most southern communities balked. Would the federal government enforce the court's order? The issue was tested before the nation in 1957. That year the school board in Little Rock, Arkansas, a moderate, emerging southern city, decided to allow a few black students to enroll in previously all-white Central High School. The decision to accede to the federal court order incensed Governor Orval Faubus, who sent troops from the Arkansas National Guard to bar blacks from the school. President Eisenhower, concerned over the threat to federal prestige, nationalized the Guard and sent a thousand paratroopers into Little Rock to escort nine black teenagers to school. The troops patrolled the school's corridors for the rest of the year. The Little Rock experience was a painful one, but it was a start.

School integration victories, however minor, encouraged other efforts toward gaining broader civil rights. Again cities provided the major theaters of action. In 1956 a young Baptist minister named Martin Luther King, Jr., led a long boycott of segregated public buses in Montgomery, Alabama. The boycott's success (the Supreme Court invalidated Alabama's segregation laws) proved to be less important than the means by which it was achieved—mass, nonviolent action. Cities now contained large enough numbers of blacks, so that collective resistance could be effective. Soon Dr. King's "weapon of love" spread to other places. In Greensboro, North Carolina, in 1960 a group of students, black and white, sat at a Woolworth's lunch counter and refused to leave after being denied service. Their tactics began a wave of passive sit-ins, lie-ins, and wade-ins at segregated restaurants, stores, and swimming pools. By the end of 1961 lunch counters had been desegregated in two hundred cities, most of them in the upper South. Then, in 1963, Dr. King, now leader of the influential Southern Christian Leadership Conference, spearheaded a massive march against discrimination by employers and merchants in Birmingham, Alabama. Although King was only partially successful in obtaining concessions, the brutal reaction by Police Commissioner Eugene "Bull" Connor, who used cattle prods, dogs, and water hoses against the demonstrators, pushed liberal public opinion toward King's forces.

By the mid-1960s the civil rights movement was reaching a climax. Under persistent prodding from President Johnson, Congress in 1964 passed a Civil Rights Act, outlawing racial discrimination in public accommodations. In the Voting Rights Act of 1965, also passed with inspiration from President Johnson, Congress authorized federal agents to register voters who had been illegally denied suffrage. Three years later, the faith of two decades of struggle lay shattered. Martin Luther King was dead, the victim of an assasssin's bullet, and the cores of a dozen cities were pocked with burned-out districts, the remnants of four of the most violent summers in the nation's modern history. The refrain of "We shall overcome" was now replaced by epithets like "Kill Whitey" and "Burn, baby, burn." Just as cities had given impetus to the integration movement, so too did they produce the violence that stalled it.

In spite of the achievements of the past, nagging frustrations continued to plague blacks, now more than ever an urban people. For one thing, blacks believed they were still being denied a fair share of social and economic progress. The concessions they had won in their quests for better jobs, housing, and education seemed to be mere tokens, insufficient compensation for three centuries of oppression. In addition, blacks faced new charges that their social and economic deprivations were self-inflicted. In a 1965 report for the Labor Department, Daniel Patrick Moynihan, who later became adviser on urban affairs to President Nixon, suggested that inequality and poverty were the results of black family instability. "The Moynihan Report," drawn from a host of census statistics, stirred black and white liberals to rapid and spirited rebuttal. Critics argued, for example, that Moynihan's figures showing illegitimate birth rates to be at least seven times higher for blacks than for whites proved not that blacks were more promiscuous or less family-oriented but that whites were better able to conceal illegitimacy because they had easier access to abortions and adoption and because they had financial resources to pay for false registration and "shotgun" marriages. Although Moynihan expressed sympathy for civil rights goals, he was accused of reversing the actual sequence of causation which placed family disorganization as the result of poverty and inequality, not the other way around.

Frustrations and debate provoked further reactions from blacks and whites, particularly in cities where numbers of blacks were large enough to exert significant pressure for greater civil rights. As the quest for equality moved into the North, it stirred white fears over sensitive issues like schools and housing. Residents of outer wards in Chicago, Detroit, and Philadelphia organized to fight open housing and school busing. Moreover, by 1965, militant declarations of "black power" were drowning out integrationist themes of "blacks and whites together." A new restlessness spread through the civil rights movement and confounded whites who had urged that blacks patiently accept slow but sure progress toward equality.

The tensions exploded during the hot summers between 1965 and 1968. Ugly riots racked scores of cities and cast a gloom that still hangs over urban America. No region of the country escaped racial outbursts. Fires, stonings, snipings, and lootings occurred in Los Angeles, San Francisco, Portland, Kansas City, Omaha, Chicago, Milwaukee, Atlanta, Miami, Nashville, Cincinnati, Dayton, Cleveland, Rochester, New York City, Philadelphia, Washington, Boston, and many other cities. During a three-week period in the summer of 1967, a riot in Newark left twenty-six dead and twelve hundred injured, and a frenzy of violence in Detroit killed forty-three and injured two thousand.

Nearly all of the seventy-five or so riots of these years followed the same general pattern. They began as minor incidents involving the police and ghetto dwellers. Crowds collected, threw bricks and bottles at the police, and tensions mounted. Then windows were broken and social control dissolved. If police could not restore order at this point, the riot exploded into arson, looting, and sniper fire. Unlike most racial violence of the past, the riots of the sixties did not involve confrontations between blacks and whites over contested neighborhoods. Instead they were what Morris Janowitz has called "commodity riots"—outbursts within the ghetto against property and retail establishments usually owned by whites. Most deaths and injuries occurred in clashes between rioters and the police, not in fighting between black and white citizens.

Although violence also struck smaller cities, conditions were most explosive in big cities. The growth of huge ghettos, with their racial homogeneity and inferior services, created large populations of distressed blacks who could spontaneously mobilize once a riot broke out. Investigators estimated that roughly 10 percent or more of the ghetto populations of Detroit, Newark, and Watts (Los Angeles) participated to some extent in the riots of those cities. In each case this would mean that tens of thousands were involved, certainly too many for any local police force to handle. Moreover in big cities blacks had frequent occasion to view the disparities between their own situations and those of the middle-class white consumer culture that they constantly confronted. This is why so many became looters when ghettos erupted. As one Detroit rioter explained, "On Twelfth Street everybody was out, the whole family, Mama, Papa, the kids, it was like an outing. . . . The rebellion—it was all caused by the commercials. I mean you saw all those things you'd never be able to get. . . . Men's clothing, furniture, appliances, color TV. All that crummy TV glamour just hanging out there."

As cities smoldered, black militancy seemed to spread with the smoke. A new breed of young black leaders rallied behind the cry of "black power," a slogan coined during a civil rights march in Mississippi in 1966. Followers of this creed rejected integration and condoned violence as a means of attaining political and economic power. In part this urge for independence reflected racial pride in the emergence of new black nations in Africa. More importantly, black nationalism in America stemmed from the urbanization experience, with its thwarted opportunities and need for self identity in a socially complex environment. By the 1930s remnants of Marcus Garvey's black nationalist crusade of the 1920s merged with religious cults like the Moorish Science Temple (a sect that, like many others, had developed to meet the needs of uprooted black migrants in the cities) to form the Black Muslims, a militant separatist organization that preached hatred of whites. Under their founder W. Fard Muhammed, and his successor Elijah Muhammed, the Muslims achieved considerable influence among urban blacks, although actual Muslim membership remained small. By the early 1960s the Muslim creed of self-help aroused a new militancy among disaffected blacks like Malcolm X (who had rejected his "slave name" of Little). "You need somebody who is going to fight," Malcolm X once asserted. "You don't need any kneeling in or crawling in."

Malcolm X was brutally assassinated in 1965, but his words foreshadowed what many would call by 1967 the collapse of the civil rights movement. Urban life had promised so much, yet allowed so little. In every city conditions seemed the same: police harassment, inadequate housing, inferior schools and municipal services, neglect by public officials, discriminatory courts, discriminatory consumer credit practices, unemployment and underemployment. Even blacks who had achieved some parcel of success were excluded from decent white neighborhoods. Blacks had always carried the burdens of inferior status in towns and countryside. But in the cities this weight became too oppressive, for here the ghetto became what Richard C. Wade describes as the mocking "symbol of the unfulfilled promise of equality." In this context, violence and black power became expressions of political and social frustration. Thus the Kerner Commission speculated in the wake of a score of riots:

> What the rioters appeared to be seeking was fuller participation in the social order and the material benefits enjoyed by the majority of American citizens. Rather than rejecting the American system, they were anxious to obtain a place for themselves in it.

As the violence subsided, a number of black leaders, many of them graduates of the civil rights movement in the cities, began to pull back from integration as the major objective of their quest of equality. Instead they turned back to the ghetto itself to try to find there a means to win a place in the American system. Racial pride, which had grown during the equal rights crusade, now blossomed as African fashions, soul music, and soul food became symbols of identity and solidarity rather than ordinary features of ghetto life. Colleges and high schools adopted black studies programs, often in response to pressure from militants. Some blacks even rejected the busing of black children to white schools to achieve racial balance and better education. Busing, still a leading cause of white liberals, had raised doubts whether black children could actually benefit from contact with white children who had all the advantages of consumer society that blacks did not. As one black professor observed, "Psychologically, it's bad to tell a kid that he'll only make it if he sits next to a white."

As an alternative, the new cohort of black leaders sought to develop independent political and economic power. This strategy aimed to utilize blacks' greatest resource in the cities—numbers. For example, in 1973, Lonnie King, director of the Atlanta branch of the NAACP, offered the city a plan that abandoned school integration and busing in return for nine black appointments to the city's seventeen-member school board. The plan so undermined the NAACP's longstanding goal to integrate schools that the organization threatened to revoke the charter of its Atlanta chapter. In many cities black political candidates were seeking offices they never would have considered a generation ago—only now they could command the votes that made their chances altogether possible. In 1970 fifty cities had black mayors, and by 1974 black men had been elected mayors of six major cities—Atlanta, Cleveland, Detroit, Gary, Los Angeles, and Newark (and two were appointed mayors—of Cincinnati and Washington, D.C.). These men were racial moderates who had promised service to all races, and they received considerable white support. But their positions reflected the emergence of black influence on local politics.

Economic power, long a goal of nationalist groups like the Garveyites and Muslims, took on a new dynamic energy as blacks turned back toward the ghetto in the late 1960s. A leader of the drive was Reverend Jesse Jackson of Chicago, a fiery young spokesman for black capitalism whose boycott campaign against the A & P food chain prodded the company to hire seven hundred black workers, market black products, deposit in black-owned banks, advertise in black media, and contract with black construction firms and service companies. Jackson's scheme, Operation Breadbasket, was used against other companies and spread to fifteen other cities by 1970. "We are going to see to it," he stated in a 1969 interview, "that the resources of the ghetto are not siphoned off by outside groups. Right now, black exterminating companies don't even get the contracts to kill the ghetto's rats. But that's going to change. If a building goes up in the black community, we're going to build it. And we're going to stop anyone else from building it." Reverend Jackson has since organized a movement called PUSH—People United to Save Humanity—that has incorporated the tactics of Operation Breadbasket with a drive to implement an "economic bill of rights" for all underprivileged people.

What Jackson was proposing was for blacks and other minorities to follow the same path that all migrants to the city had followed—only he knew all too well how blacks were different. "I hear that melting pot stuff a lot," he stated.

and all I can say is that we haven't been melted. We've been getting burned on the bottom of the pot. We don't want anything that's different from the experience of other ethnic groups. If you go into an Irish neighborhood, most of the businesses are run by Irishmen. The same is true in a Chinese or Jewish or Italian neighborhood. The difference between all of them and us is that they are all separate and independent groups, while we are separate and *dependent*. We want to control the vital elements of our lives: the school boards, the churches, the businesses, the police. . . . we must fight for our independence.

This attitude of militant self-help also won favor among Mexicans and Puerto Ricans in the cities. But a nagging difficulty remained: the fact, as Martin Luther King had observed, that racial minorities could not pull themselves up by their bootstraps as long as they were barefoot. Poverty and discrimination have separated these groups from the housing, jobs, and education afforded white groups. And the amelioration of these conditions has become a principal task of local and federal governments.

THE DIRECTIONS OF FEDERAL ACTIVITY

Since the end of World War II, all the failures of modern American society seem to have gathered in cities. Street crime has reached fearful proportions and now penetrates "respectable" neighborhoods; poverty, physical and personal, blights the inner city; governments grope for relief to their financial stringency; traffic snarls streets and expressways; and pollution darkens the air and waters. Although we have been haunted by an "urban crisis" ever since the 1670s when fires almost destroyed the young town of Boston, the dilemmas of urban life appear more acute today, if only in magnitude. Yet these problems are no longer strictly urban or even metropolitan. Rather, they are national, and their solution demands a national urban policy. Significantly, however, the federal government's measures toward and affecting cities have rarely fulfilled expectations. In fact critics have justly accused Washington of aggravating, or even causing, many of the problems that plague cities today.

Although outwardly, federal policies toward cities in the postwar era appear to have vacillated between encouraging cities to solve their own problems, on the one hand, and assuming federal responsibility for urban affairs, on the other, in actuality the federal stance has been quite consistent. It has always followed and reinforced private markets. Government programs have encouraged private investment when it has focused on suburbs and when it has shown interest in central city land. This assistance has boosted prosperity in outer districts and has reinvigorated downtown areas—but at severe social costs. For federal policy has rarely been able to transcend a narrow focus that viewed people, particularly poor people, as social statistics to be moved around like checkers.

The crucial event in the evolution of modern federal-city relationships occurred in 1949 when Congress passed, and President Truman signed, the Wagner-Taft-Ellender Housing Act. By 1945 a decade of depression followed by five years of war had left acute housing shortages in the nation's cities. A new wave of farm-to-city migration pressed against housing markets and left between 20 and 30 percent of the nation's population housed in physically substandard quarters. Mortgage insurance and G.I. loans enabled middle-class families to find better housing through private markets, but the only measure that could help the millions of poor was public housing. In 1945 Senators Robert F. Wagner of New York, Allen J. Ellender of Louisiana, and Robert A. Taft of Ohio cosponsored a bill that set a goal of 1.25 million new housing units a year (for all classes) for the next ten years with liberal government loans and subsidies for the construction of 810,000 public housing units (for low-income groups) in four years. Real estate and construction interests prevented the bill from passing, but four years later, after a determined campaign, the champions of public housing squeezed their measure through Congress. The act of 1949 was an omnibus bill, combining several types of measures—principally slum clearance, public housing, and expanded mortgage insurance (through FHA). Contrary to the expectations of liberal supporters of the bill, these three emphases were never connected or coordinated, and herein lay the seeds for future frustration.

Title I of the Housing Act of 1949 established the principle of urban redevelopment, a principle that has since been the cause of considerable misinterpretation. In essence the provision committed federal funds to the clearance of slums by local redevelopment agencies. The law mandated that redevelopment programs be predominantly residential. But this meant either that areas earmarked for redevelopment had to be at least 50 percent residential in character before they were cleared; or that new construction in cleared, residential areas had to include 50 percent residential units—*but not necessarily both*. Thus most redevelopment projects removed blighted slums (predominantly residential) and replaced them with factories, shopping complexes, luxury apartments, and parking lots—land uses that would boost property values, assist private investment, increase tax revenues, and restore economic viability. Urban redevelopment brought revitalization to former slum areas in cities such as Pittsburgh, Boston, Cincinnati, and Chicago, but it did not help rehouse low-income slum dwellers—nor did it necessarily mean to rehouse them.

The goal of the 1949 Housing Act was to provide "a decent home and a suitable living environment for every American family." The goal effectively applied to high- and middle-income families as well as to the poor. In fact very little money was appropriated under the act for public housing, and it took twenty years, not four, for cities to construct the 810,000 public housing units that Wagner, Taft, and Ellender had envisioned. Redevelopment projects under the act furnished relocation funds for displaced families, but in many places rehousing provisions were deemed unnecessary because the exodus of affluent whites had created high vacancy rates in existing inner-city dwelling units. Officials simply assumed that these quarters would filter down to the more disadvantaged who had been displaced.

In 1954 Congress, backed by the Eisenhower administration, amended the 1949 provisions, and urban renewal replaced urban redevelopment. The amended Housing Act now recognized the need for rehabilitation of dilapidated structures rather than massive slum clearance, although provisions for clearance were retained—thus redevelopment and renewal were usually combined into the latter term. The amendments included a new provision that allocated 10 percent of federal grants-in-aid for projects in nonresidential areas. That is, localities could now use a tenth of federal funds for projects that did not fit the loose, "predominantly residential" criterion of the 1949 act. Further amendments in 1961 boosted the proportion of nonresidential funds to 30 percent, removing redevelopment farther from the solution of housing problems.

Although those concerned with the interests of disadvantaged groups have expected more, the principle objectives of urban renewal and redevelopment have been renovation of inner-city neighborhoods to attract middle- and high-income residents and revitalization of business districts for the benefit of private investment. During the 1950s this was a consistent federal policy. Its emphases on economics and aesthetics ignored social issues; it simply assumed that with the help of a gentle nudge poor people could redistribute themselves in the city and make way for economic progress that eventually would trickle down to them. Thus whole neighborhoods, such as Boston's West End, were leveled without regard for the beneficial functions that the shops and apartment houses served for working-class residents. Renewal and redevelopment were particularly hard on blacks who lived in districts most often renewed and who were given little assistance in finding new homes. Al-

The Impact of Urban Renewal and Redevelopment

Left, Demolition of a slum. This photograph shows the systematic destruction of a so-called blighted area of Providence, Rhode Island, in the early 1950s. A neighborhood consisting of over a thousand structures—mostly multiple-family dwellings—was completely leveled and replaced by a shopping center, school, apartment houses, and town houses.

Right, The new neighborhood. These apartments were built on some of the cleared land depicted at left. The redevelopment project represented here included both low- and medium-priced rental units, but not all projects were as diversified. Often lower-class homes were removed and replaced by more costly housing designed to attract middle- and upper-income families back into the city. *Both photographs, Providence Journal-Bulletin.*

though redevelopment laws specified that housing assisted by federal funds could not discriminate by race, creed, or color, most blacks were excluded from the new housing constructed on cleared land because rents were too high. Experts estimated that as a result of slum clearance and urban renewal programs, the United States *lost* a net of 200,000 housing units a year between 1950 and 1956, and 475,000 a year between 1957 and 1959. No wonder critics charged that urban renewal was really "Negro removal."

Implementation, though not the intent, of the government's home financing and highway construction policies also worked against the interest of blacks and of poor people in general. Since its creation in 1934 the Federal Housing Authority has offered generous mortgage insurance to middle-class whites, thereby encouraging banks to grant mortgage loans to the groups who have been fleeing central cities. But, until recently, it has denied such advantages to the least affluent groups by enforcing income requirements for families receiving insurance. FHA guarantees, Veterans Administration loan programs, and income tax deductions for mortgage interest and real estate property taxes have in effect subsidized middle-class suburbanization while leaving the poor behind.

Moreover highway construction has been as responsible as urban renewal for displacing the poor from their homes. Expressways and interchanges, particularly those planned as part of the Interstate Highway System, sliced through low-rent districts where, planners argued, dilapidated buildings needed to be torn down anyway. Highway builders did not intentionally seek out slums to destroy, but they carefully avoided high-rent areas where construction would most disrupt private investment. Land in the path of a proposed highway rapidly declined in value and its residents were uprooted. Although the government offered minimal relocation assistance, most displaced businessmen (usually owners of small, neighborhood-oriented establishments) never reopened, and most displaced families only fled to more crowded slums.

Thus during the 1950s the promise of a strong federal policy toward cities generated new favors for special interests with the poor again receiving little attention. Postwar national prosperity, particularly during the first Eisenhower administration, deflected direct concern with the total problems of cities. The emphases on local initiative and economic rejuvenation resulted in renovation of downtowns in many cities, and local leaders assumed that the benefits of good times would eventually reach the poor. Federal leaders seemed insensitive to the huge inmigrations of poor people who were pressing against all the facilities of central cities.

In 1960 the trend changed. Both candidates in that year's presidential election, Richard M. Nixon and John F. Kennedy, directed much of their attention to urban problems. Kennedy's reference to a New Frontier and his promise of federal support for schools, medical care, urban transportation, and planning particularly caught the interest of civic leaders. Kennedy revealed a concern for city and metropolitan problems, and once elected he sought to fulfill his commitments by pumping new funds into old programs for housing, renewal, pollution control, and mass transit. His President's Committee on Juvenile Delinquency initiated several projects that organized slum communities to work out solutions to their own problems, a tactic that later became central to the War on Poverty. These policies and the metropolitan emphases of cabinet members such as Arthur Goldberg and Abraham Ribicoff were directed at inner cities and inner suburbs where Kennedy had elicited considerable voter support. Kennedy's attempt, however, to create a cabinet department of urban affairs failed when southern Congressmen balked at his intention to nominate a distinguished black housing expert, Robert C.

Weaver, as secretary. Creation of the department of Housing and Urban Development was delayed until 1966.

President Lyndon Johnson and his advisers mounted an even greater attack against urban problems, particularly against poverty, in their attempt to build a Great Society. In 1964 Johnson pressed Congress to pass the Economic Opportunity Act, creating an Office of Economic Opportunity (O.E.O.) that directed a number of programs designed to end domestic poverty: Job Corps, a community work-training program to teach skills to young people; Head Start, an educational boost for preschool children with disadvantaged backgrounds; Volunteers in Service to America (VISTA), a domestic Peace Corps; Legal Aid; and the Community Action Program (C.A.P.), to encourage "maximum feasible involvement" of neighborhood residents in policy planning. Other legislation expanded the food stamp program, funded old and new housing programs, and provided federal monies to modernize hospitals. In 1966 the Johnson administration launched the Model Cities program, a new variant of renewal that targeted federal funds to special districts where locally elected boards had hammered out a coordinated plan for the improvement of housing, health, education, employment, and welfare. Like War on Poverty measures, Model Cities emphasized neighborhood participation in community projects, an objective that often stirred conflict between community organizations and outside caretakers—the planners, social workers, scholars, and politicians who tried to apply their expertise to a project. And in practice federal officials approved only those model cities projects that would not undermine locally elected officials. In housing Johnson retreated slightly from public housing and instead offered rent supplements (1966) and subsidies to low-income families who wished to buy their own homes.

The election of Richard Nixon in 1968 brought a new bearing to the lofty promises, but frustrating results, of urban policies in the 1960s. Disturbed by the fiscal waste and bureaucratic red tape of Kennedy and Johnson programs, Nixon sought to reduce the roles of federal government and citizen participation in urban affairs and strengthen control by local officials. The new Republican administration slashed budgets of Great Society agencies and prepared to phase out Model Cities. In addition in 1973 the President impounded funds from federal housing and rehabilitation projects and cut back appropriations for solid waste removal. In place of these programs, Nixon proposed to establish a New Federalism, the return of policy-making decisions to state and local levels. The keystone of this policy was revenue sharing, the distribution of federal funds directly to local governments rather than through federal agencies. Despite strong opposition the State and Local Fiscal Assistance Act passed Congress in 1972, and during the succeeding winter, checks totaling $5.3 billion were distributed to 38,000 state and local governments. Two-thirds of the money went directly to cities and towns to be used in nine possible areas: public safety, administration, transportation, health, environmental protection, capital expenditures, libraries, recreation, and social services for the poor and aged. Beyond these priority identifications the money could be spent without federal guidelines—except that discrimination by race, sex, ethnicity, and religion was prohibited. Nixon also proposed measures of special revenue sharing, block grants to be distributed explicitly for use in education, law enforcement, manpower training, and urban community development.

The goal of reinforcing local autonomy reflected new metropolitan facts of life, but it also revealed a misinterpretation of local needs. During the early 1960s the U.S. Supreme Court had upheld the principle of equal representation in legislative bodies (one man-one vote) and had mandated reapportionment of congressional and state legislative districts. This ruling at last gave cities more equitable representation, but it came too late. Reapportionment actually strengthened suburbs, fast becoming the new centers of population, and it gave them political strength to secure federal funds at the expense of cities. By 1970 only about twenty of the nation's 247 metropolitan areas were managed by fewer than ten local governmental bodies. Suburbanization and the proliferation of urban services had spawned thousands of new, independent administrative authorities (municipalities, townships, school districts, and utilities districts). The Chicago area alone had over eleven hundred separate governments; Philadelphia, almost nine hundred; New York, almost six hundred. Not all of these bodies qualified for revenue sharing, but their numbers raised fears among big city officials that revenues would not be distributed according to need. Thus cities comprised of poverty-stricken racial minorities would not receive proportionally more than suburbs inhabited by affluent whites. Moreover critics have charged that the New Federalism simply makes the federal government a tax collector, allowing Washington to distribute revenues without injecting incentives and guidelines for how the money should be spent in the national interest.

In practice revenue sharing has not yet proved to be the bonus that some had expected. Although funds have been distributed according to a complex formula which grants more money to areas with higher population densities, disparities remain. Smaller cities—particularly suburbs—have benefited; federal grants have prevented local tax rates from rising, have kept municipal salaries high and have funded new projects such as roads and sewage disposal plants. But for most of the nation's twenty-six cities with populations above five hundred thousand, the New Federalism has brought little relief to social and economic crises. Local

officials have been forced to spend most of their grants to avoid severe
budget cuts and to sustain Great Society programs threatened by curtailment or impoundment of direct federal funds. As one big city mayor
lamented,

> In area after area, we are having to end successful programs. Cuts in model
> cities mean hundreds of minority jobs will be eliminated. We are not going
> to get the federal help we've had in the past. It's a retreat, a failure to
> recognize needs of cities. The Administration measures the urban crisis as
> how many windows were broken, how much fire-bombing was done. That is
> erroneous. The urban crisis is still there.

Moreover, some people wondered how seriously the President supported
his own idea. At a meeting of the U.S. Conference of Mayors in June,
1974, Henry W. Maier, mayor of Milwaukee, charged that President
Nixon had undercut the New Federalism by impounding urban program funds appropriated by Congress.

In addressing urban problems President Nixon also determined to
clear up the "welfare mess." During the 1960s the number of welfare
recipients in this country literally mushroomed, even though the number
of people actually defined as poor decreased. Much of the new pressure
on the welfare system resulted from the government's own urban policy.
The community action programs of the Kennedy and, particularly, the
Johnson administrations had encouraged poor people to organize in their
own interest. Welfare rights movements, plus continuing in-migrations of
poverty-stricken rural and minority families forced a tremendous welfare
expansion, especially in big cities. Moreover, as Frances Fox Piven and
Richard A. Cloward have asserted in *Regulating the Poor*, fears of racial
violence in the mid-sixties moved local officials to expand welfare rolls as
a means of soothing tensions. As a result, relief cases tripled in many
cities between 1960 and 1970. By 1970 New York City welfare rolls
contained a million people, a population larger than that of fifteen states.
In 1971 one out of every ten residents of the nation's twenty largest
metropolitan areas depended on some form of public relief. The most
common forms of welfare included Aid to Families with Dependent
Children (A.D.C.), unemployment compensation, food stamps, housing
supplements or public housing, and free medical care. Although state
and federal agencies supported some of these programs, local government carried most of the burdens. In 1970 the welfare budget of New
York City alone was $1.4 billion. Cities also received most of the criti-
cism for sustaining welfare cheaters. Sometimes charges were warranted
—such as when it was discovered that New York was supporting a number of families in $40-a-day rooms in the luxurious Waldorf Astoria
Hotel. But more often, the needs of the poor overwhelmed cities, strain-

ing local revenues with millions of cases like that of a nineteen year old New York girl who wrote on her welfare application, "I have no one to help me. I was living with my grandmother, but she put me out on the street with my two children."

Frequently the burdens of poverty have fallen most heavily upon women—the "welfare mothers" who have become a vocal pressure group in many big cities. These women—black and white, married and unmarried—have been caught between the self-help ethic on one side and requisites of family support on the other. They have also received considerable abuse from welfare critics on one side and are urged to join the equal rights crusade by middle-class feminists on the other. Civil rights activities and community action programs have brought these women together, so that they now comprise the vanguard of welfare rights and tenants' organizations. Welfare mothers participate actively in local hearings and lobby forcefully for day-care centers, housing reform, job training, fairer relief allotments, and more humane treatment by public officials. Such women have often adopted these immediate goals rather than the broader issues of education and human rights espoused by their wealthier counterparts. When feminist leader Gloria Steinem told a 1971 meeting of the National Welfare Rights Organization that white women and black welfare mothers were similarly exploited, she was swiftly challenged. "We're not the same as white women," complained one delegate. "We don't get the chance to be."

The Nixon administration correctly realized that municipalities should not be held responsible for financing relief of a problem that is created by national migration trends. Cities have not in themselves caused poverty; rather they have enticed impoverished persons who were seeking opportunity and security. By assuming responsibility for relief of those who failed, cities had only attracted more poor people. In the late sixties, if you needed help in Mississippi, you could get $55 a month; in New York, you could get $278. Thus Nixon hoped to remove some of the disparities that had loaded many cities with extra problems. The President linked his plan for federal welfare reform to the work ethic by proposing a family assistance program that offered incentives in the form of income supplements to families who joined the work force and tried to earn their way out of poverty. Although this plan ensured a minimum income for all families, it discriminated against the largest segments of urban poor: the aged, the handicapped, and mothers who have no way to care for their dependent children. As Raymond A. Mohl has written,

What emerged clearly from the Nixon plan is the idea that work—any work at whatever pay—is important for character and self-esteem and that it is somehow unfair, unethical, and un-American for society to assume responsibility for those who are poor or near starvation because they are unable to compete with the rest of us.

On the surface, the activities of the federal government on behalf of cities over the past three decades appear limited at best. Public housing never reached its goals and left a legacy of concrete jungles, high-rise slums that only added a further stigma to being poor. Urban renewal and redevelopment enhanced city landscapes but at the expense of the powerless who were pushed out of their shops and homes. The war on poverty put more people on the welfare rolls and created a huge new bureaucracy (white-collar welfare, some called it) to administer a frightening maze of government programs. And welfare reform and the New Federalism harkened back to a mythical past when self-help and local autonomy supposedly made America great.

Yet none of these policies is intrinsically evil, and all are logical extensions of the urban historical experience. Public housing is the culmination of a long battle against decay, dating from the model tenement schemes of the mid-nineteenth century. Rehabilitation of blighted areas has been a major objective of building code reforms and of city planning schemes that have ranged from park landscaping and the City Beautiful to regional planning and greenbelt towns. And public responsibility for the relief of poverty ratifies the recognition that some people are unable to improve their conditions not because such people are sinful or lazy,

An American City at Mid-Century
This view of San Diego emphasizes the gridiron street pattern surrounding the huge park in the center of the city. *U.S. Army Air Forces, The National Archives.*

but because they lack sufficient incomes. Over the past half-century, and certainly since World War II, urban problems have become national problems, and it is no longer feasible to expect municipalities and private interests to solve social and environmental problems. Only the federal government has the regulatory powers and innovative resources to direct a national urban strategy. That strategy calls for both a sensitivity to, and a break with, the past.

THE PROSPECT FOR URBAN AMERICA

The American metropolis today is caught between conflicting pressures. On one side stand the forces of the past, a century of decentralization that has fractured social and economic bonds within cities and between cities and suburbs. The emergence of the suburban nation has ratified the triumph of these forces. Ours is now a polynucleated society; the centrifugal dynamics of urbanization have prevailed over the centripetal. But the results have been dangerous. The exodus of affluent whites has left central cities with huge burdens. Spiraling costs for services and for municipal salaries have forced city tax rates skyward and have encouraged more businesses and homeowners to leave. Moreover by using zoning laws to exclude "undesirables," suburbanites have prevented blacks, Chicanos, Indians, and poor people in general from partaking of the residential mobility that has been so integral to the urban experience of white groups.

On the other hand, federal policy, when it has operated, has followed the assumption that cities should have some centrality. Although federal mortgage insurance and highway construction have nurtured suburbanization, most government attention has focused on revitalizing urban cores to make them healthier places for economic progress. From the City Beautiful through urban renewal, the emphasis has been on restoring the downtown. Slum clearance and public housing are part of this process of reclamation. But here too the poor have suffered. Programs that targeted a decent home for every American destroyed twice as many dwellings as they built.

Prescriptions for how to save urban America have included both preserving the center and encouraging further decentralization. Experts on urban affairs continue to press the federal government for more funds to restore central city vitality through land rehabilitation, community organization, manpower training programs, and pollution control. Although central business districts have lost much of their traditional retail functions, they retain increasing importance as locations for management, bureaucratic, and professional sectors of business and government. Today, over forty million Americans work in offices, and in spite of sophisticated communications systems, most white-collar operations still demand close proximity to each other. Thus there is new impetus for movements to save the city's center among private as well as public interests. In Detroit, for example, private businesses are sponsoring a $500 million project called "Renaissance Center," a cluster of office towers, apartments, and a hotel along the city's riverfront. Their objective is to recycle downtown, but whether the project will furnish revenues for starved municipal services and generate jobs and housing for the city's emerging black majority remains to be seen.

Other planners, however, propose to fuel decentralization by helping formerly excluded groups to board the mobility train outward. By planting low-cost housing in suburbs and by providing low-income families with rent subsidies and income supplements, it would be possible to make the suburban dream possible for almost all Americans. Moreover many advocates of decentralization would invest faith in "new towns," like Reston, Virginia, Columbia, Maryland, and Jonathan, Minnesota— protogreenbelt communities that have been totally planned in an attempt to avoid all the problems of big cities. New towns offer more orderly land use, but to date they have done little to help the poor because their housing costs and job opportunities remain outside the capabilities of low-income families.

Whatever urban policy or combination of urban policies the nation follows, it will be forced to overcome two serious obstacles that are legacies of our history. One is the notion of land as a civil right of private exploitation; the other is the tradition of local autonomy. Speculative enterprise has been a predominant strain in our urban past. It has created cities, fostered their unplanned growth, given them their dynamic prosperity, and left them with their blight. As one expert has asserted, no policy "can succeed while the public power is so limited and the market in capital and land is free to determine new growth and, through lack of maintenance, the decline of old growth." Nor can any policy succeed while cities and suburbs vie with each other over metropolitan issues. The growth of freely incorporated municipalities has given metropolitan areas so many independent, overlapping and competing governmental jurisdictions that comprehensive planning and coordination are impossible. Here is where a New Federalism is needed to bring order to the chaos of the fragmented metropolis—a federalism between all the independent communities within a metropolitan area, not between local governments and the federal government. The establishment of forms of metropolitan government (consolidation of the various city, suburban, and county administrations) in the Miami area in 1957, the

Nashville area in 1962, and the Indianapolis area in 1969 has been promising and frustrating. These metro governments have created the broad powers over traffic, sanitation, taxing, and zoning that regional planners have advocated for most of this century. But they have still not overcome the jealousies that have always splintered urban areas; localities, protective of their self-interest, have remained suspicious about the exercise and implementation of metropolitan powers. Thus a national policy carries two prerequisites foreign to the past: land as a public resource not as a private right; and the metropolis as a forum for confederates, not as an arena for combatants.

"Do we really care about our cities?" Scott Greer, one of the nation's leading experts on urban affairs, posed this question in 1965, before the worst riots, before the dismantling of the Great Society, and before the energy crisis. Then, most Americans would probably have answered Greer with a half-hearted affirmative. Today, even a reluctant, "Yes, I guess so" may be rare. In spite of three centuries of criticism, the American city has never received such a "bad press" as it has in the recent past. Today, nostalgia for a mythical, idyllic Arcadia is rampant. Popular journals feature articles about city-bred families who foresake the urban rat race and move to a rural retreat in uncluttered Vermont or Oregon. Makers of foods with "natural" ingredients advertise their products with bucolic scenes and nostalgic slogans ("One taste and all the flavor of the past comes flooding back"). Some critics even predict that we are rushing toward an American Necropolis, city of the dead.

Yet a recurrent theme of American urban history is that cities have proved to be remarkably resilient in the face of crisis and catastrophe. Urban dwellers have emerged from wars, fires, floods, epidemics, and civil disorders eager to rebuild and ready to reform. In spite of all our problems, urban life today is considerably safer and healthier than it was a century ago. No one can predict if cities will survive their present predicaments, particularly as shortages in materials and energy loom as serious threats and as feverish inflation scorches the national economy. Still the eulogies for urban America seem premature. Cities today remain what they have always been—the centers of economic, social, and cultural opportunity. As Mr. Dooley once reasoned,

> Ye might say as Hogan does, that we're ladin' an artyficyal life, but, be Hivins, ye might as well tell me I ought to be paradin' up and down a hillside in a suit iv skins, shootin' the antylope an' the moose, be gory, an' livin' in a cave as to make me believe I ought to get along without sthreet cars an' ilictric lights an' illyvators an' sody wather an' ice. "We ought to live where all the good things iv life comes from," says Hogan. "No," says I. "Th' place to live is where all the good things iv life goes to."

BIBLIOGRAPHY

Because the literature on recent urban developments is so voluminous, only a few of the most notable works can be mentioned here. For general analyses and prognoses see Blake McKelvey, *The Emergence of Metropolitan America, 1915–1966* (New Brunswick, N.J.: Rutgers University Press, 1968); Sam Bass Warner, Jr., *The Urban Wilderness* (New York: Harper and Row 1973); Bayard Still, *Urban America: A History With Documents* (Boston: Little, Brown, 1974); Leonard J. Duhl, ed., *The Urban Condition* (New York: Basic Books, Inc., 1963); Jack Tager and Park Dixon Goist, eds., *The Urban Vision* (Homewood, Ill.: Dorsey Press, 1970); Lewis Mumford, *The Urban Prospect* (New York: Harcourt Brace, 1968); Melvin Urofsky, ed., *Perspectives on Urban America* (Garden City: Doubleday, 1973); and Jean Lowe, *Cities in a Race With Time* (New York: Random House, 1967).

Harlan Paul Douglass's *The Suburban Trend* (New York: Century and Co., 1925) was one of the earliest systematic studies of modern suburbanization. More recently, analysts have produced a wide variety of works on the nature of suburban and metropolitan growth. These works include Herbert J. Gans, "Urbanism and Suburbanism as Ways of Life: A Re-evaluation of Definitions" in Arnold Rose, ed., *Human Behavior and Social Process* (Boston: Houghton-Mifflin, 1962), pp. 625–48; The Editors of Fortune Magazine, *The Exploding Metropolis* (Garden City, N.Y.: Doubleday, 1958); Jean Gottman, *Megalopolis: The Urbanized Northeastern Seaboard of the United States* (Cambridge: M.I.T. Press, 1961); Herbert J. Gans, *The Levittowners: Ways of Life and Politics in a New Suburban Community* (New York: Pantheon, 1967); Robert Wood, *Suburbia: Its People and Their Politics* (Boston: Houghton-Mifflin, 1958); Bennett M. Berger, *Working Class Suburbs: A Study of Auto Workers in Suburbia* (Berkeley: University of California Press, 1968); Scott Donaldson, *The Suburban Myth* (New York: Columbia University Press, 1969); William H. Whyte, Jr., *The Organization Man* (Garden City: Doubleday, 1957); and Kenneth T. Jackson, "The Crabgrass Frontier: 150 Years of Suburban Growth in America," in Raymond A. Mohl and James F. Richardson, eds., *The Urban Experience: Themes in American History* (Belmont, Cal.: Wadsworth Publishing Co., 1973), pp. 196–221. David Karp's *Leave Me Alone* (New York: Knopf, 1957) is representative of the many fictional attacks on modern suburban society during the 1950s.

Among a large body of works on ethnicity, race, class, and poverty in modern urban areas, particularly see Nathan Glazer and Daniel Patrick Moynihan, *Beyond the Melting Pot: The Negroes, Puetro Ricans, Jews, Italians, and Irish of New York City* (Cambridge: M.I.T. Press, 2nd ed., 1970); Karl E. and Alma F. Taeuber, *Negroes in Cities: Residential Segregation and Neighborhood Change* (Chicago: Aldine Press, 1965); Herbert J. Gans, *The Urban Villagers: Group and Class in the Life of Italian Americans* (New York: The Free Press, 1962); Charles Silberman, *Crisis in Black and White* (New York: Knopf, 1967); *The Report of the National Advisory Commission on Civil Disorders* (New York: Praeger, 1968); Morris Janowitz, "Patterns of Collective Racial Violence," in Hugh D. Graham and Ted R. Gurr, eds., *Violence in America*, Vol. 2 (Washington: Government Printing Office, 1969); Michael Harrington, *The Other Americans: Poverty in the United States* (New

York: Macmillan, 1962); Frances Fox Piven and Richard A. Cloward, *Regulating the Poor: Functions of Public Welfare* (New York: Pantheon, 1971); and Edward C. Banfield's updated and provocative *The Unheavenly City Revisited* (Boston: Little Brown, 1974). For a glimpse at one of the more dynamic urban personalities of recent years, see the interview with Rev. Jesse Jackson in *Playboy*, 16 (November 1969).

Studies of urban housing, planning and education include Richard O. Davies, *Housing Reform During the Truman Administration* (Columbia: University of Missouri Press, 1966); Sam Bass Warner, Jr., *Planning for a Nation of Cities* (Cambridge: M.I.T. Press, 1967); Jane Jacobs, *The Death and Life of Great American Cities* (New York: Knopf, 1961); and Colin Greer, *The Great School Legend: A Revisionist Interpretation of American Education* (New York: Basic Books, Inc., 1973). Recent urban politics are treated in Edward C. Banfield and James Q. Wilson, *City Politics* (Cambridge: Harvard University Press, 1963); Robert A. Dahl, *Who Governs: Democracy and Power in an American City* (New Haven: Yale University Press, 1961); and Mike Royko, *Boss: Richard J. Daley of Chicago* (New York: Dutton, 1971). For the impact of, and proposals for, national urban policy, see Herbert J. Gans, "The Failure of Urban Renewal: A Critique and Some Proposals," *Commentary*, 39 (April 1965), 29–37; Scott A. Greer, *Urban Renewal and American Cities: The Dilemmas of Democratic Intervention* (Indianapolis: Bobbs-Merrill, 1965); and Daniel Patrick Moynihan, ed., *Toward a National Urban Policy* (New York: Basic Books, Inc., 1970), especially Chapter 23 by Scott Greer.

INDEX

Harris, William T., 164
Harrison, Carter (I and II), 140
Hartford, Conn., 4
Hawthorne, Nathaniel, 44
Hays, Samuel P., 155
Head Start, 260
Health. *See* Public health
Hearst, William Randolph, 157–58
Heinz, H. J., 145
Hendrick, Burton J., 159
Henretta, James, 14, 15
High schools, 165. *See also* Education
  and schools
Highway Act of 1956, 240
Highways, 194–95, 239–41, 259. *See also*
  Streets and bridges
Hoan, Daniel W., 212
Holiness churches, 200–201, 228
Holli, Melvin, 154
Holt, Glen, 70, 75
Holyoke, Mass., 35
Home Owners Loan Corporation (HOLC),
  218–19
Home ownership, 181, 219
Home rule movement, 152–53, 172, 175
Hoover, Herbert, 206, 210, 213, 214,
  215, 229, 230
Hopkins, Harry, 215, 216, 217, 230
Hopkins, Mark, 72
Horse cars (horse railways), 70–72
Hough (Cleveland), 249
Household, urban, 53, 111
Housing, urban:
  in early nineteenth century, 82
  and New Deal, 218–21, 224
  in 1920s, 180–81
  in post-World War II cities and sub-
    urbs, 238–39
  and reform (1850–1920), 101–7
Housing Act of 1949, 256
Housing Act of 1954, 257
Housing Division of Public Works Ad-
  ministration, 219–20
Houston, Tex., 87, 100
Howard, Ebenezer, 106, 203, 222
Howe, Frederick C., 154, 171
Hughes, Langston, 187
Hull House, 166
Human ecology, 202–3
Hungarians, 95
Huntington, Collis P., 72
Hutchinson, Thomas, 22, 24
Huthmacher, J. Joseph, 145, 174, 177

Ickes, Harold, 216, 217, 230
Illinois Central Railroad, 60
Immigrants, 92–98, 113–16, 119, 165,
  166, 174, 205, 206, 230. *See also*
  individual immigrant groups
  and crime, 197–98
  and the New Deal, 229
  and urban politics, 126–27, 129, 130–
    32, 143–44, 175–77
Immigration, foreign, 91, 92–98, 183, 205
  "new," 94–97

Immigration, foreign (*Cont.*)
  "old," 92–94
  return, 98
Immigration restriction, 12, 171, 183–84
Impressment, 23
Indianapolis, Ind., 92, 119, 180, 206
  Ku Klux Klan in, 199
  metropolitan government, 267
Indians, 15, 249
Industrial parks, 241–42
Industrialization:
  before 1860, 35–36, 49–52, 55
  1860–1920, 84–88, 112
  in 1920s, 187–88
  in post-World War II era, 241–42
Inland trade, 4 .
Institutional church, 161
Interstate Highway Act (1956), 240
Ireland, John, 96
Irish, 46, 48, 65, 93, 94, 95, 96, 97, 98,
  112, 113, 117, 120, 127, 145, 197
Italians, 94, 95, 96, 97, 111, 113, 114,
  115, 117, 119, 145, 197

Jackson, Jesse, 254–55
Jackson, Kenneth T., 198–99, 244
Janowitz, Morris, 252
Jazz, 187
Jersey City, N.J., 58, 126, 141, 176, 206
Jews and Judaism, 94, 96–97, 111, 113,
  117, 119, 197
Job Corps, 260
Johnson, James Weldon, 187
Johnson, Lyndon B.:
  and civil rights, 250
  election of, 245
  policies toward cities, 260, 262
Johnson, Thomas L., 153, 154–55, 205,
  232
Jonathan, Minn., 266
Jones, Samuel, 153, 154–55, 232
Journalism, 157–58

Kalamazoo, Mich., 92
Kansas City, Mo., 73, 74, 93, 106, 151,
  180, 188, 204, 206, 252
  boss politics in, 141
  crime in, 196, 197
  during 1930s, 217
  and railroads, 85
Karp, David, 243
Katz, Michael, 42
Kellogg, Paul U., 159
Kelly, Edward, 230
Kelly, Florence, 166, 173
Kelly, John, 136
Kenna, Michael "Hinky Dink", 140
Kennedy, John F.:
  election of, 245
  policies toward cities, 259–60, 262
Kerner Commission. *See* National Advis-
  ory Commission on Civil Disorders
Kindergartens, 164, 166
King, Lonnie, 254
King, Martin Luther, Jr., 250, 251, 255
Knights, Peter R., 46, 101

Spokane, Wash., 85
Sports. *See* Leisure activities, urban
Sprague, Frank J., 73
Springfield, Mass., 4, 46
Stamp Act (1765), 21–22, 24
Stanford, Leland, 72
Starr, Ellen Gates, 166
State and Local Fiscal Assistance Act (1972), 260
Staunton, Va., 151
Stave, Bruce, 231
Steamboats, 31, 59–60
Steffens, Lincoln, 136, 157–58, 159
Stein, Clarence, 181, 203
Storey, Moorfield, 149
Stowe, Calvin, 41
Street lighting, 8
Street railways. *See* Electric railways
Streets and bridges, 6–8. *See also* Highways
Strong, George Templeton, 55
Strong, Josiah, 117, 148, 160, 161
Strong, William, 137
Suburbs and suburbanization:
    in 1920s, 181–83
    in 1930s, 222–24
    in nineteenth century, 67, 79–80, 82, 238
    post-World War II, 237–47, 261, 266
Subways, 74–75
Sugar Act (1764), 21
Sullivan, Louis, 168
Sullivan, Roger, 141
Sullivan, Timothy D., 138–39, 142, 143–44, 144–45, 229
Sunnyside, N. Y., 203, 222
Swedes, 93
Sweeney, Peter, 134
Swift, Gustavus, 149–50
Syracuse, N. Y., 183

Tacoma, Wash., 85
Taft, Robert A., 256
Tammany Hall, 103, 129, 133–34, 136, 137–38, 144, 175, 177, 205, 232
Tampa, Fla., 180
Tarbell, Ida, 159
Taverns:
    in colonial cities, 19–20
    in modern cities, 110, 161–62, 231
Taxation, 21–22, 172, 176, 211
Taylor, Frederick W., 149, 173
Taylor, Graham R., 166
Tea Act (1773), 24–25
Technology, 86, 107
Telegraph, 172
Telephone, 163, 172, 188
Temperance movement, 161–62. *See also* Prohibition
Tenements, 105–6
Tennessee Valley Authority, 214, 221
Thelen, David, 172
Thernstrom, Stephan, 46, 101, 122, 226
Thompson, William Hale, 146
Thoreau, Henry David, 44
Thrasher, Frederick, 202

Three deckers, 102. *See also* Housing, urban
Tilden, Samuel J., 135
Tocqueville, Alexis de, 45, 46
Toledo, Ohio, 60, 92, 95, 154
Torrio, Johnny, 197
Townshend Acts, 22, 24
Toynbee Hall (London), 165–66
Traffic regulation, 65, 193
Transit, mass, 67–84
Triangle Shirtwaist Company Fire (1911), 175, 206
Trolleys. *See* Electric railways
Troy, N. Y., 58
Truman, Harry S, 256
Tuckerman, Joseph, 40, 44–45
Tucson, Ariz., 184
Tugwell, Rexford G., 222–24, 230
Tulsa, Okla., 180, 183
Turner, Frederick Jackson, 31, 122
Tweed, William Marcy, 103, 133–36, 137

Unemployment, 210
United States Conference of Mayors, 262
United States Housing Authority, 220–21, 228
United States Shipping Board, Emergency Fleet Corporation, 181
Universal Negro Improvement Association, 187
University of Chicago, 202
University Settlement, 166
Urban liberalism, 145, 174–77, 229
Urban population. *See* Population, urban
Urban redevelopment, 256–57, 261
Urban renewal, 257–58, 264, 265
Urban rivalry, 33–35
Urbanism Committee of the National Resources Committee, 233
Urbanization:
    before 1860, 29–31, 52, 55, 56
    1860–1920, 87–88, 91, 112
    in 1920s, 180–82
    in post-World War II era, 238

Van Doeple, Charles J., 73
Van Wyck, Robert, 138
Vaux, Calvert, 43–44
Veiller, Lawrence, 105, 106, 166, 173
Veterans Administration, 238, 259
Vice. *See* Crime and vice
Vocational education, 164–65
Volstead Act, 195, 196
Volunteers in Service to America (VISTA), 260

Wade, Richard C., 25, 31, 32, 33, 52, 53, 67, 253
Wagner, Robert F., 175, 176, 206, 220, 230, 256
Wagner National Labor Relations Act, 224, 231
Wagner-Steagall Housing Bill (1937), 220, 221
Wald, Lillian, 166
Walgreen's, 188

Walker, Jimmy, 142, 232
"Walking city," 64–67
Waltham, Mass., 47
War on Poverty, 259, 260
Warden, G. B., 25
Waring, George E., Jr., 108
Warner, Samuel Bass, Jr., 37, 78, 82, 109, 128
Washington, D.C., 29, 42, 68, 69, 73, 106, 241
  blacks in, 99, 116, 247, 254
  planning in, 168
  riots in, 186, 252
Waste removal, 8, 10, 109
Water supply, 36–37, 109
Watts (Los Angeles), 249, 252
Weaver, Robert C., 259–60
Weiss, Hymie, 197
Welfare, 262–64. *See also* Poverty and relief
Welfare mothers, 263
Wentworth, "Long John," 60
White, William Allen, 125
Whitier, John Greenleaf, 54
Whitlock, Brand, 154, 155
Whitney, Henry M., 74, 75
Whyte, William H., Jr., 245
Wiebe, Robert, 155, 157, 165
Wilmington, Del., 122
Wilson, Sloan, 243
Wilson, Woodrow, 193, 201
Winthrop, John, 2
Wirth, Louis, 202
Wise, Isaac Mayer, 96
Women:
  in cities (1790–1860), 54–55

Women (*Cont.*)
  in cities (1860–1920), 110, 113
  in cities in 1920s, 189–90
  in cities in 1930s, 226–27
  in colonial cities, 17–18
  in post-World War II era, 244–45, 263
  in settlements, 166
  social mobility of, 120
Women's Christian Temperance Union, 162
Women's liberation movement, 244
Wood, Fernando, 38
Wood, Gordon, 24
Woods, Robert A., 166, 173
Woolworth's, 188
Worcester, Mass., 102
Works Progress Administration (WPA), 217, 221, 228
  Historical Records Survey, 224
  Writers Project, 224
World War I, 167, 181
World War II, 234
World's Columbian Exposition of 1893, 44, 167–68
Wright, Henry B., 181, 203

Yellow fever, 36, 108
Yerkes, Charles Tyson, 75, 141
Youngstown, Ohio, 95, 180, 230

Zenger, Ann, 17
Zone of emergence, 82
Zoning, 204, 265
Zorbaugh, Harvey, 202